Co-ordinated SCIENCE

The Earth

Peter Whitehead

Oxford University Press

Oxford University Press
Walton Street
Oxford OX2 6DP

Oxford   New York   Toronto
Delhi   Bombay   Calcutta   Madras   Karachi
Kuala Lumpur   Singapore   Hong Kong   Tokyo
Nairobi   Dar es Salaam   Cape Town
Melbourne   Auckland   Madrid
and associated comapanies in
Berlin   Ibadan

© Peter Whitehead 1992

First Published 1992
Reprinted 1993

Oxford is a trade mark of Oxford University Press

ISBN 019 914372 2

All rights reserved. No part of this publication may be
reproduced, stored in a retrieval system, or transmitted, in any
form or by any means, without the prior permission in writing
of Oxford University Press. Within the U.K., exceptions are
allowed in respect of any fair dealing for the purpose of
research or private study, or criticism or review, as permitted
under the Copyright, Designs and Patents Act, 1988, or in
the case of reprographic reproduction in accordance with the
terms of licences issued by the Copyright Licensing Agency.
Enquiries concerning reproduction outside those terms and in
other countries should be sent to the Rights Department,
Oxford University Press, at the address above.

Typeset by MS Filmsetting Limited, Frome, Somerset
Printed in Hong Kong

Quotation from Herodotus (used on page 33): *Herodotus, the
Histories*; Trans. Aubrey de Selincourt (Penguin Classics,
1954).

The illustrations are by:
Harriet Dell, Michael Eaton, Nick Hawken, Ben Manchipp,
Mark Oliver, Tony Simpson, Julie Tolliday and
Galina Zolfaghari.

The publishers wish to thank the following for permission to reproduce photographs:
Air Products/J Abbott: p 28; Ancient Art & Architecture Collection: pp 66 (bottom left, bottom
middle, bottom right), 68 (centre); British Coal: p 71 (top right and right); British Geological
Survey: p 62; J Allan Cash: pp 9 (centre), 25, 47, 52 (centre), 75 (bottom left), 77; Mary Evans:
pp 18 (bottom left), 65; G. S. F: pp 9 (bottom left), 11 (top left), 35 (top right), 44 (bottom), 49
(bottom), 50 bottom left), 101, 103, 109; The Geological Society: pp 31 (top right and top left),
33, 34; Hulton: pp 76, 84; M. Mason's Pictures: p 97; Met. Office: (c) ESA pp 14, (c) Crown 26;
Nasa: pp 6 (top right), 87 (centre), 93 (bottom right); Natural History Museum: pp 30 (top right
and centre and bottom right), 35 (top right), 85 (bottom left, centre, right); Photo Library Int:
p 93 (bottom left); Science Photo Library: pp 6 (centre), 7 (top right, bottom left, centre), 8 (top
right), 9 (top right), 10 (top right), 18 (top left), 20 (top right), 48 (bottom left), 49 (top right),
58, 66 (top right), 75 (centre), 83 (bottom left and bottom right), 85 (top right), 87 (bottom
left), 88 (bottom right), 90 (top right and bottom right), 91, 92 (right); Shell: p 73 (centre,
bottom left); Telegraph Colour Library: pp 6 (bottom left), 90 (top left); TRH Pictures: pp 8
(bottom left), 67 (bottom right), 92 (top left), 93 (top right), 108; Zefa: pp 16, 43.
Additional photographs by T Waltham: pp 10 (centre, bottom right), 11 (top right, bottom (4)),
13 (bottom, right), 36 (bottom left, centre, bottom right), 38 (bottom), 40 (top right, bottom
right), 41, 42, 44 (top right), 45 (top right, bottom), 48 (centre (2), bottom right), 50 (top right,
right, centre, bottom, left), 52 (top), 53, 55, 56 (top right, centre), 60, 61, 68 (top right, bottom
left), 74 (bottom (3)).

For advice and help in writing this book the author would like to thank David Thompson,
Dr A L Graham and *Antarctic Science*, Dr Keith Westhead and the British Geological Survey,
Mike Boston and the British Coal Opencast Executive (West Central Region), the Science teaching
and technical staff of Blue Coat Comprehensive School, Walsall, and Davina Whitehead.

Introduction

This book is about our planet and its place in space.

For thousands of years people have been fascinated by the Earth and sky. Their discoveries have completely changed the way that we think about our place in the Universe.

We all need the Earth. We have nowhere else to live. If we are to survive on our home planet, we need to understand it. That is why Earth Science is so important.

The book is divided into sections, each covering a different main theme in the study of the Earth Sciences.

Each section is made up of double-page-spreads, which include questions and investigations to help you to understand the theme. We have included many photographs and illustrations to show you some of the evidence about the Earth and the Universe, and to help you to see how scientists try to explain these observations.

At the end of most of the sections are questions which you can use to help you to revise the ideas you have studied, and which may help you to investigate topics further. Some questions are intended to be answered by using other books in libraries, or by searching for information on databases such as NERIS.

This book will help you in your study of the Earth and its place in the Universe, but you should also look at specimens of rocks, minerals and fossils, and visit some of the places where they are found in the real world outside your laboratory. Please visit museums which have collections of these specimens – some of them have things you might never find yourself in a lifetime of searching. Look at buildings around your school to see how earth materials are used. As for the Universe, remember to look up into the sky on dark, clear nights. You can see some of the greatest natural wonders just by lifting your eyes.

Peter Whitehead

Contents

Section 1: Expedition to Earth
1.1	The Blue Planet	6
1.2	Anyone at home?	8
1.3	The changing face of Earth	10
1.4	The main features of Earth	12

Section 2: Wind and Rain
2.1	Measuring weather	14
2.2	Moving air	16
2.3	Winds around the world	18
2.4	Around the water cycle	20
2.5	The Sun and the seasons	22
2.6	Climate and crops	24
2.7	Stormy weather	26
2.8	The atmosphere	28
	Questions	29

Section 3: The time detectives
3.1	The fossil hunters	30
3.2	Layers of Earth history	32
3.3	How old is the Earth?	34

Section 4: Shaping the Earth
4.1	Weathering	36
4.2	Soils and sediment transport	38
4.3	Transport and rock formation	40
4.4	Sedimentary environments	42
4.5	Interpreting sedimentary rocks	44
4.6	Interpreting a sedimentary sequence	46
	Questions	47

Section 5: Our active planet
5.1	Volcanic eruptions	48
5.2	Igneous rocks	50
5.3	More about igneous rocks	52
5.4	Zones of volcanoes and earthquakes	54
5.5	The effects of earthquakes	56
5.6	Seismic waves	58
5.7	Faults and folds	60
5.8	Metamorphic rocks	62
	Questions	64

Summary: The Rock Cycle   65

Section 6: The Earth – used and abused

6.1	The Earth-shapers	66
6.2	Building materials	68
6.3	Extracting coal	70
6.4	Oil and gas	72
6.5	Ores, metals and chemicals	74
6.6	Some pollution problems	76
6.7	Our throwaway world	78
	Questions	79

Section 7: Worlds beyond the sky

7.1	Our round world	80
7.2	Patterns in the sky	82
7.3	Evidence from the sky	84
7.4	Space technology	86
7.5	Our neighbour in space	88
7.6	The inner planets	90
7.7	The gas giants and their moons	92
7.8	The solar system	94
7.9	Stars and galaxies	96
7.10	Back to the Big Bang	97
	Questions	98

Summary: The scale of the Universe   99

Section 8: Eggshell Earth

8.1	Continental drift and sea-floor spreading	100
8.2	Shrinking oceans and colliding continents	102
8.3	The theory of plates	104
8.4	Looking through the Earth	106
8.5	At the beginning	108
	Questions	110

Summary: An overview of plate tectonics and Earth processes   111

Index   112

SECTION ONE

EXPEDITION TO EARTH

1.1 The Blue Planet

We are all in this photograph; every human, every other kind of animal, and every kind of plant. The photograph was taken by a spaceprobe and shows the Earth and the Moon from far away in space.

1 The Earth has a diameter of about 13 000 km. Estimate the diameter of the Moon.

Both Earth and Moon are round. In the picture they do not look round because only the sides facing the Sun are lit up, and the sides facing away from the Sun are dark. We only see the light sides.

Our spaceprobe is now passing the Moon.

2 List three differences you see between Moon and Earth.

The spaceprobe is getting closer to us. It shows us that our planet has oceans, clouds and land. Clouds are white, the ocean is blue. The other colours are areas of land. Overall, about 70 per cent of the Earth is covered by ocean.

3 What do we call these areas of land?

4 What do we call the main ocean seen here?

5 Why might 'The Blue Planet' be a good name for Earth?

Look at the edge of Earth. You might be able to see the **atmosphere**. This is a thin layer made of a mixture of gases. The Moon has a sharp edge in photographs because it has no atmosphere.

The spaceprobe is flying round Earth. Here we see two **continents**. Continents are large rocky areas, mainly above the level of the oceans. One of these continents is covered by ice.

6 Name the two continents in the photograph.

Earth is a planet of water. It is the only planet with water in all three states of matter: solid, liquid and gas. This is because the temperature of our planet is usually in the range from $-20°C$ to $+40°C$.

7 What do we call 'solid' water?

The oceans contain most of Earth's liquid water. Under the oceans there is solid rock.

Our spaceprobe is moving further around Earth. The clouds are made of millions of tiny drops of water. They are spread in patterns by moving air.

8 Is the air moving *clockwise* or *anticlockwise* in the spiral pattern of clouds?

Moving air, or **wind** brings changes in the weather. The air moves as it is heated by the Sun, and as the Earth spins. Some planets have stronger winds because they spin faster, or are heated more by the Sun.

The spaceprobe is now over the British Isles.

9 Do you live on this picture? Trace an outline of the islands and mark where you live.

10 Label your blank outline to show the following places: Wales; Scotland; Ireland; Cornwall; the Hebrides; the English Channel; the North Sea.

We have been given an outsider's view of our home planet. Our Earth is a planet of water, ice, clouds and rocks. To find out that it has life, including people, a visitor from space would have to look very carefully.

7

SECTION ONE

EXPEDITION TO EARTH

1.2 Anyone at home?

A visiting spaceprobe would not find it easy to tell that we live on the Earth. Most of what we do hardly shows up from space.

If the spaceprobe flew over the dark side of the Earth, away from the Sun, it would detect more signs of life than on the daylit side.

The bright lights of our cities show up clearly (white). Some of the brightest lights are from gas burning on oil rigs (yellow). The red lights show areas where vegetation is being burnt. Other bright lights are carried by large fleets of fishing boats.

1 What part of the world does this photograph show?

2 A city from a satellite. The colours are not natural, but produced by a computer. Buildings are shown in blue. Can you identify rivers, bridges, roads, and an airport in the picture?

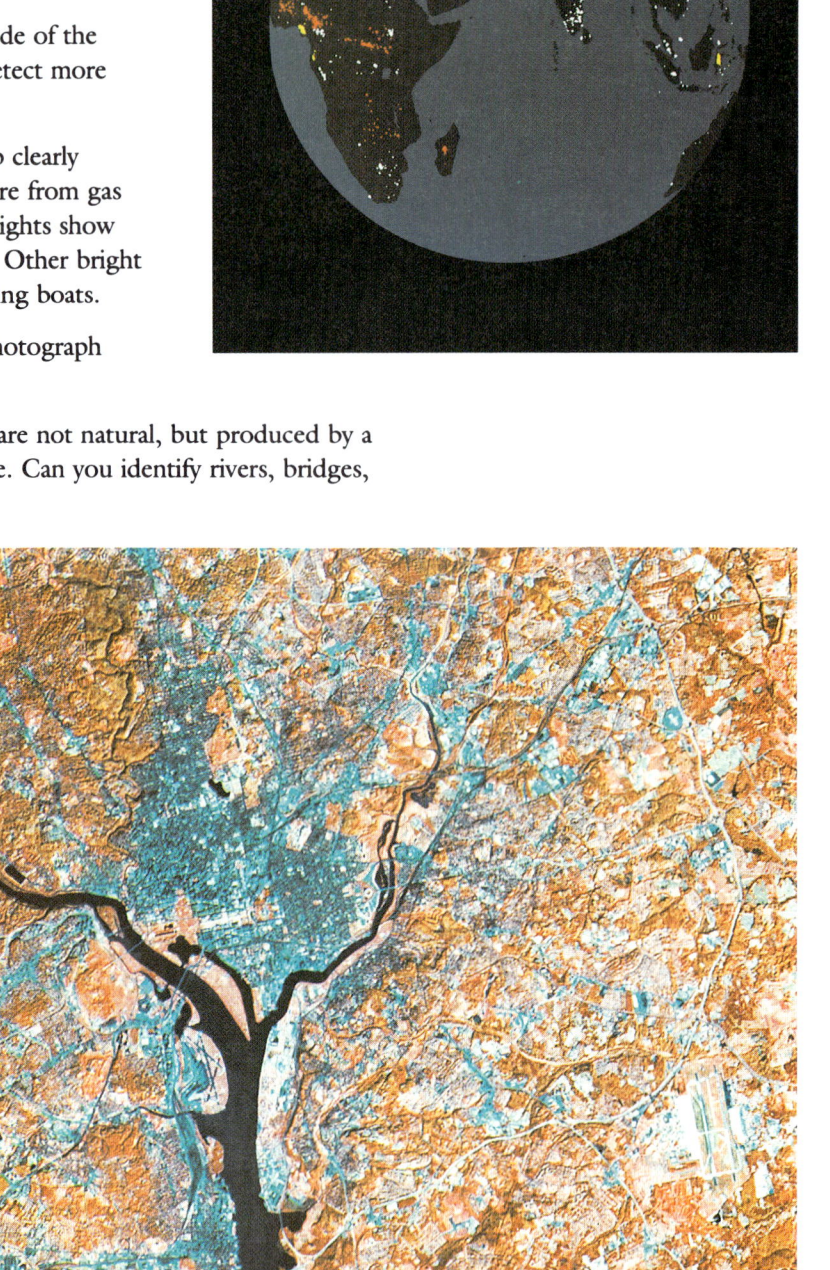

From space our visitor can see some evidence of the way we use our planet. Here, over South America, great clouds of smoke are rising up from the tropical rainforests.

3 What is causing these clouds?

This large hole is not natural. Humans are digging into the Earth for its raw materials.

4 Make a list of twenty different natural materials that we get by digging in the Earth.

Even in the atmosphere there is evidence of human activity. This haze is over a large city. If our spaceprobe could find out what gases were in the air here, it would find human-made chemicals not usually found in the Earth's atmosphere.

5 What gases might be causing the haze?

6 How might humans have made these gases?

From a distance, Earth appeared as a clean, blue, natural planet. As the spaceprobe approached, it found that the planet was covered by evidence of human activity.

1.3 The changing face of Earth

A visiting spaceprobe flying low across our planet would find that the surface of the Earth has many different features. Here, a mountain is throwing out clouds of dust, fragments of rock and very hot liquid rock from a hole in its top. It would be obvious that our planet has energy inside it.

1 What do we call this kind of mountain?

The materials thrown out by these fiery eruptions make new rocks, called **igneous** rocks. This means they needed heat to make them.

Our spaceprobe has seen land being built up around a volcano. In other places, the land is being worn away.

Here in the Grand Canyon, layers of rocks are being worn down, or **eroded**, by a river. Bits of rock are being carried away by water.

This river is flowing into the sea. The river is carrying lots of mud and sand.

2 Where has the mud and sand come from?

When the river flows into a lake or the sea, the water slows down. The mud and sand sink to the bottom, and will slowly become harder. The mud and sand will become new layers of rocks. These **sedimentary** rocks are made of recycled material from older rocks.

Most of the old rocks of the Grand Canyon are sedimentary rocks made in the past. They have fossils of sea animals in them. Now those layers are a long way above the sea.

3 Write down two ways that could explain how this happened.

4 If you walked down into the Grand Canyon, where do you think you would find the oldest rocks? Give a reason for your answer.

Mud and sand being washed into a lake by a river.

These layers of sedimentary rocks have been squashed, or **buckled** up and broken.

5 Draw a diagram from the photograph and mark places where the rocks have been (a) buckled up and (b) broken.

The Earth must have plenty of energy to create forces that can lift rock layers out of the sea and buckle or break them.

6 What do we call sudden violent earth movements that break rocks?

These mountains are made of rocks that have been buckled up and heated while they were buried quite deeply under other rocks. They were sedimentary rocks in the past, but have now changed into new, harder rock types. They are examples of the third main kind of rock, **metamorphic** rocks. Metamorphic means *changed*, by heat, pressure from rocks lying above, and pressure from earth movements.

Sedimentary | **Igneous** | **Metamorphic** | **Quartz**

All **rocks** are mixtures of different **minerals**. Each mineral is made of one or more chemical elements. Here are three different rocks, one sedimentary, one igneous and one metamorphic. All of them are mixtures of different minerals, but one mineral is found in all of them. It is quartz. The sand on most beaches is nearly pure quartz.

7 Examine examples of earth materials and sort them into *minerals* and *rocks* (mixtures of minerals).

8 Examine examples of igneous, metamorphic and sedimentary rocks. List the main differences between the three classes of rock.

1.4 The main features of Earth

More than half of the Earth's surface is made of the *igneous* rock **basalt**, which makes up the ocean floors. The basalt is often covered by sands and mud, but it forms a solid shell around most of our planet under the oceans.

Underwater mountain chains run across the ocean floors, linking to make a network around the Earth. These **mid-ocean ridges** have deep central rift valleys, where molten basalt keeps erupting from underwater volcanoes.

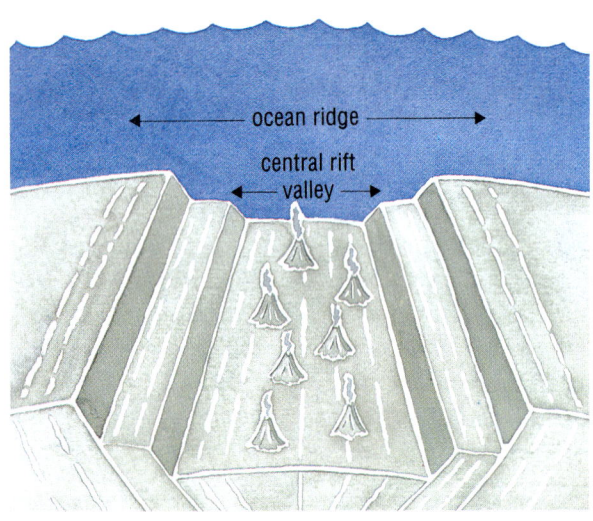

The structure of an ocean ridge

At many places around the Earth the ocean floor drops to form long narrow **ocean trenches**. Mud and sand flow into these to make layers of sediment.

Running alongside these trenches we often find chains of volcanoes, either in **island arcs**, or on the nearest continent.

The continents have many mountain chains, but not made of basalt. They are made of folded layers of *sedimentary* and *metamorphic* rocks. These must have been squeezed in from the sides, and folded. *Igneous* rocks such as granite have often pushed up through these **fold mountains**.

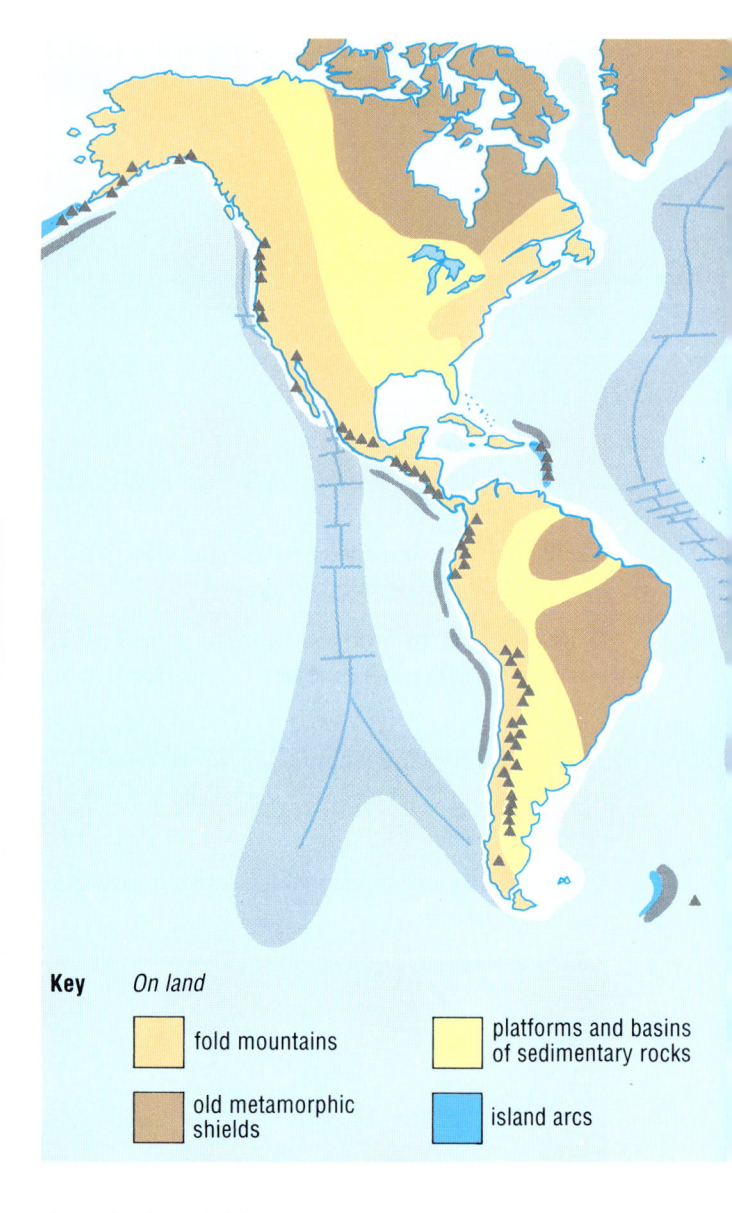

The fold mountains are the highest parts of the continents. The lower-lying areas are of two types.

Some central low-lying areas of the continents are made of metamorphic and igneous rocks. These ancient areas are called **shields**. Scientists have tested them to find their age. The rocks are from about 1000 million years old up to about 4000 million years old.

Key *On land*

- fold mountains
- old metamorphic shields
- platforms and basins of sedimentary rocks
- island arcs

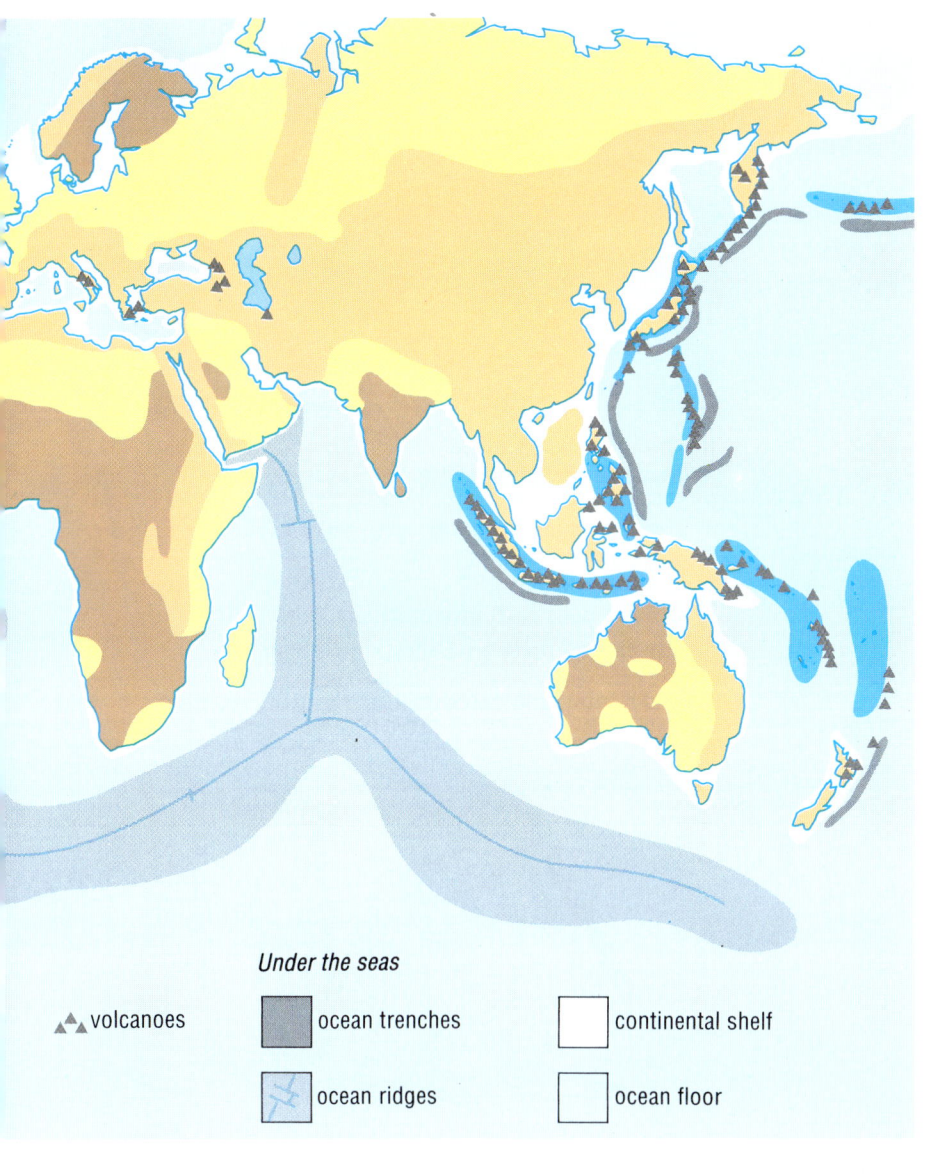

The other low-lying parts of continents are made of layers of sedimentary rocks. These are called **platforms** where the layers are flat, and **basins** where they are gently folded.

The Cotswolds

Under the seas

▲▲ volcanoes

ocean trenches

ocean ridges

continental shelf

ocean floor

1 Make a list of the main features of the earth's surface described on this page and add the rocks found making up each feature.

The Scottish Highlands

13

SECTION TWO

WIND AND RAIN

2.1 Measuring weather

A spaceprobe approaching Earth would find many satellites in orbit around the planet. Many of them are recording changes in the weather.

Satellites check the weather from space, and send information and photographs to Earth. Weather records are also made by aircraft, ships and land stations. Earth is surrounded by a web of weather-watchers, some human and some machine.

1 Make a list of facts about the weather that the weather-watchers could be recording.

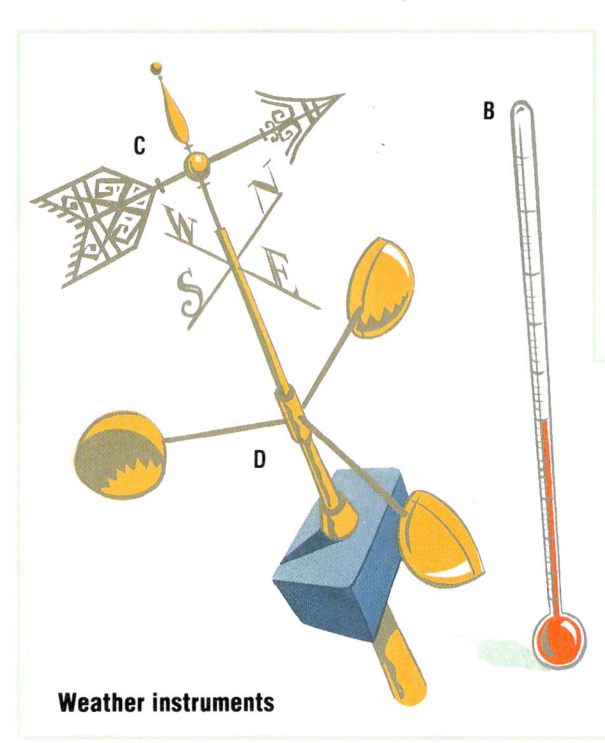

Weather instruments

Weather instruments

These instruments are used to record different things about the weather.

2 What does each instrument record? Your list of answers to Question 1 should help you.

3 Describe how you think each instrument works.

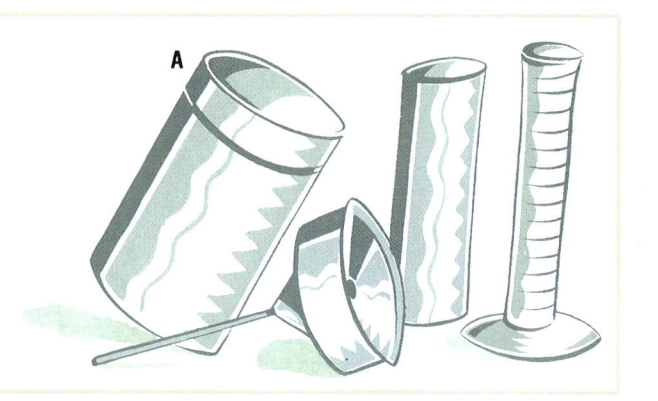

Air pressure

One of the most useful weather instruments is the *barometer* which measures air pressure. You will have heard weather reporters talking about areas of high and low pressure. These are important because changes in air pressure produce changes in the weather.

Earth is surrounded by a deep ocean of air called the *atmosphere*. The pressure that this produces is measured in *millibars*. It increases as you get closer to the Earth's surface.

Even near sea-level, air pressure changes from place to place and from time to time.

An aneroid barometer

Air pressure in mb

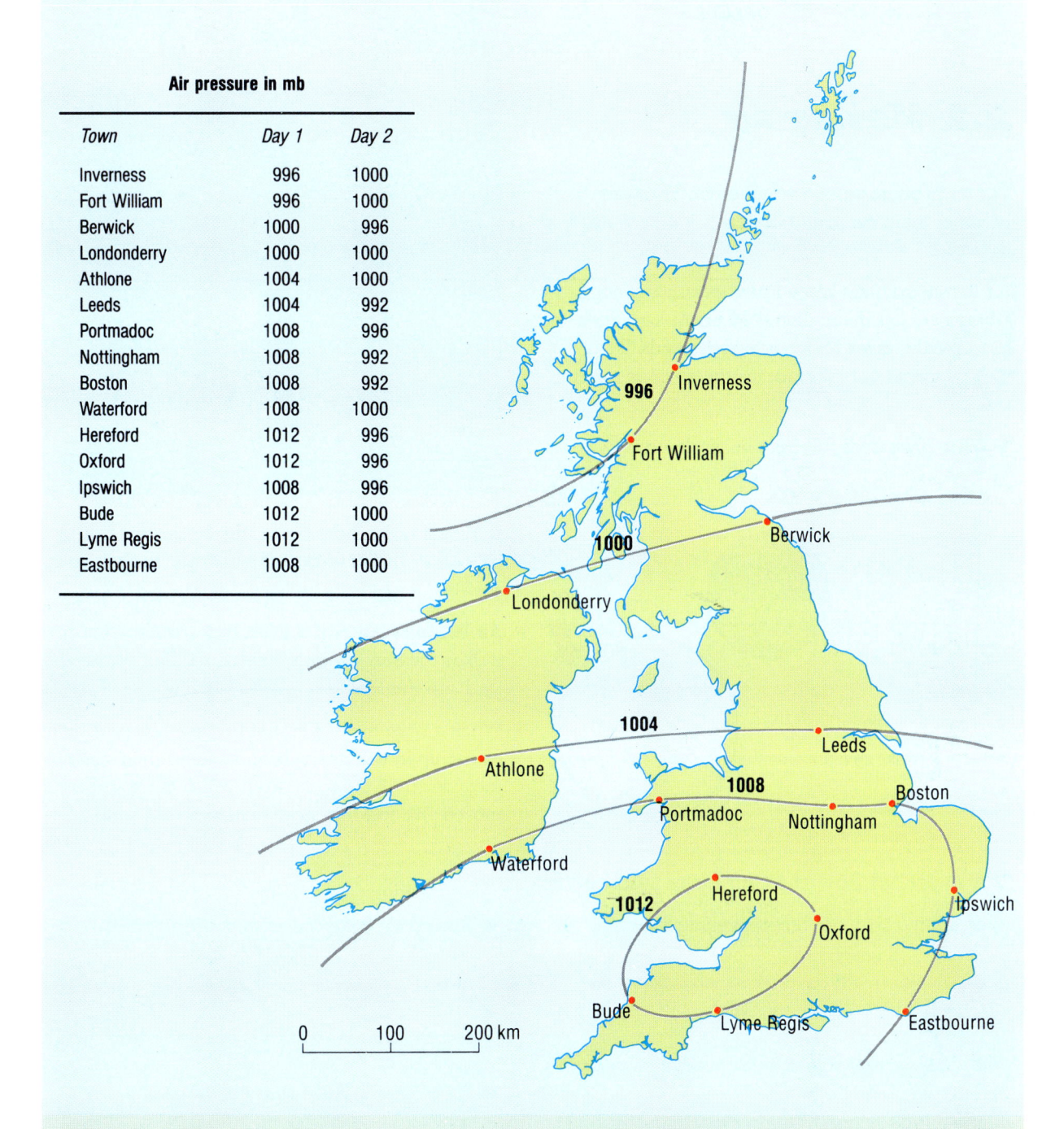

Town	Day 1	Day 2
Inverness	996	1000
Fort William	996	1000
Berwick	1000	996
Londonderry	1000	1000
Athlone	1004	1000
Leeds	1004	992
Portmadoc	1008	996
Nottingham	1008	992
Boston	1008	992
Waterford	1008	1000
Hereford	1012	996
Oxford	1012	996
Ipswich	1008	996
Bude	1012	1000
Lyme Regis	1012	1000
Eastbourne	1008	1000

Plotting pressure on maps

The map shows towns where barometers recorded the air pressure in *millibars* (mb) on two different days.

The Day 1 readings have been recorded on the map by drawing lines, or **isobars**, between towns with the same air pressure.

- Trace a copy of this map, without the isobars.
- Mark the Day 2 set of readings on the map copy.
- Join matching numbers to make isobars, which are lines of equal pressure. It is easiest if you start with the biggest numbers. Mark each complete line with the pressure in millibars.

4 a) On Day 1, was there a centre of high pressure or low pressure over the British Isles?

b) On Day 2, was there a centre of high pressure or low pressure over the British Isles?

2.2 Moving air

The air pressure around you increases if the air becomes more dense and decreases if it becomes less dense.

Air density changes when its temperature changes. Warm air is less dense than cold air. As air warms up, its molecules move about at higher speeds. They start to spread out. This means the air takes up more space.

1 What effect does this have on air density?

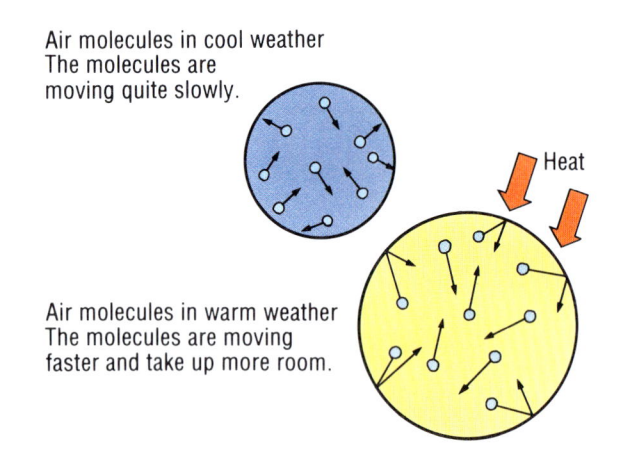

Air molecules in cool weather
The molecules are moving quite slowly.

Air molecules in warm weather
The molecules are moving faster and take up more room.

2 Which is the more dense, the air *inside* a hot air balloon or the air *outside* the balloon? Explain your answer.

Air becomes hotter if it gains heat from the Earth as well as the Sun. During the day, the Sun warms the land and the sea.

When a large mass of air has become heated it tends to rise up in the atmosphere. Cold air then starts to move in to fill the space from which the warm air has moved. We feel this movement as a cold wind.

A model of how the Sun heats land and sea

- Set up two trays, one containing water and one containing soil.
- Arrange two thermometers in clamp stands with their bulbs just above the surface of the two materials.
- Put a powerful light bulb above the two trays to represent the Sun.
- Record the temperatures every minute for 20 minutes, and then switch off the light bulb.
- Record the temperatures over another 20 minute period as the two materials cool down.
- What conclusions can you draw from your results about how the soil and water heat the air?
- How did you make sure that this was a *fair test*?

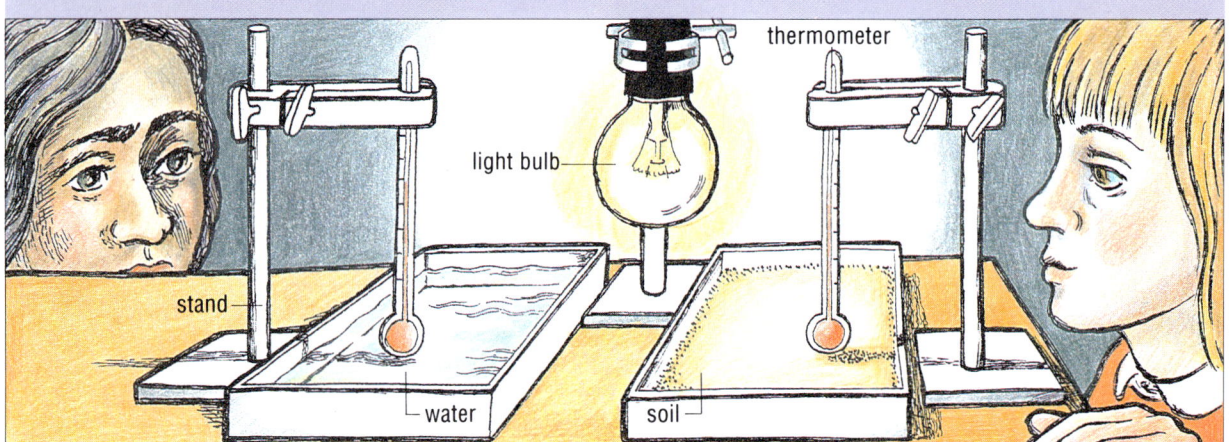

Moving air masses and fronts

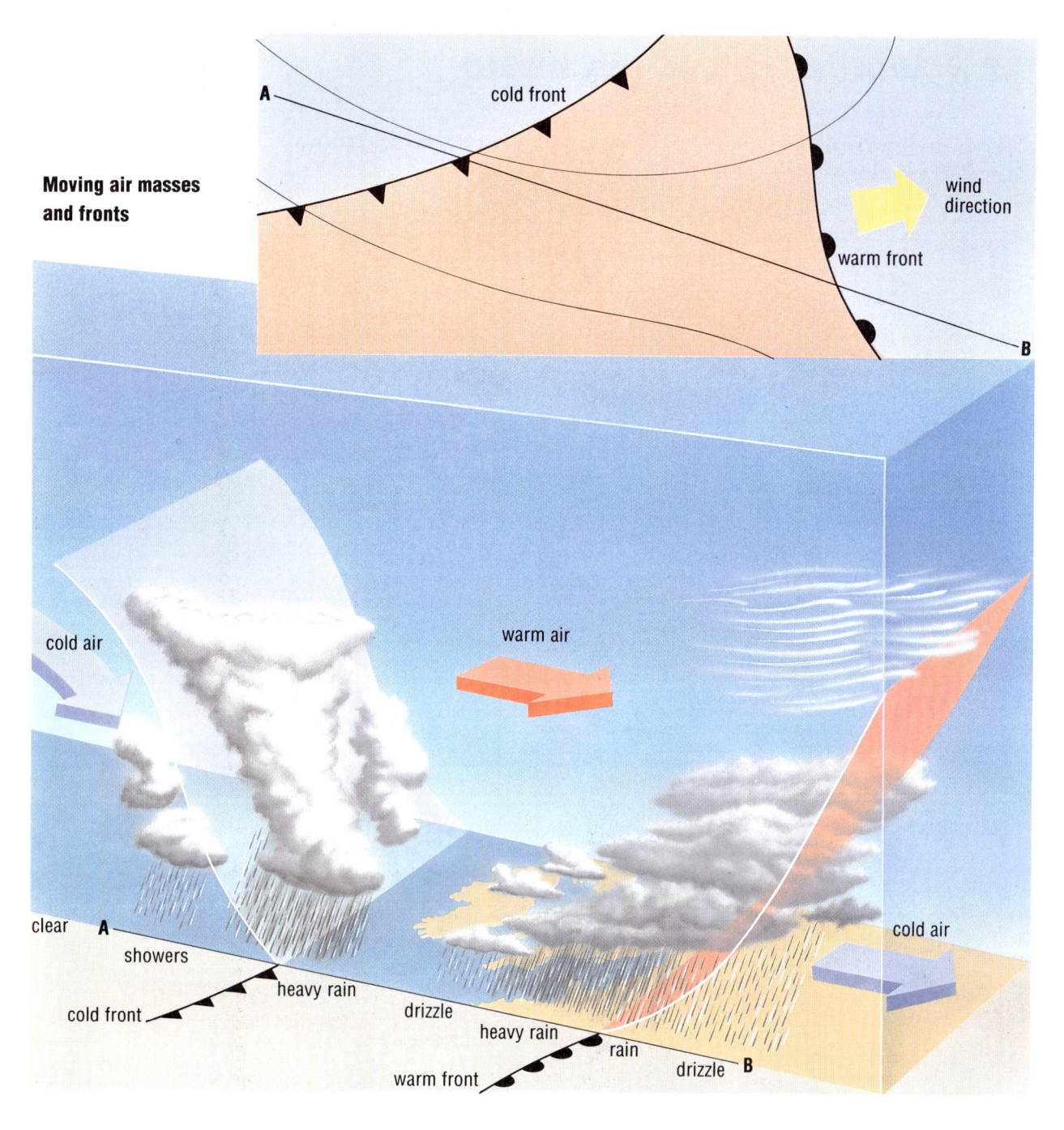

This weather map shows masses of cold air and warm air moving. Air masses of different temperature push each other across the surface of the Earth. Where they meet there are sharp temperature changes marked by **fronts**.

The cross-section shows how one cold mass of air is pushing under warm air. The warm air is pushed over another cold air mass, which is forced forwards in its turn.

4 From the diagram, make a list of differences between **warm fronts** and **cold fronts**.

Warm air can hold lots of water vapour, but when warm air is made to rise by cold air the water vapour turns into water droplets or ice crystals. **Clouds** are masses of air full of these droplets and crystals. The water droplets in clouds can collide and join to make drops heavy enough to fall as rain.

5 From the diagram of warm and cold fronts, describe how the weather would change as a pair of fronts passed across your home.

2.3 Winds around the world

Winds travel across the Earth from high to low pressure, but not in straight lines. This satellite photograph shows that the winds travel in a spiral pattern. The spin of the Earth affects the moving air.

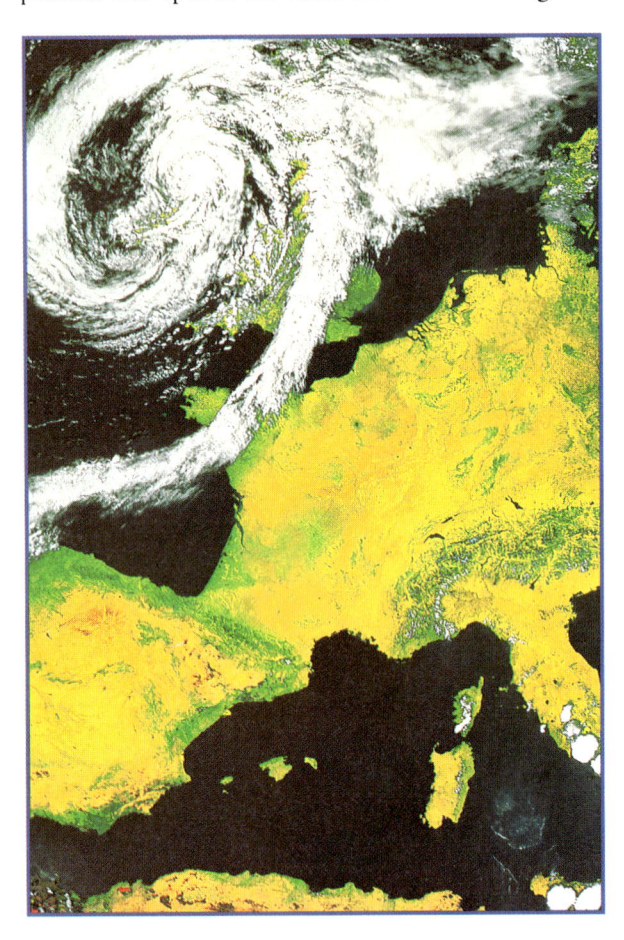

Lines on a spinning surface

- Put a round sheet of paper on an old turntable from a record player.
- Spin the turntable and, while it is still spinning, use a felt pen to draw a straight line from the edge to the centre of the paper.
- Stop the turntable and examine your result.
- Repeat the experiment spinning the turntable the other way.

Winds try to move directly from areas of high pressure to areas of low pressure but the spin of the earth makes them go in a spiral instead.

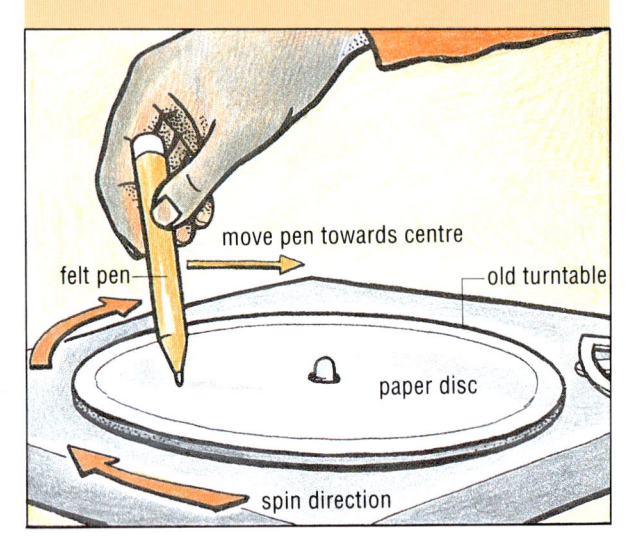

Regular patterns of pressure appear in some places. In summer, there is a regular spiral cloud pattern over the North Atlantic. This spiral is the North Atlantic High. It is caused when warm air rises over the sea.

The North Atlantic High has *clockwise* winds blowing from it which have helped sailing boats for hundreds of years.

1 If you sailed from Portugal using these winds, what would be your likely destination?

These winds helped explorers like Christopher Columbus. They are known as **Trade Winds**.

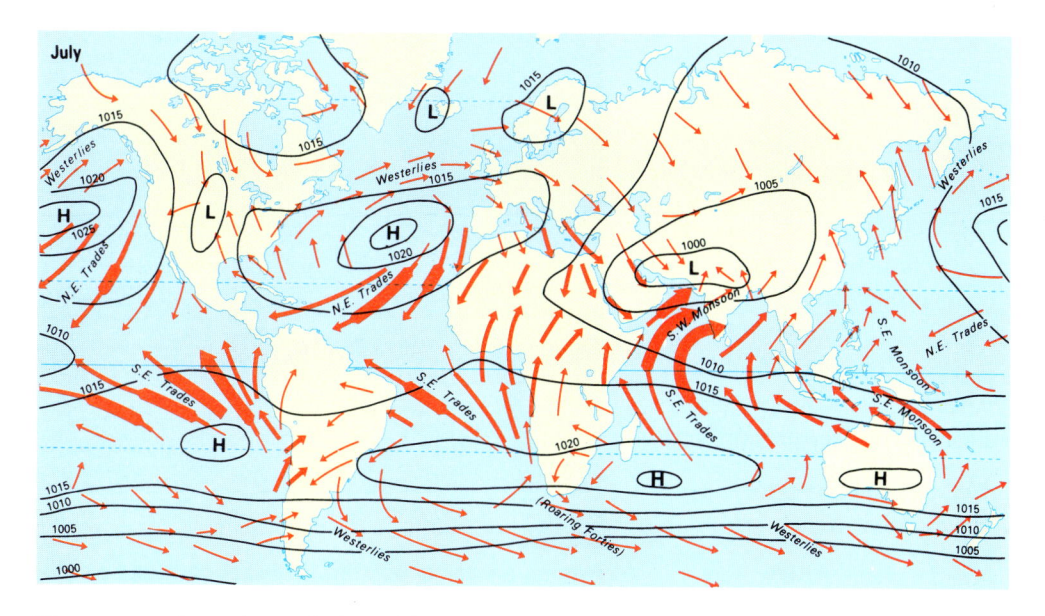

These maps show the typical world pattern of high and low pressure areas, and their surrounding wind patterns, in July and in January.

2 What differences can you see between the two maps? Make a list.

3 What similarities can you see between the two maps? Make a list.

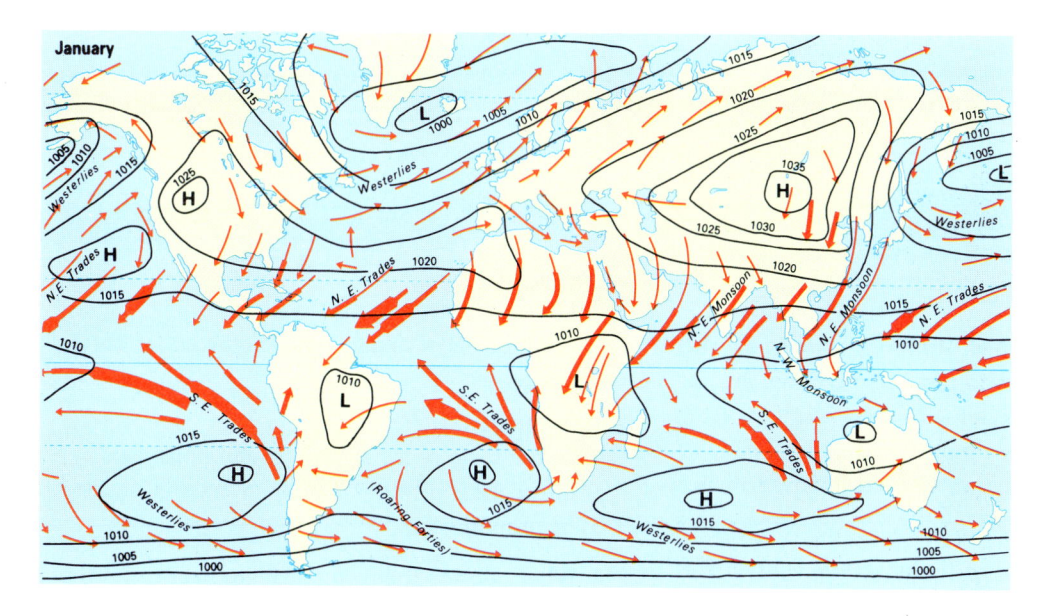

4 Copy and complete this set of rules about how air pressure systems produce winds in the northern and southern hemispheres:

High pressure areas in the northern hemisphere produce clockwise winds.

Low pressure areas in the northern hemisphere produce _____ winds.

_____ pressure areas in the southern hemisphere produce clockwise winds.

_____ pressure areas in the southern hemisphere produce anticlockwise winds.

19

2.4 Around the water cycle

A visitor from space arriving near the Earth would make a strange discovery: Earth has one very important chemical, *water*, in all three states – solid, liquid and gas.

This does not happen on all planets. Most are too hot or too cold. Our home planet happens to have temperatures which allow ice, liquid water and water vapour (gas) to exist. A space visitor would probably think that our watery coatings, the oceans, icecaps and clouds, were the most amazing features of Earth.

1 What temperature would a planet have to stay below if its water was *always* solid?

2 What temperature would a planet have to stay above if its water was *never* liquid or solid?

Europa, a moon of Jupiter, is always covered by a shell of ice.

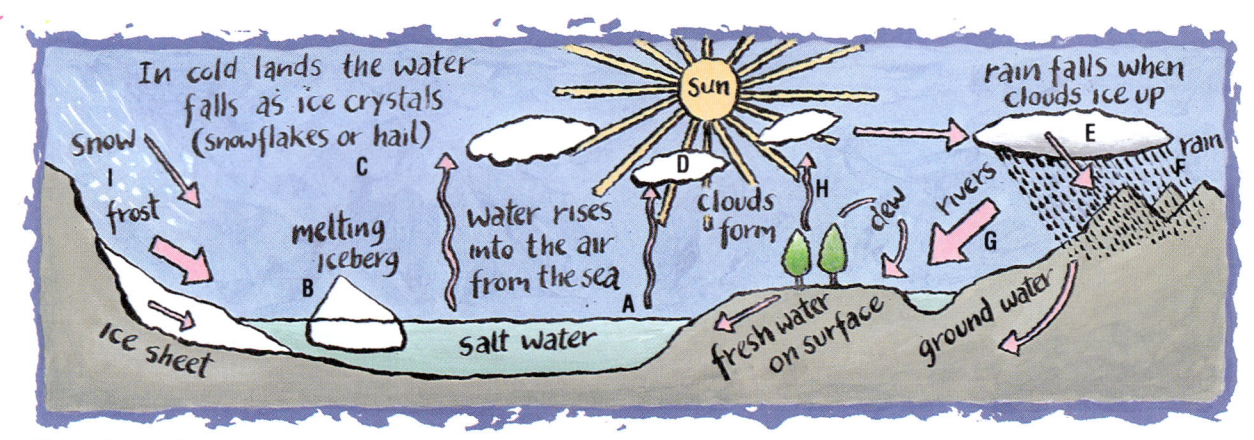

The water cycle

Water constantly changes from one state to another and moves from place to place. We call this the **water cycle**. To make some of these changes, water must *gain* energy. When other changes happen, water *loses* energy. The **water cycle** is driven by heat from the Sun.

Our planet has a total of about 1400 million cubic kilometers of water.

About 97 per cent of the water is seawater.

About 2.25 per cent is ice in the polar caps and glaciers.

About 0.01 per cent is in rivers and lakes as fresh water, and in the air as water vapour.

The remainder, 0.74 per cent, is soaked into spaces inside the rocks of the earth, as groundwater.

3 Work out how many cubic kilometers of water there are:

a) in the oceans
b) in the form of ice in glaciers and polar caps
c) in the form of water vapour, rivers and lakes
d) as groundwater.

4 Where do the following changes happen on the picture of the water cycle? Answer by choosing letters. You might choose more than one letter for some answers.

a) Water changing from liquid to gas.
b) Water changing from gas to liquid.
c) Water changing from solid to liquid.
d) Water changing from liquid to solid.
e) Water losing energy.
f) Water gaining energy.

Models of the water cycle

Try these investigations. Plan ahead to decide what observations and recordings you will make. How will you ensure that your tests are fair? Decide where each fits into the water cycle. Draw diagrams and label parts of the experiment that represent
clouds   icebergs   oceans   the Sun   wind.

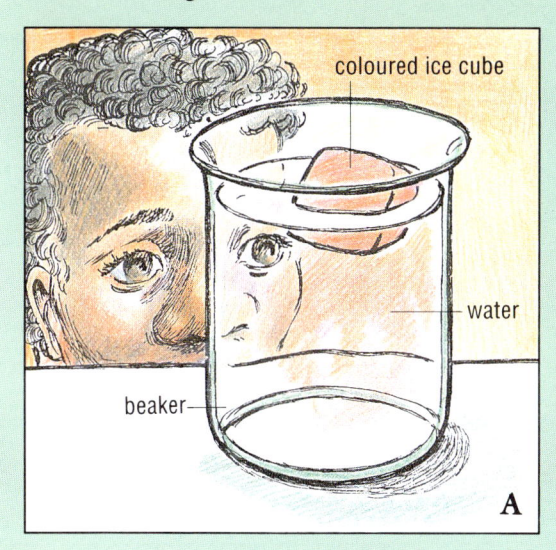

A

Make ice cubes of potassium permanganate solution, and then gently put a cube in a beaker of water. Try beakers with (a) tap water (b) salt water (c) warm tap water (d) warm salt water.

B

Fill a large tray with sand. Use a watering can to sprinkle water on to the sand. Repeat this with similar trays of soil, mud, and gravel. Make as many observations as you can.

C

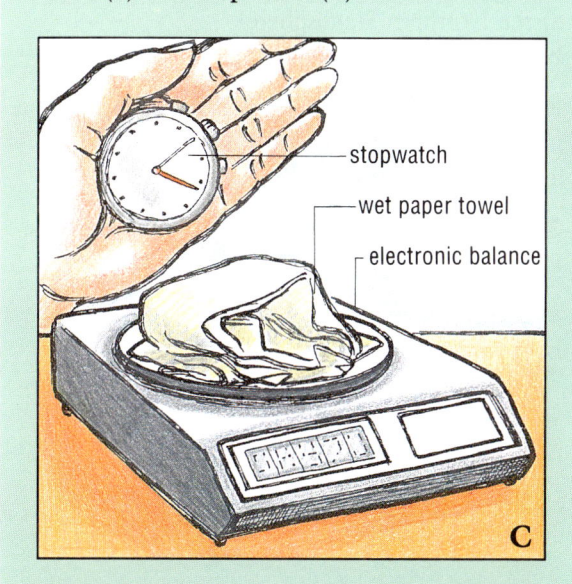

Soak a paper towel with water. Put it on a top-pan electronic balance and note its mass every 15 seconds for 5 minutes. Repeat the experiment with a fan blowing over the towel, then with a lamp over the towel, then with both. List your results in a table.

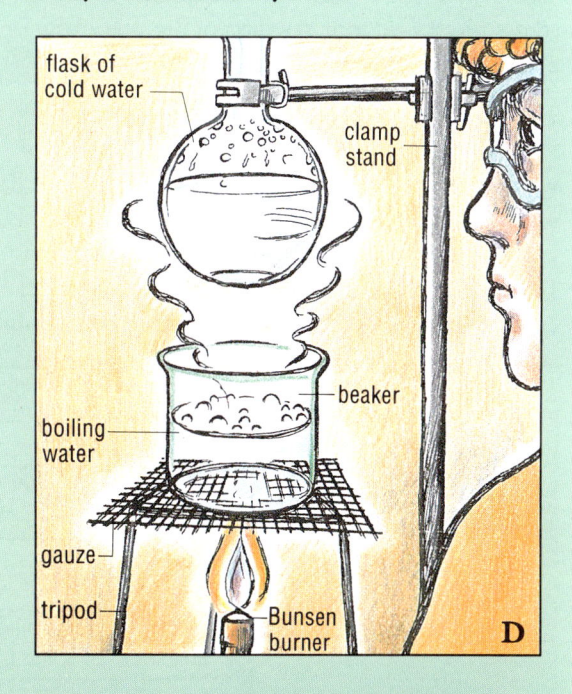

D

Clamp a flask of cold water about 40 cm above boiling water in a beaker. Make as many observations as you can.

2.5 The Sun and the seasons

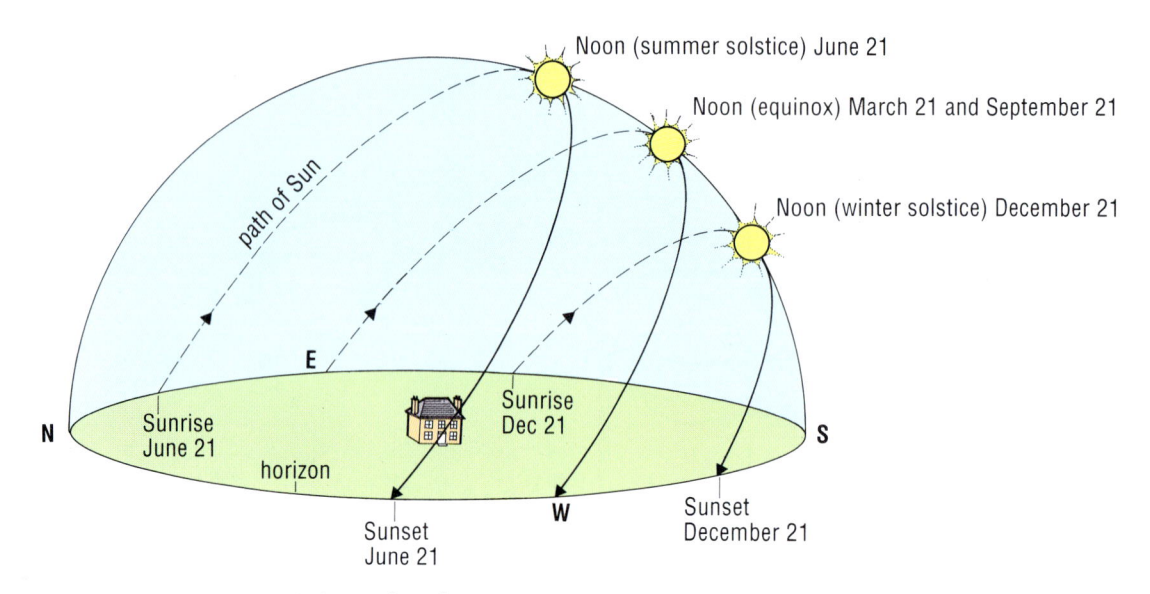

The path of the Sun across the sky at solstice and equinox

Our weather is solar-powered. The energy of the Sun drives the water cycle. Without the Sun our planet would be a frozen ball.

The seasons

This picture shows how the Sun appears to move across the sky on four key days of the year, from one place on the surface of the Earth.

The surface of the Earth gains most heat when the Sun is above the horizon for the most hours, *and* when it reaches the highest angle in the sky. The day when this happens is June 21st in the Northern Hemisphere, and December 21st in the Southern Hemisphere. This **Midsummer Day** is sometimes called **summer solstice**. Solstice means 'Sun standing still'.

The surface gains the least heat exactly half a year after summer solstice, when the Sun is at its lowest angle above the horizon *and* stays above the horizon for the fewest hours. This is **Midwinter Day**, or **winter solstice**.

1 What date is the winter solstice in:

a) the Northern Hemisphere?
b) the Southern Hemisphere?

2 On the days of the two **equinoxes** the days and nights are equal in length. For how long is the Sun in the sky on those days?

3 On which day will the Sun give this part of the Earth the *least* energy?

4 On which day will the Sun give this part of the Earth the *most* energy?

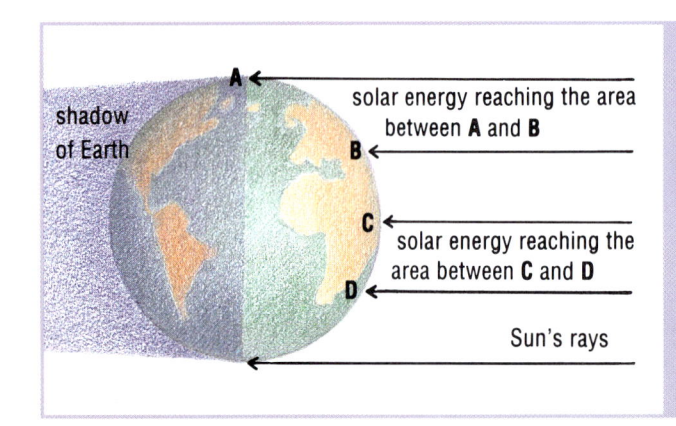

This picture helps to show why some parts of the Earth's surface are cooler than other parts. The energy from the Sun reaching the area between A and B is the same as the energy reaching the area between C and D.

5 Where is the energy more concentrated? Is it between A and B or between C and D? Test your answer using a globe, a torch and a dark room.

Solar heating

Looking at the seasons

It is easier to see why the seasons exist by making a model as shown in the picture. Hold the rod so that it is about 20° from vertical. (The exact figure is $23\frac{1}{2}°$, and you could model this by mounting the rod in a wooden block measured to this angle.) Mark a green line around the 'equator' of the model, and a blue dot where you live.

Set your model with its tilt towards a model 'Sun' – a small electric bulb about 0.5 m away. Use a 0.5 m string to keep the distance fixed as you slowly move your 'Earth' around the 'Sun'. Move around *anticlockwise*.

6 What do we call the time it takes the Earth to make one orbit of the Sun?

7 At which positions do all parts of the Earth get day and night of exactly equal lengths?

8 Are these statements true or false?

a) When the Earth is at position C it is winter in the southern hemisphere.
b) When the Earth is at position B it is spring in the southern hemisphere.
c) When the Earth is at position A there will be 24 hours of daylight at the north pole.

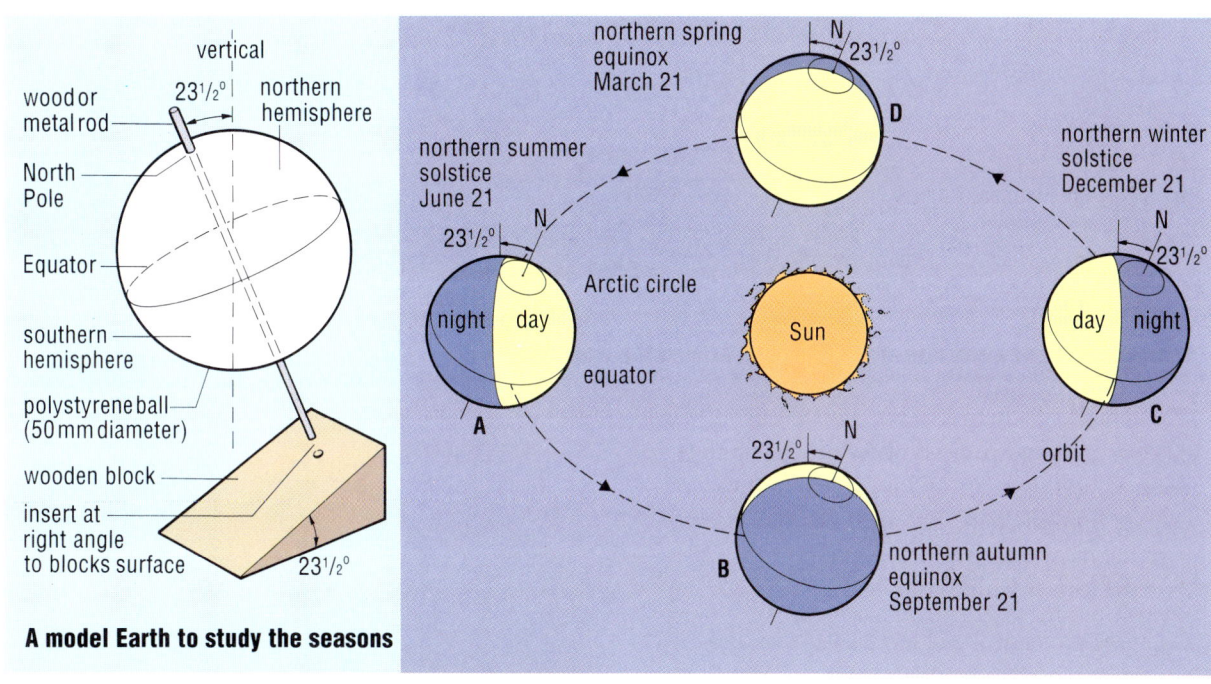

A model Earth to study the seasons

Stonehenge, in Wiltshire, was built about 5000 years ago. In 1771, Dr John Smith studied the stone positions at Stonehenge. He suggested the theory that Stones 92 and 91 pointed to the sunrise position at Summer Solstice. In 1846, Rev Edward Duke added to the theory by suggesting that Stones 94 and 93 pointed to the sunset position at Winter Solstice.

These important lines had been marked by stones set on the circular bank long before the famous central stone circles were built.

9 List reasons why seasons were even more important to people 5000 years ago than today.

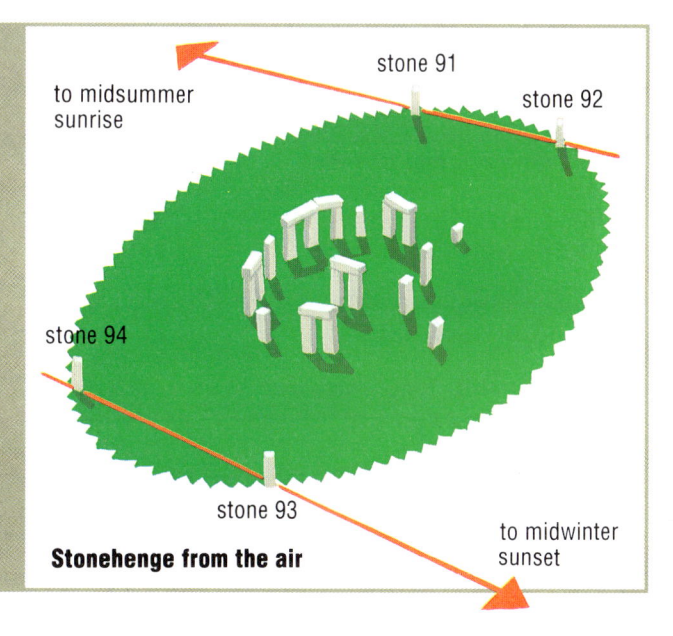

Stonehenge from the air

SECTION TWO
WIND AND RAIN

2.6 Climate and crops

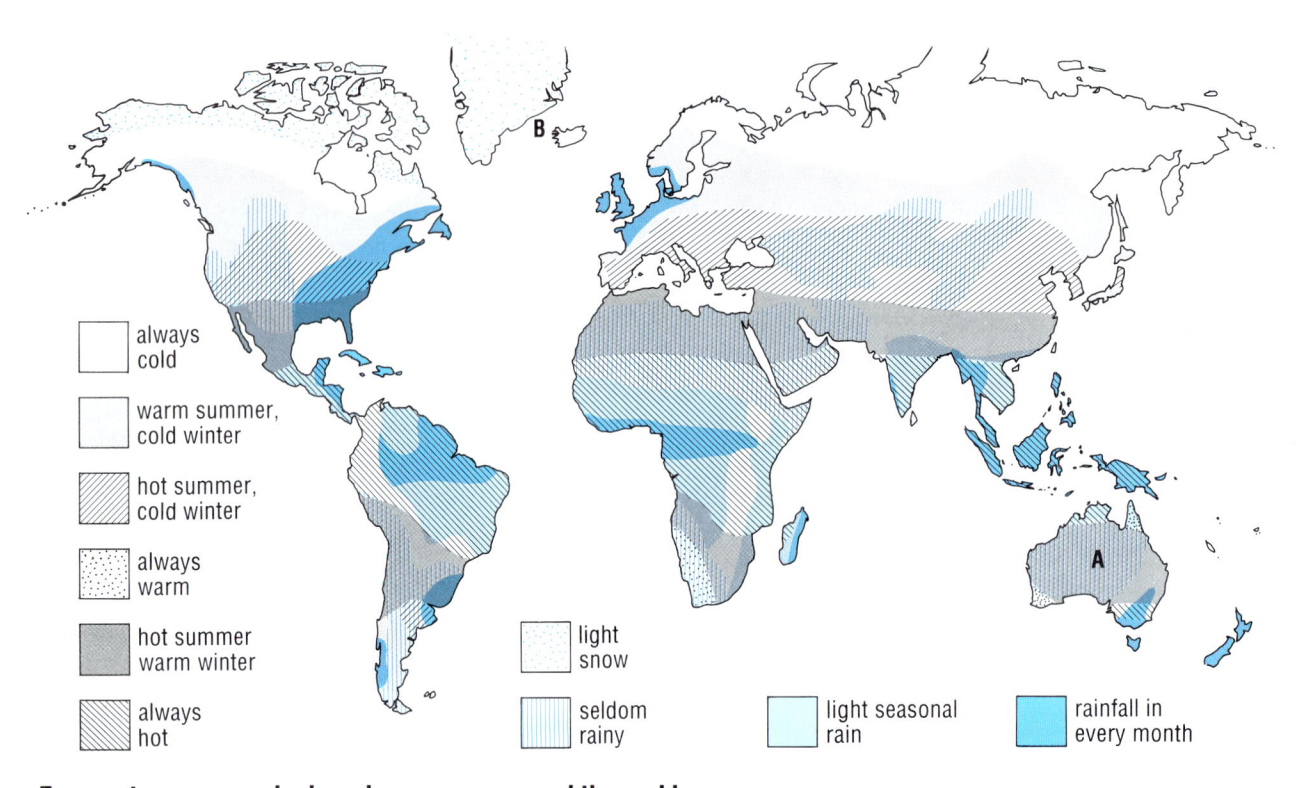

Temperature zones and rain and snow zones around the world

Legend:
- always cold
- warm summer, cold winter
- hot summer, cold winter
- always warm
- hot summer warm winter
- always hot
- light snow
- seldom rainy
- light seasonal rain
- rainfall in every month

The climate of any part of the world depends partly on the winds and partly on how much rain they bring. It also depends on how much heat the area collects from the Sun. The areas near the equator have the most solar heating. Areas near the poles have the least solar heating.

Compare the rainfall and temperature on the map above.

Deserts are mostly found in areas where it hardly ever rains and it is hot, especially in summer.

1 On a blank map of the world, mark in where you would expect to find deserts.

Tropical rainforests mostly grow where there is rainfall every month and where it is always hot.

2 Mark on your map where you would expect to find tropical rainforests.

Ice sheets mostly form where there is snow, not rain, and where it is always cold.

3 Mark on your map where you would expect ice sheets to form.

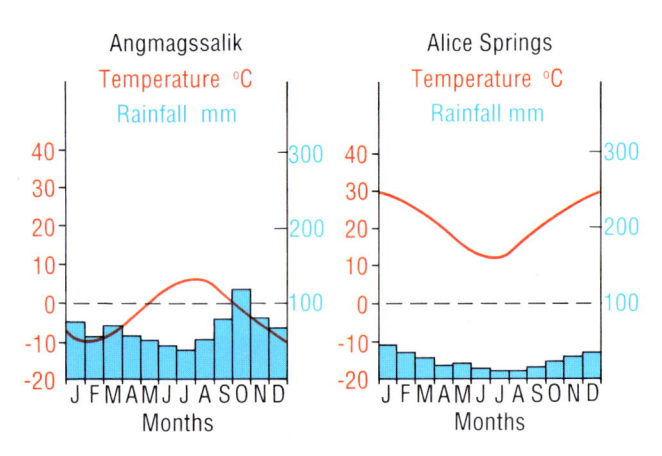

These graphs show how temperature and rainfall change during an average year at two towns around the Earth.

4 Which town is often at temperatures below the freezing point of water?

5 Which town has midwinter in June?

6 Which town has the most rain?

7 Which town is in a desert?

8 The two towns are marked by letters A and B on the map. Which letter marks which town?

24

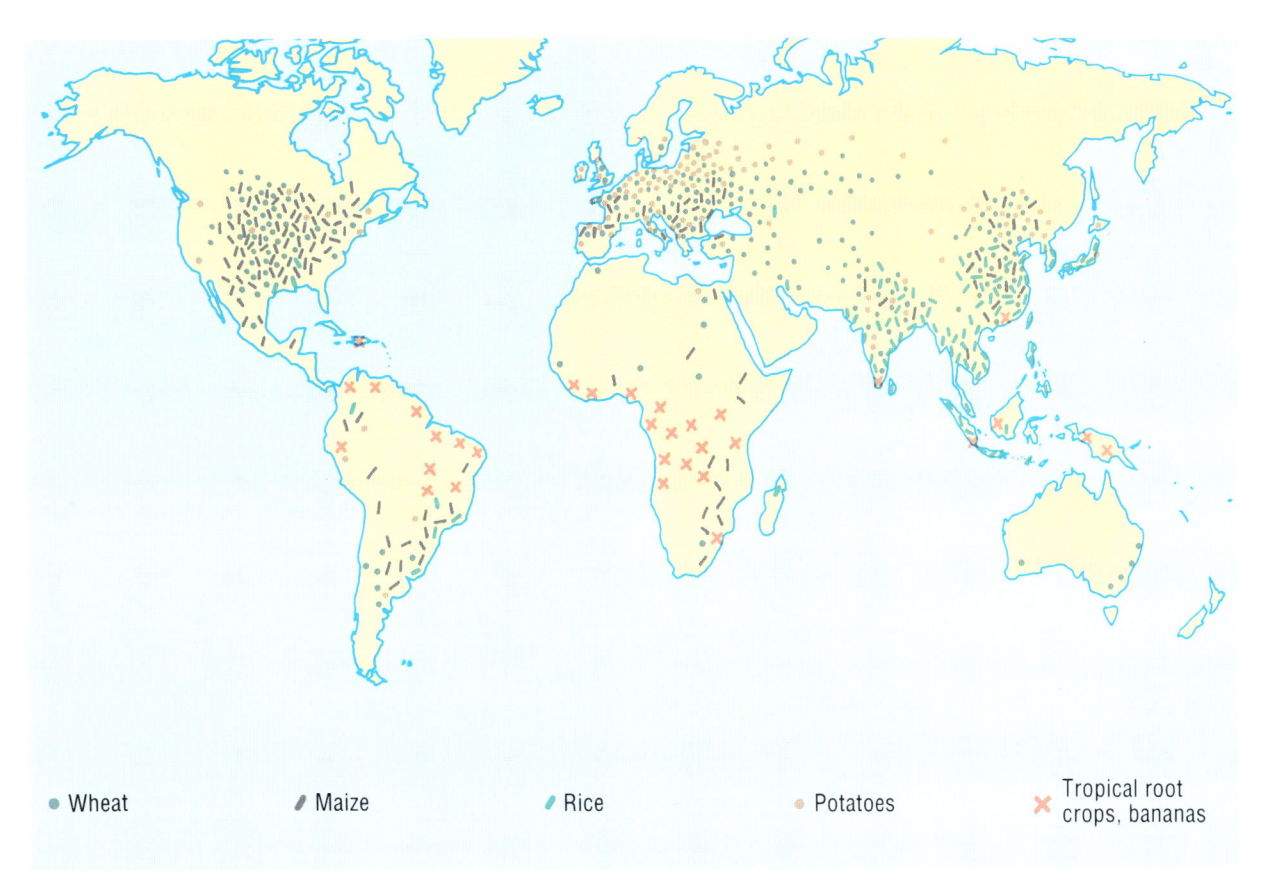

● Wheat ／ Maize ／ Rice ● Potatoes ✗ Tropical root crops, bananas

Food crops around the world

This map shows where some main kinds of food crops are grown.

9 Draw up a chart to show the kinds of climate that each food crop prefers, by comparing this map with the one on the opposite page.

Investigating crops

Use seeds of some of these food crops to devise an investigation of the conditions they prefer.

You need to think about ways of modelling different types of climate. Make the investigation fair. For example you will need: (a) to plant a reasonable number of each type of seed; (b) to choose suitable equipment to control your 'artificial climates'; (c) to decide how to tell if a crop is 'successful'.

This kind of experiment is done by organisations such as the United Nations to help advise farmers about new crops.

Climate is only one factor influencing which crops are grown in an area. People may prefer other foods, or may be able to sell other crops for more money.

Farming in Nigeria

Section Two

Wind and Rain

2.7 Stormy weather

In September 1989, Hurricane Hugo, a powerful tropical storm, swept across the islands of the Caribbean and across the sea to hit the coast of the State of Carolina. It caused large-scale damage and many casualties.

H at the start of *Hugo* tells us that it was the eighth hurricane of 1989. Hurricane names start from *A* each year, so the eighth hurricane has a name starting with *H*, the eighth letter of the alphabet. The name **hurricane** is used for tropical storms in the Atlantic Ocean. Tropical storms in the Pacific are called **typhoons** and in the Indian Ocean they are called **cyclones**.

The energy of hurricanes comes from the Sun's heat, like all weather energy. Hurricanes start over warm, tropical oceans, where the temperature is over 27°C. They begin as seawater takes in heat from the Sun and turns to water vapour. This becomes a very low pressure spinning whirlpool of wind, cloud and rain.

1 Why does water need energy to turn into water vapour? Explain, using ideas about *molecules*.

To turn 1 kg of water into water vapour takes about 2000 kJ of energy. Warm air carries this water vapour up until it reaches a height of about 1 km. There, the water vapour turns back to water droplets, starting a cloud. This gives *out* heat into the air.

2 What happens to the air molecules when they gain this heat energy?

2000 kJ given out by condensing water vapour will raise the temperature of 1 kg of air by about 2°C.

3 If air becomes warmer, does it rise or fall?

The rising warm air allows cool air to flow into the area below, starting spiral winds.

4 Why does the wind start to spin around the centre of the hurricane? (See page 18.)

Speeding up the wind

Spin a small object on a string around your hand, then let the string wind around your hand. As the string gets shorter, what happens to the speed of the object?

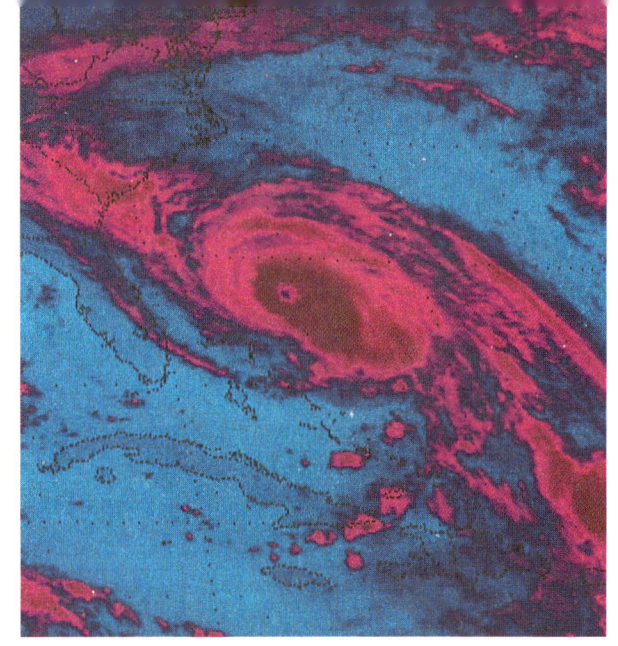

Hurricane Hugo photographed by a satellite. The false colours are made by a computer.

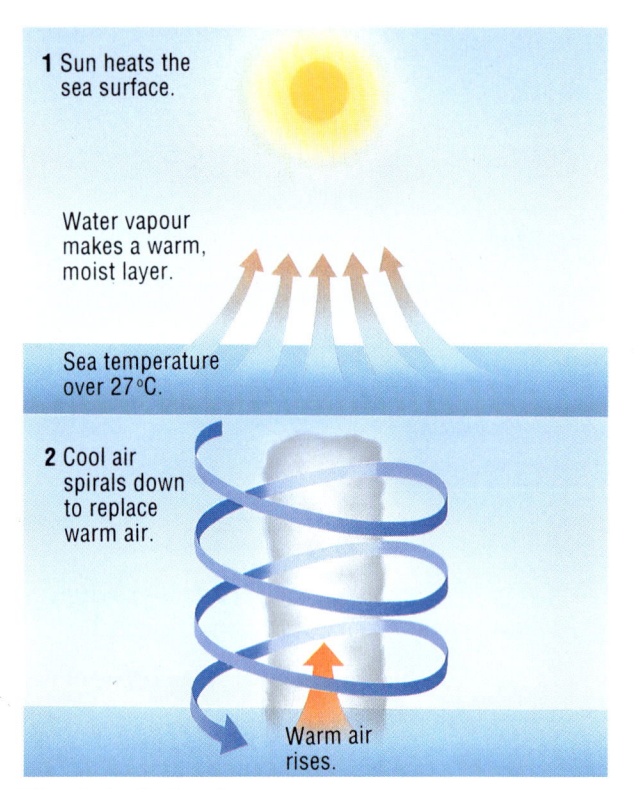

1 Sun heats the sea surface.

Water vapour makes a warm, moist layer.

Sea temperature over 27°C.

2 Cool air spirals down to replace warm air.

Warm air rises.

The start of a hurricane

The air spiralling into a hurricane speeds up in the same way. Eventually it cannot speed up any more because of friction with the sea. Then it has to rise up, leaving a still centre about 25 km across. This is the **eye** of the storm.

The winds in hurricanes can reach speeds of over 300 km/hour.

5 Imagine you are on a tropical island. Describe how you might experience a hurricane as it came towards you, as it went past, and as it moved away.

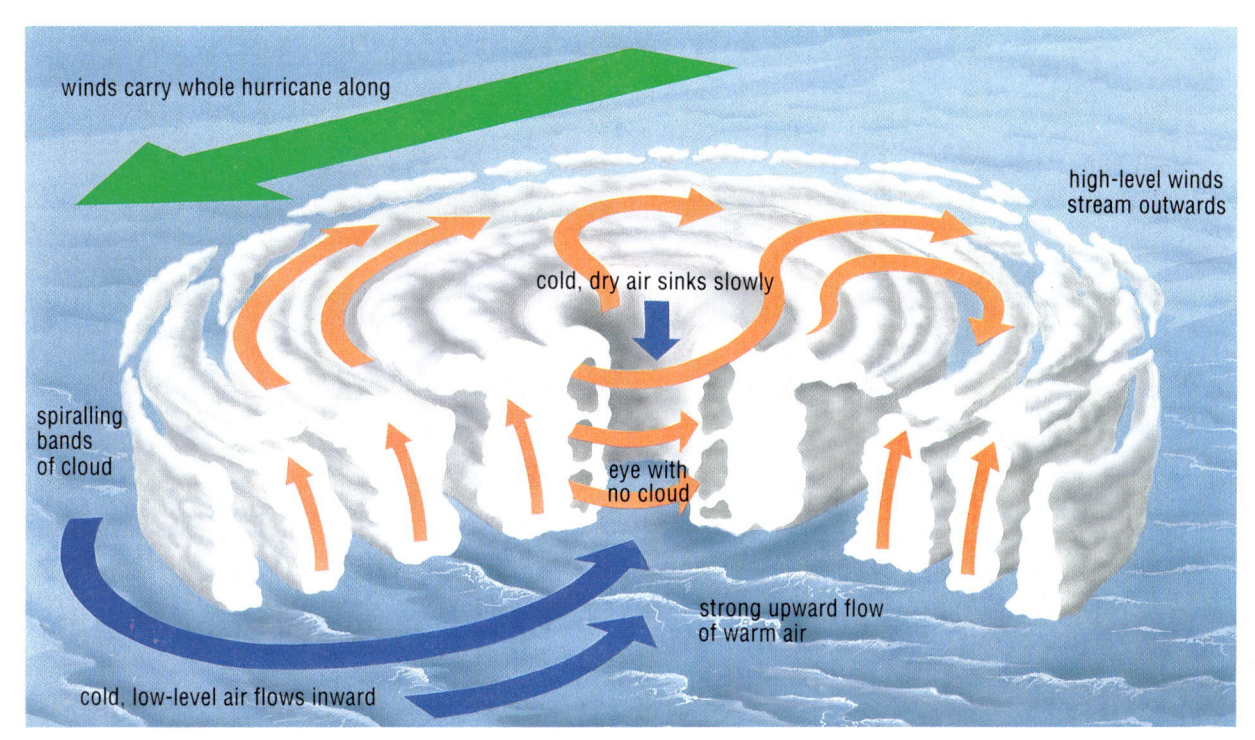

The structure of a hurricane

Thunderstorms, lightning and hail.

Thunderstorms happen when large deep clouds build up over areas of warm, moist, rising air. This may happen over hills or over a cold front.

The moist air rises to about 2 km where the air temperature is about 0°C. In this cold air, the water vapour turns to water droplets which are heavier than air and start to fall. As they fall, they cool the air, and so the cloud is full of both warm rising and cool falling air currents. Some droplets are caught in rising currents and go round the cycle again.

They may go up and down repeatedly and become coated with many layers of ice, making **hailstones**. Hailstones up to 13 cm diameter form in this way, even in summer. The inside of the hailstone has a negative charge, and the outside has a positive charge.

Water droplets freeze from the outside. When the centre of the drop freezes, it expands and the outer coat of ice can be shattered. The heavier centre falls, carrying its negative charge. The lighter outer fragments rise up with their positive charges. Electrical charges build up in the cloud: negative charges at the base of the cloud and positive charges at the top.

When the electrical charge is large enough, a sudden electric current jumps from the cloud to another cloud or to the earth. This is seen as a flash of **lightning**. It instantly heats the air alongs its path and so that air expands violently, making a **thunderclap**.

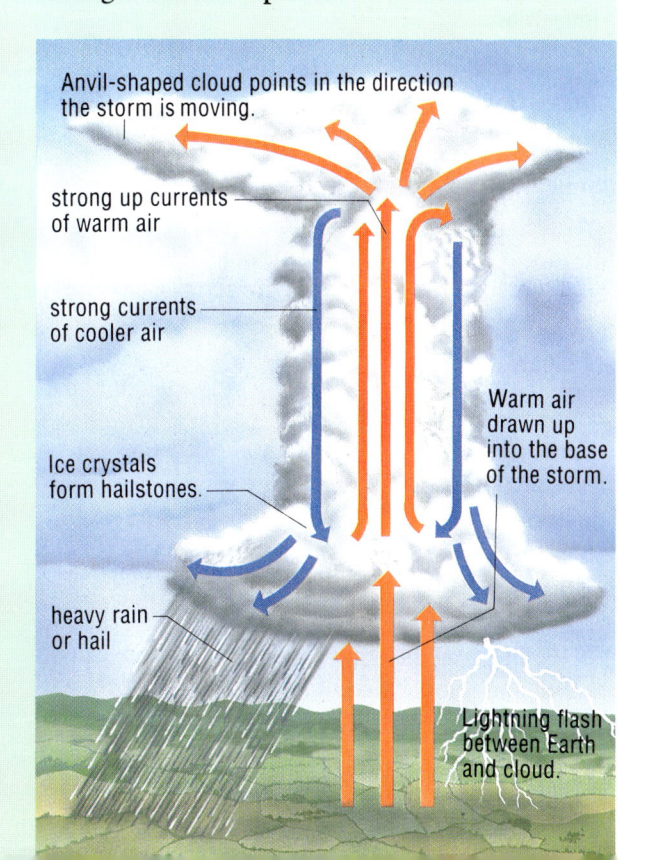

27

Section Two

2.8 The atmosphere

The atmosphere, or layer of gas around our planet, is a complicated mixture. One way to separate the different gases in the mixture we call air is to cool it down to a liquid. Because the different components of air have different boiling points, gentle warming of liquid air releases one gas at a time. Many industries use liquid air or one of the different gases it contains.

Liquid air is a valuable commercial product for many industries.

At $-200°C$ dry air becomes a liquid. If this liquid is heated gently to $-196°C$, about 78 per cent of it turns to gas again. This gas is **nitrogen**.

If the remaining liquid is heated to $-190°C$, another 1 per cent of the liquid turns to gas. This is **argon**.

The 21 per cent that is left is nearly all **oxygen**.

1 Draw a pie chart to show the *percentage composition* of the three main gases in air.

Carbon dioxide makes up only about 0.033 per cent of air but this amount is increasing. It is more important than it appears from the percentage alone.

2 Out of 10,000 molecules of air, how many are there of each of the four gases mentioned so far?

3 We began by thinking about *dry* air. What other important gas must have been taken out first?

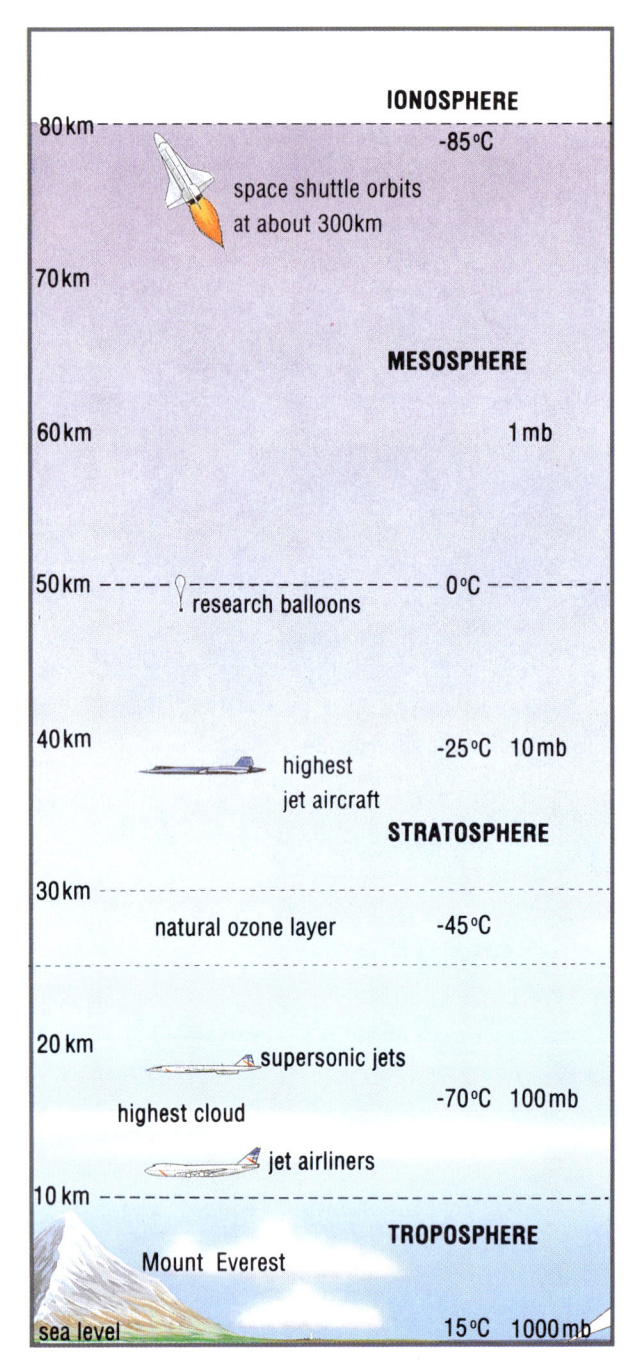

The atmosphere of the Earth

The weight of the atmosphere pressing down on us at sea level is enormous – about 10,000 kilograms on every square metre. At the top of Mount Everest this pressure is reduced to about a third.

The structure of the atmosphere

4 Use this diagram of the atmosphere to make a table to describe the various layers. You will need columns for name, height, temperature and pressure.

Section 2 questions

1 Match these instruments to their correct use: barometer, thermometer, anemometer; temperature, pressure, wind speed.

2 In what way is the flight of a hot air balloon similar to the way winds are generated? Explain your answer in terms of how air molecules behave when the temperature changes.

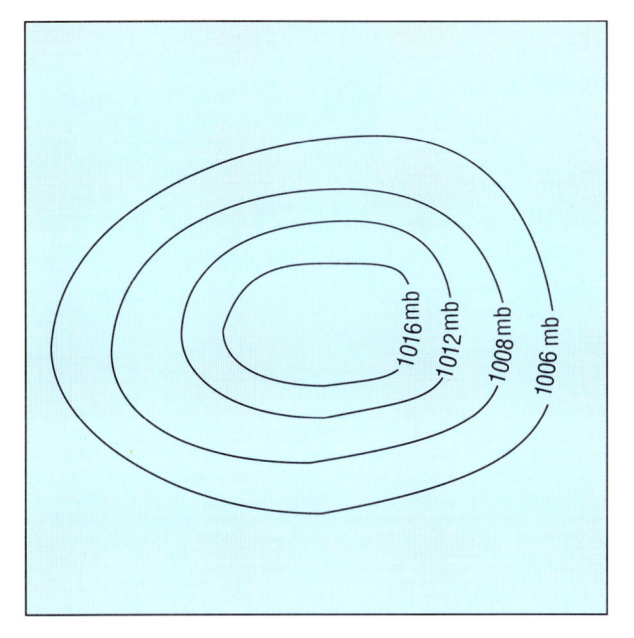

3 Does this diagram show a high pressure area or a low pressure area? Which way would the wind go around it if it was: a) in the northern hemisphere; b) in the southern hemisphere?

4 Draw a labelled cross-section to show how cold and warm fronts affect the weather.

5 Put the following parts of the water cycle in order in a circle, with arrows to show direction:
*evaporating oceans   running rivers
falling rain   condensing clouds*

6 Draw a diagram to show why areas near the Earth's poles are cooler than areas near the equator.

7 Explain, using a diagram, how the position of the Sun in the sky changes throughout the year.

8 What differences would you find between the climate of deserts and the climate of rain forests?

9 What kind of climate conditions are preferred by: a) maize b) wheat c) rice d) potatoes?

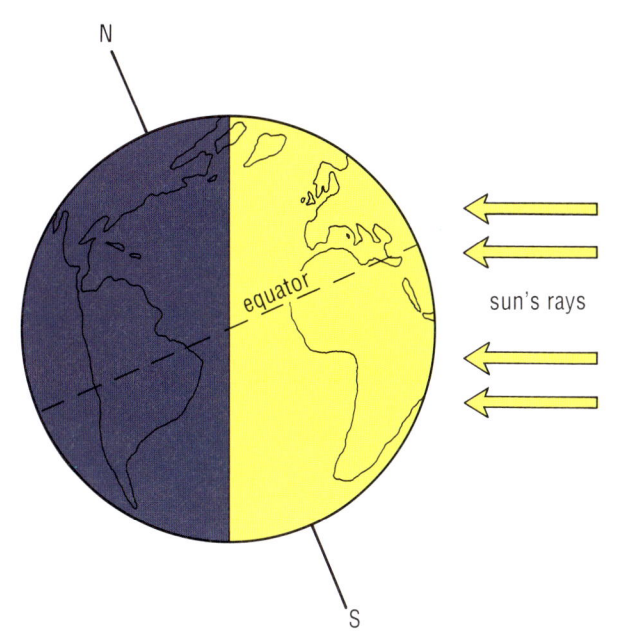

10 In this diagram of the Earth, is it winter or summer in the northern hemisphere?

11 What would you need to know if you were an African farming expert about to introduce new crops in a particular area? Make a list.

12 Draw labelled diagrams to show the structure of: a) hurricanes b) thunderstorms. List the hazards of these two kinds of storm.

13 Copy and complete this chart about the gases in the air:

Gas	% in air	Symbol
Oxygen		O_2
	78%	
		Ar

14 What differences would there have been if Stonehenge had been built in Australia?

15 Collect newspaper weather reports giving temperatures in different cities around the world during a week. Use a suitable computer program to display this information.

16 Using weather satellite photographs, make a display of how the weather changed in Britain during one week. If possible, collect weather maps from newspapers from the same period and show how the maps relate to the photographs. Add notes on the actual weather for each day.

SECTION THREE
THE TIME DETECTIVES

3.1 The fossil hunters

Fossils are one of the keys to Earth history. Layers of rocks are like the pages of a book telling the story of the Earth. Fossils act as page numbers to put the story in order.

Leonardo da Vinci was one of the first to see that fossils are remains of ancient life.

Famous fossil collectors

Mary Anning lived in Lyme Regis in the early nineteenth century. At the age of 12 she found a new fossil animal, the *Ichthyosaurus*.

Mary Anning made her living selling fossils to museums and to royal customers across Europe. The tongue-twister "She sells sea-shells by the sea shore." is thought to be about Mary Anning.

Mary Anning

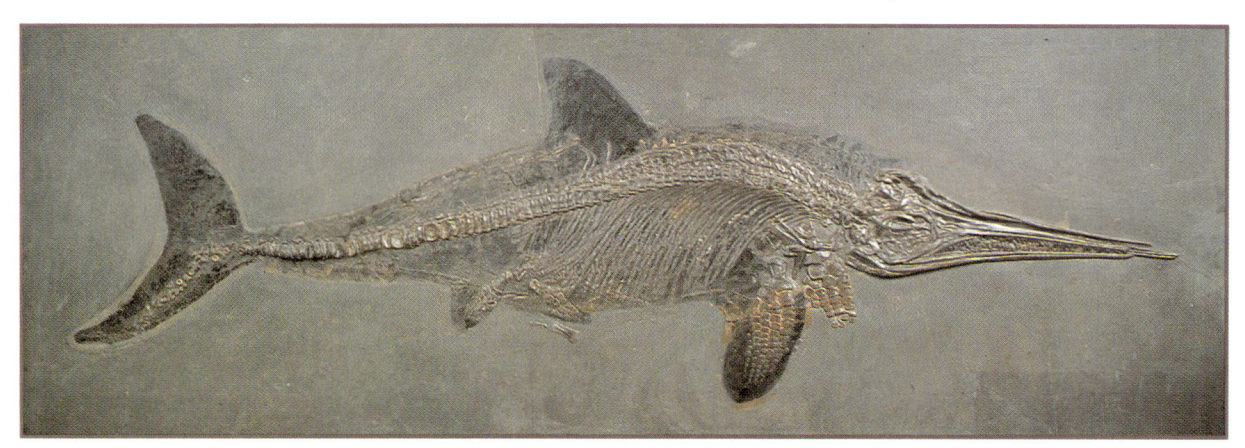

An *Ichthyosaurus*

The *Ichthyosaurus* was one of many new kinds of fossil found during the eighteenth and nineteenth centuries. These fossils showed that life had been different in the past. Eventually this discovery led to the **theory of evolution**. New kinds of living things have *evolved and then become extinct* during the history of the Earth.

1 Trace a diagram of the Ichthyosaurus, and add labels to show these parts of its skeleton: skull; backbone; flippers; tail; ribs.

> **William Walker**, a plumber and amateur scientist, was looking for fossils in a claypit in southern England in 1984. He found a fossil claw from a previously unknown dinosaur. It is now called *Baryonyx walkeri*. *Baryonyx* means 'heavy claw'. New fossils are found every year, giving more clues about the history of life.

30

Many fossils were found when canals were dug across England in the eighteenth century. One canal engineer, **William Smith**, noticed that each rock layer had its own special set of fossils. Deeper layers were assumed to be older than those formed above them.

By recording rock layers and their fossils, Smith drew a cross-section across England and Wales.

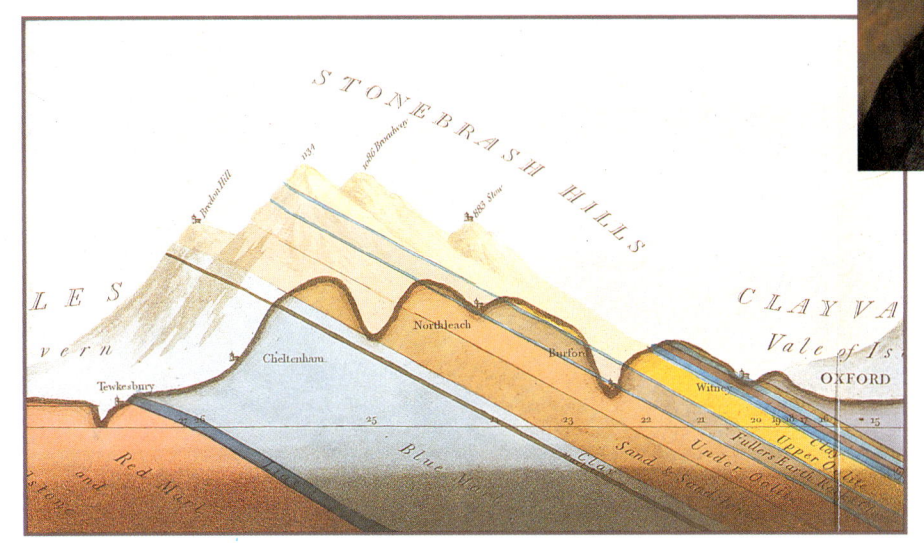

William Smith

The hills and layers are not this steep. The vertical scale has been exaggerated.

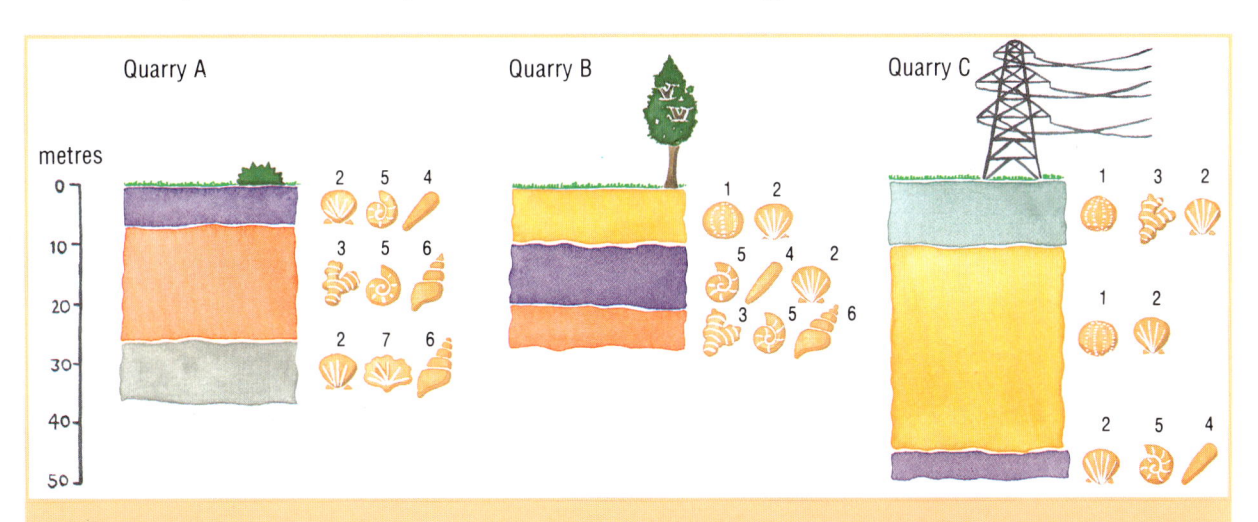

Correlation of rock layers

These columns are records of rock layers found in quarries a few kilometers apart.

- Trace copies of the columns.
- Cut out your copies as separate strips.
- Lay them out to overlap where the same layer appears in more than one column.
- Draw a single column to show the complete sequence in the area around the quarries.

2 Answer these questions about the sequence:

a) Which type of fossil lived first?
b) Which type of fossil changed least during the time these layers were forming?
c) Which type of creature only lived during the time one layer was forming?

3 On your column, mark when fossil 5
a) evolved and b) became extinct.

31

3.2 Layers of Earth history

During the nineteenth century scientists who followed William Smith divided up the sequence of rocks into sections. They drew boundaries at points where the fossils showed major changes. They produced the **geological column**. This divides time into **geological time periods**. The question still remained: how long had all these rocks taken to form?

The Geological Column

William Smith's labels	Time periods	Some typical British fossils
	Quaternary	human skull, mammoth (tooth)
London clay	Tertiary	snail, bivalve shellfish
chalk / clunch clay	Cretaceous	ammonite, lampshell, sea urchin
oolite series / blue marl	Jurassic	lampshell, ammonite, sea urchin, coral
red marl	Triassic	bivalve shellfish, fish (tooth)
	Permian	bivalve shellfish, fish (tail), lampshell
coal measures	Carboniferous	tree root, coral, amphibian (skull)
red rhab	Devonian	lampshell, fish
killas, slates	Silurian	coral, trilobite, lampshell, graptolite
killas, slates	Ordovician	graptolite, lampshell, trilobite
killas, slates	Cambrian	lampshell, trilobite, trilobite
	Precambrian	Fossils hardly ever found in Precambrian rocks

Scale: 0 1cm

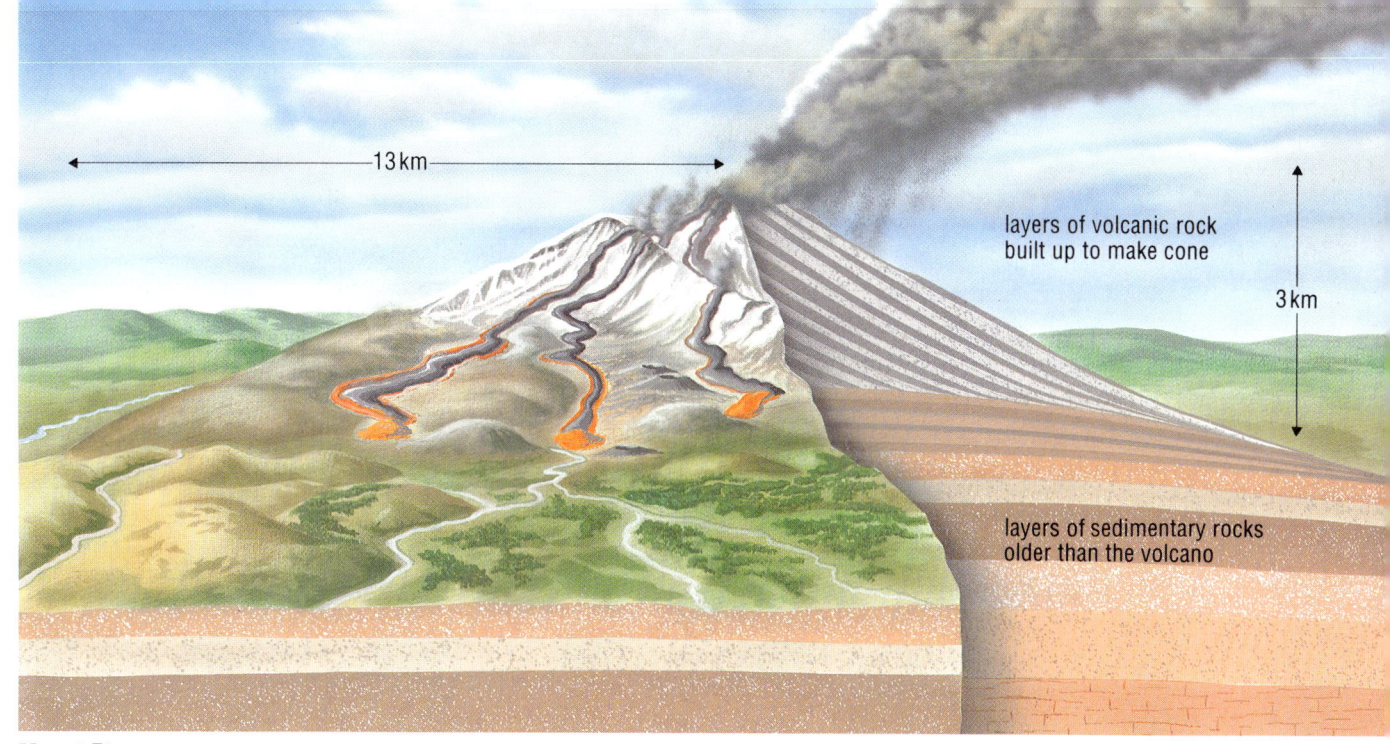

Mount Etna

Thousands of years ago, the Chaldean people of Iraq believed Earth to be 21,500,000 years old. Hindu thinkers in India decided Earth was created in 1,972,947,101 BC.

In the fifth century BC, the Greek **Herodotus** wrote about the delta of the River Nile. He decided that it was made of mud washed down the river. Even if this took tens of thousands of years, it could happen in 'the vast stretch of time which has passed before I was born'.

In later times, in Europe, ideas about the age of the Earth had to fit the creation story in Genesis, the first book of the Christian Bible.

In seventeeth-century England people tried to find a date for creation using lifespans of people in the Bible. October 23rd, 4004 BC was Archbishop Ussher's answer, and it became the official view of many Christians.

Charles Lyell

It was hard to explain the many layers of rocks, and fossil evidence of slowly changing life, within only six thousand years of time.

In the 1830s, the Scot **Charles Lyell** studied the volcano Mount Etna in Sicily. Mount Etna is roughly cone-shaped, with a height of 3 km. Lyell discovered that it had erupted 2 km³ of rock in 200 years.

1 How much rock does Etna erupt in a year?

2 Find the total volume of rock in Mount Etna; use the formula:

Volume of cone $= \frac{1}{3} \times$ (radius)$^2 \times$ height $\times \pi$
(where $\pi = 3.14$)

To find the age of Mount Etna, Lyell needed to divide the second answer by the first answer.

3 Find the age of Mount Etna.

Having put a date on Mount Etna, Lyell looked at the fossil shells in the sedimentary rock beneath the oldest lava. They were identical to the seashells found on the Sicilian beaches at the time. He concluded that although the sedimentary rocks below the volcano must be at least 50,000 years old, they were still only from the most recent geological time period, the **Quaternary**. This suggested that the Earth could be millions of years old.

The thickness of the sedimentary layers of the geological column could be a clue. In the 1870s **Samuel Haughton** of Ireland estimated that 1 m of sediment took about 25,000 years to form. He calculated that the Cambrian part of the geological column was 60 km deep.

4 Find the time from the start of the Cambrian period to the present using Haughton's figures.

3.3 How old is the Earth?

In 1862 **Lord Kelvin** worked out an age for Earth assuming it had started as a hot molten ball and cooled down to its present state. He calculated an age of between 20 and 400 million years. He pointed out that this could be wrong if the Earth had some extra source of heat.

Radioactivity was the real key to time, and the source of extra heat. Radioactivity was discovered in 1895 by **Henri Becquerel**. In 1902 **Ernest Rutherford** discovered the idea of **half-life**. This is the time taken by half of any sample of radioactive atoms to change to another kind of atom. For example, **uranium** changes through a series of other atoms to **lead** with a half-life of 4510 million years. Radioactive decay is a key source of the Earth's heat.

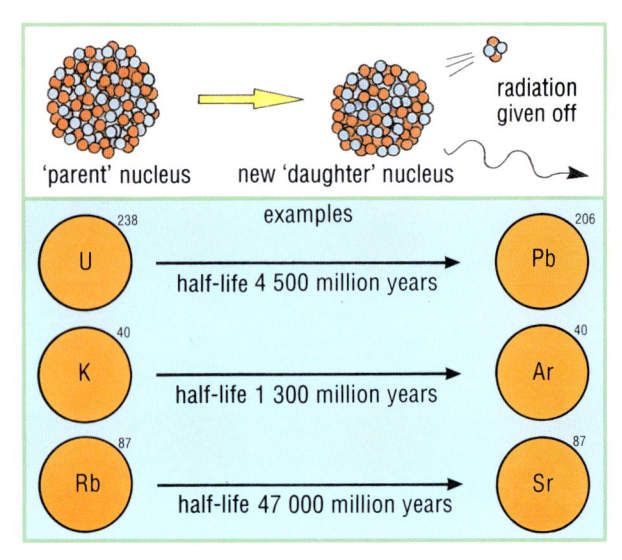

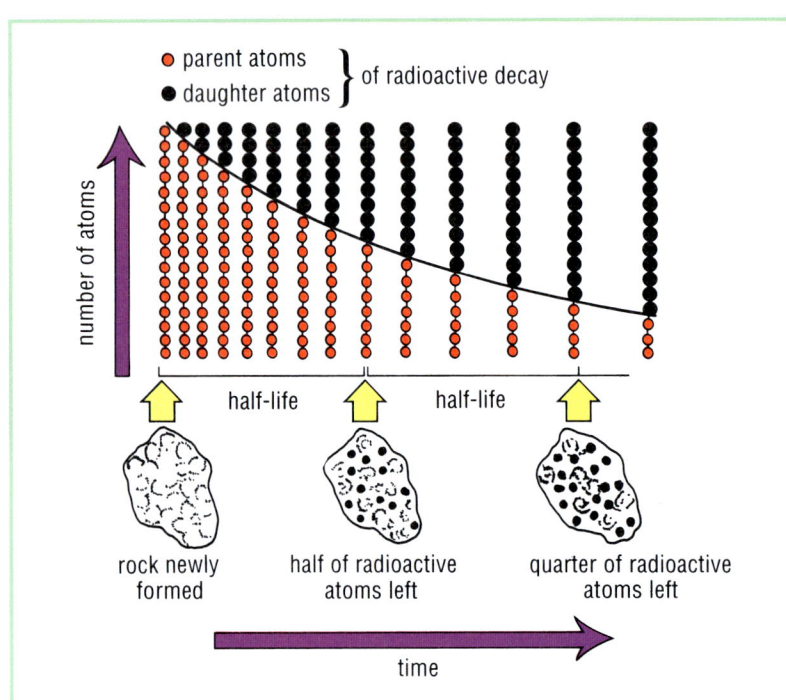

Many rocks contain small amounts of uranium. By measuring uranium and lead in rocks, in 1913 **Arthur Holmes** finally found ages of some rocks. This method is called **radiometric dating**. It can mainly be used on igneous and metamorphic rocks.

Radiometric dating

Accurate dating involves other elements. The best are **potassium** which changes to **argon** with a half-life of 1300 million years, and **rubidium** which changes to **strontium** with a half-life of 47,000 million years.

1 After three half-lives have passed, what fraction of a sample of radioactive atoms would still be unchanged?

2 A rock sample is found to have only 25 per cent of its radioactive potassium left, the other 75 per cent has turned to argon. How old is the rock?

Arthur Holmes

So far the oldest rocks found on Earth come from Greenland; they are metamorphic rocks and are 4000 million years old. Ocean floor rocks are up to 200 million years old. Moonrocks 4200 million years old were collected by the *Apollo* crews. Meteorites are up to 4600 years old. This is probably the age of the planets, including Earth.

Earth history is divided into four **eras**, and each of these is divided into **periods**. The time-scale is hard to imagine, but the diagram will give you some idea.

Gneiss (2700 million years old)

Moon rock

Present day

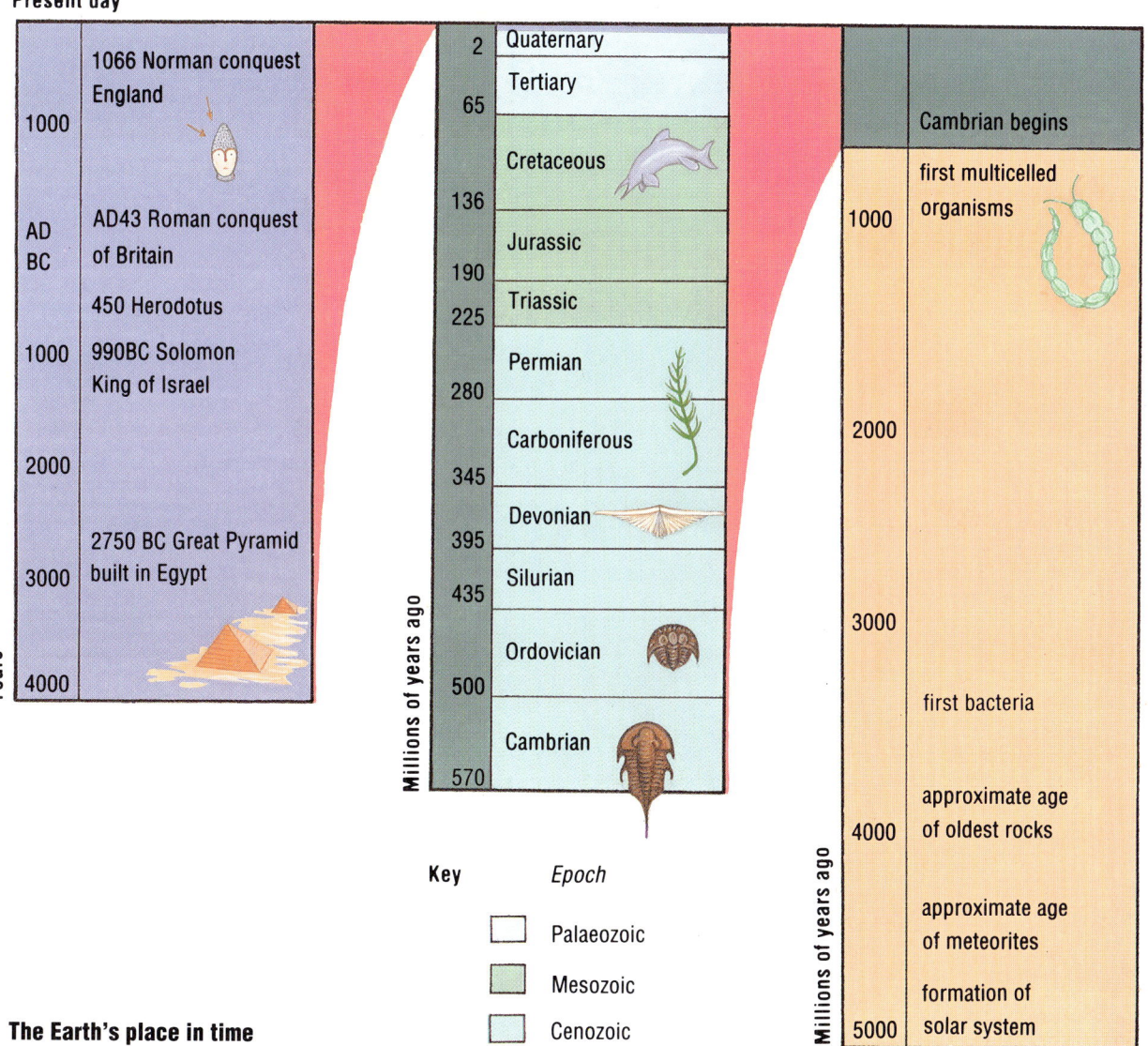

Years	Events
1000	1066 Norman conquest England
AD / BC	AD43 Roman conquest of Britain
	450 Herodotus
1000	990BC Solomon King of Israel
2000	
3000	2750 BC Great Pyramid built in Egypt
4000	

Millions of years ago	Period
2	Quaternary
65	Tertiary
136	Cretaceous
190	Jurassic
225	Triassic
280	Permian
345	Carboniferous
395	Devonian
435	Silurian
500	Ordovician
570	Cambrian

Key *Epoch*
- Palaeozoic
- Mesozoic
- Cenozoic

Millions of years ago	Event
	Cambrian begins
1000	first multicelled organisms
2000	
3000	first bacteria
4000	approximate age of oldest rocks
	approximate age of meteorites
5000	formation of solar system

The Earth's place in time

SHAPING THE EARTH

4.1 Weathering

The rocks at the surface of our planet are under attack. Too slowly for us to notice in everyday life, rocks are *broken down* into smaller bits or *dissolved* in the water around them. The processes which cause this are called **weathering processes**.

Weathering processes cause *changes* to the rocks, and these changes are either *physical* or *chemical*.

Physical weathering happens when *forces* open up any weak points in the rock.

Chemical weathering happens when there is a *chemical reaction* between the rock and its surroundings.

Which of these examples are physical weathering? Which are chemical weathering?

1 When a seed falls into a crack in a rock it may find conditions good enough to allow germination. A stem grows upwards from the crack and a root grows down. The growing plant forces the crack to widen.

2 Some rocks contain *iron compounds*. The oxygen and water in the environment can react with the iron to make *rust*.

3 Rainwater is slightly *acidic* because it picks up *carbon dioxide* from the air as it falls. This weak *carbonic acid* can attack some rocks, especially *limestones*.

4 Groundwater becomes *acidic* if it runs through soil containing rotting plants. These make *humic acid* which also attacks limestones.

5 When water turns to ice it expands. If this happens in cracks in rocks, the crack widens.

6 Rocks are mixtures of different minerals. When they are heated by the sun, these minerals expand by different amounts. Each grain pushes against the next, making the rock weaker.

Investigating weathering

- Weathering processes can be shown in these activities. Decide whether each activity is about physical or chemical weathering.

- Each of these can be developed into a more accurate investigation of a weathering process. Equipment that you might use to do this is listed in brackets.

- Fill a plastic bottle with water and put it in a freezer overnight. *(large graduated plastic syringe)*

- Wearing goggles, heat a granite lump in a bunsen flame for two minutes, then plunge it into cold water. Repeat this six times. *(filter paper, microscope)*

- Put equal volumes of dilute hydrochloric acid in three test tubes. Add equal masses of limestone to each, one as a single lump, one as small grains and one as powder. Compare the rate of production of bubbles. *(electronic balances, stopwatch)*

- Put some iron filings in a test tube with water. Leave them to stand for a few days. *(iron wool, iron nail)*

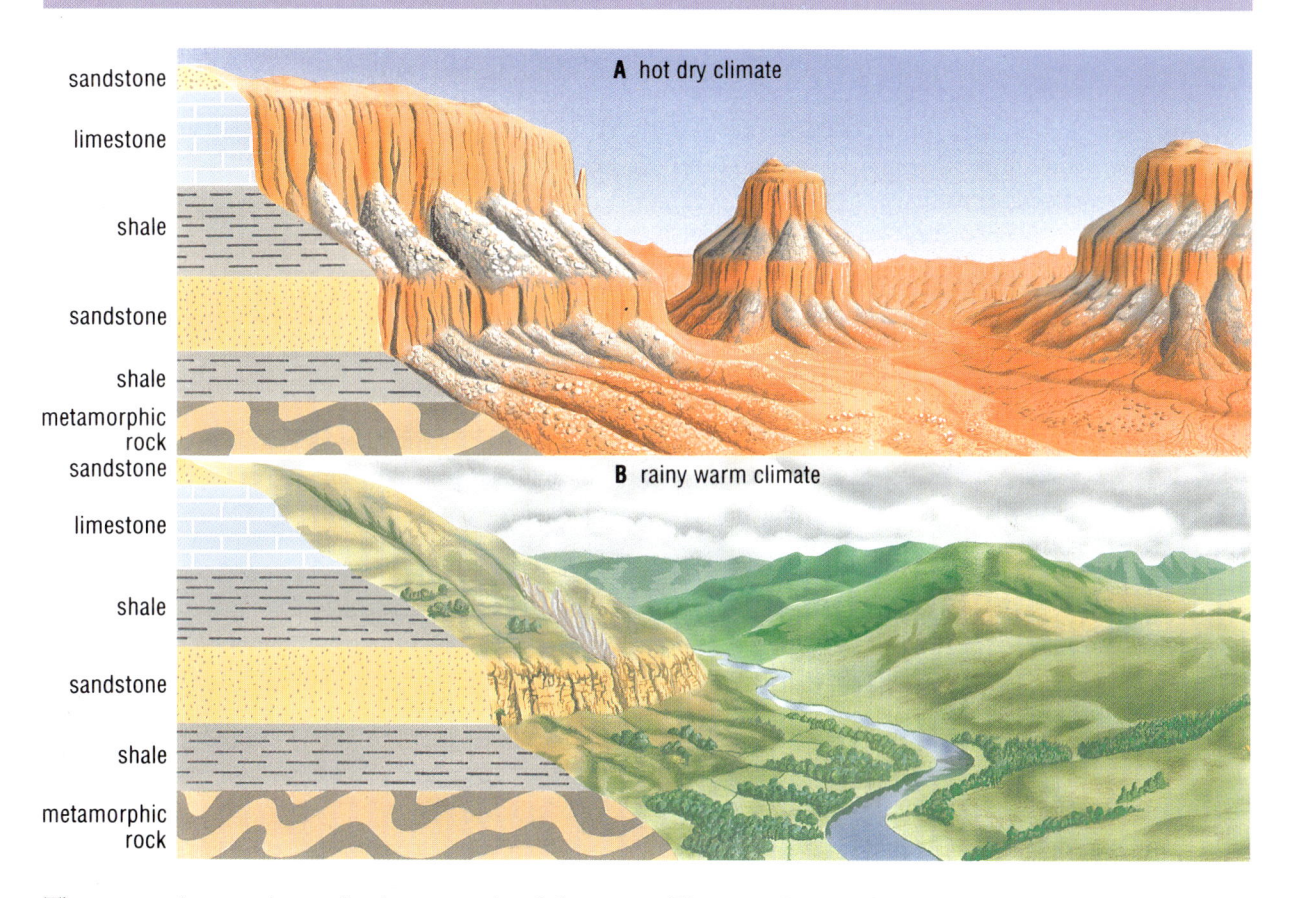

A hot dry climate

sandstone
limestone
shale
sandstone
shale
metamorphic rock

B rainy warm climate

sandstone
limestone
shale
sandstone
shale
metamorphic rock

These two pictures show a landscape made of the same layers of rock, but in different climates. The rocks have weathered differently.

1 Which rock types tend to form steep cliffs in a) wet, warm climates b) hot, dry climates?

2 In which climate does chemical weathering seem to have most effect? Explain why.

The products of weathering

Weathering produces *rock fragments* of all sizes and *chemical solutions* in groundwater. If the rock fragments stay in place, they form the starting material for **soils**. The type of weathering, and how quickly it happens, depends on the climate.

4.2 Soils and sediment transport

If rock fragments produced by weathering stay in place they form soils.

Looking at soils

- Study a variety of soil types and produce a report on the differences between the soils.
- Examine each soil under a microscope.
- Shake up each soil in water and leave to stand.
- Compare each soil with the rocks found under it. What evidence is there that the soil is made partly from weathered rock?
- Cut a **soil profile** in a suitable place. It needs to be about 1 metre deep.
- Compare the soil (a) in the top 15 cm (b) at about 50 cm down (c) below 75 cm.

A soil profile

From bare rock, soil takes about 1000 years to form by the action of weathering processes and the effects of plants and animals.

Transport of weathering products

If enough *force* acts on the products of weathering, they move.

To move rock fragments or solutions takes energy. The energy starts as potential energy.

1 What force pulls rock fragments downhill?

2 What type of energy do the fragments gain as they start moving?

If gravity is the only force acting, then rock fragments on a flat surface stay in place. On slopes they may be held in place by friction. If the slope is steep enough, friction cannot hold the fragments. **Landslips** happen when loose material moves under the effect of gravity.

Gravity may act on its own, but *water*, *wind* and *ice* are the main **transport agents** for sediment. Transport agents remove fragments, causing **erosion** of the landscape.

This road has collapsed because the underlying rock is unable to support the load placed on it.

Water transport

Water can carry sediment over the land either in **channels** or in **sheet wash**. Chemical solutions can be transported by channels and sheet wash, and also by groundwater.

This graph shows the results of experiments on sediment movement in water. The top curve shows the speeds at which sediment is *removed* from the point being studied. The bottom curve shows the speeds at which sediment is *deposited* on to the bed of the channel.

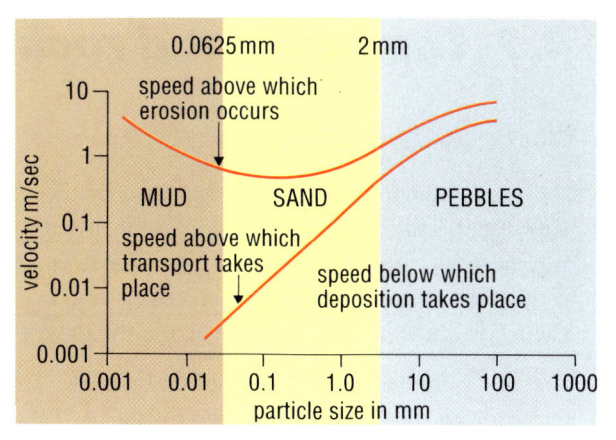

How moving water affects mud, sand and pebbles

3 a) What is the slowest water speed which can lift 1 mm sand grains from stream beds?
b) What size of particles could be picked up by a river flowing at 1 m/s?
c) If particles of mud with sizes about 0.01 mm have settled on a stream bed, what can you say about the speed of the water?

Pebbles, sand and mud only move if they have enough energy. The larger the particle, the more energy is needed to transport it.

Rivers and streams usually develop curved channels, or **meanders**. Water goes fast at the outside of the bends, slow on the inside.

4 a) Will the banks be worn away on the outside or the inside of bends in rivers?
b) Will sand be dropped on the inside or the outside of bends in rivers?

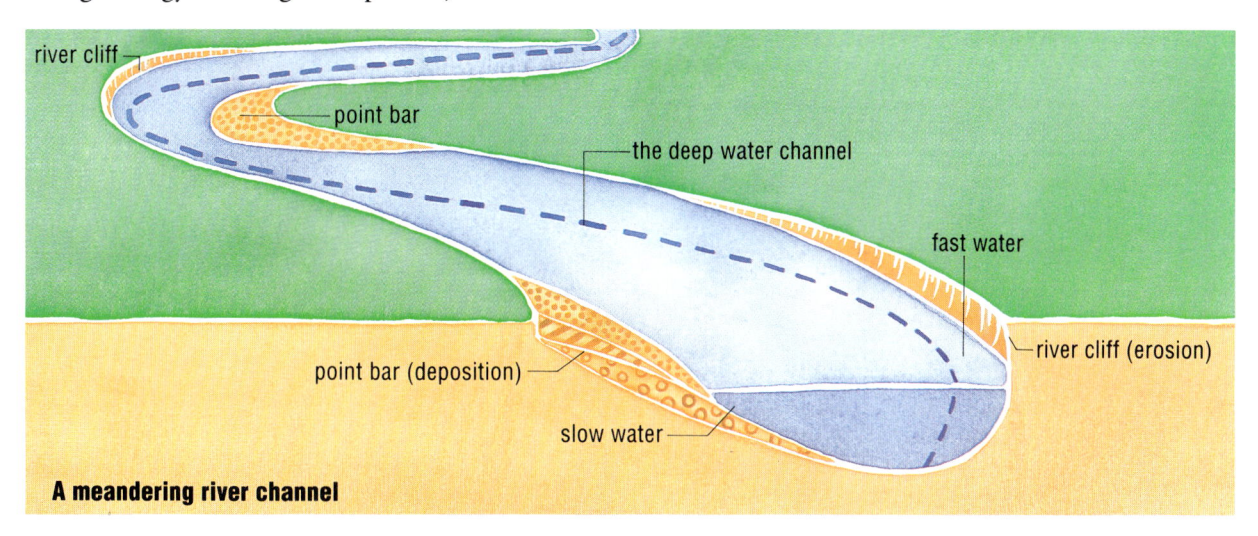

A meandering river channel

Investigating rivers

Test your answers by making a model river in a circular glass bowl.

- Fill a beaker with water and stand it in the centre of the bowl. The space between the beaker and the bowl will be your river channel.
- Put sand and water in the channel.
- Sweep the water around the channel with a watchglass.
- Write a report of what you do and see.

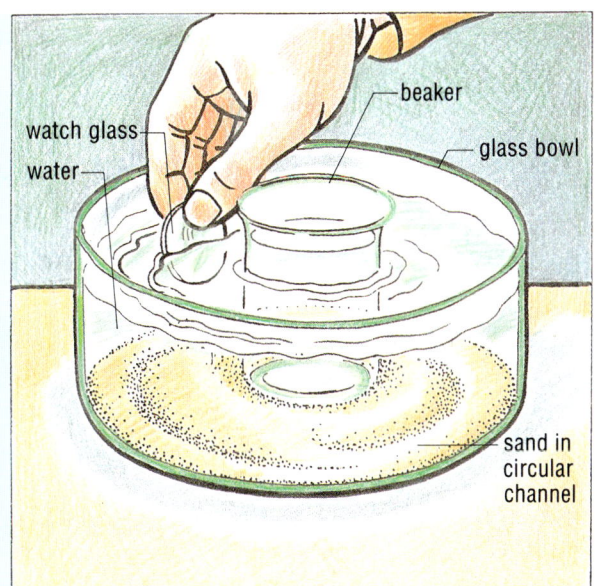

SECTION FOUR

SHAPING THE EARTH

4.3 Transport and rock formation

Wind transport

This **sand dune** in a desert is being blown by the wind. Sand is lifted off the back slope and carried over the top. It then drops down on to the steep front of the dune making a layer at a steep angle. The whole dune is slowly moving across the desert.

The sand in dunes is often made of tiny round grains, much rounder than river sand grains.

1 Suggest some possible reasons for dune sand grains being round.

Investigating sediment transport

A
Use a fan to blow mixed sand along a line of sticky carpet tape. Examine the tape with a lens. Repeat the experiment using different mixtures of sand, gravel and dry mud powder. What could this tell you about sand transport deposition?

B
Half-fill a tumble polisher drum with broken rock fragments and add water. Roll the drum for a week and compare the fragments with one of the original fragments. Try using different rock types in different drums.

Ice transport

Glaciers and **ice sheets** collect frost-shattered fragments from the rocks around them. As they move slowly downhill, they carry the fragments along. The fragments can fall through cracks into the ice. As the ice moves, it wears more fragments out of the rocks below. These add to the 'ice file' rubbing away at the Earth.

When the ice melts, the rock materials in the ice begin to wash out.

2 Suggest some possible reasons why most rock fragments dropped by ice have sharp corners and many are scratched.

Rock fragments come out of this glacier as it starts to melt.

Rock fragments and chemical solutions may turn into **sedimentary rocks** when deposited. This may happen in deserts, seas, or rivers, or other **depositional environments**.

Rock fragments may move around for some time before being deposited, or they may have settled quickly in the place where we find them.

A closer look at the way in which fragments are deposited can give us clues about how different sedimentary rocks were formed.

The graphs beneath show the results of sieving beach sand and glacial sand. The glacial sand is **badly sorted** – it has a wide range of sediment sizes. The beach sand is **well sorted**.

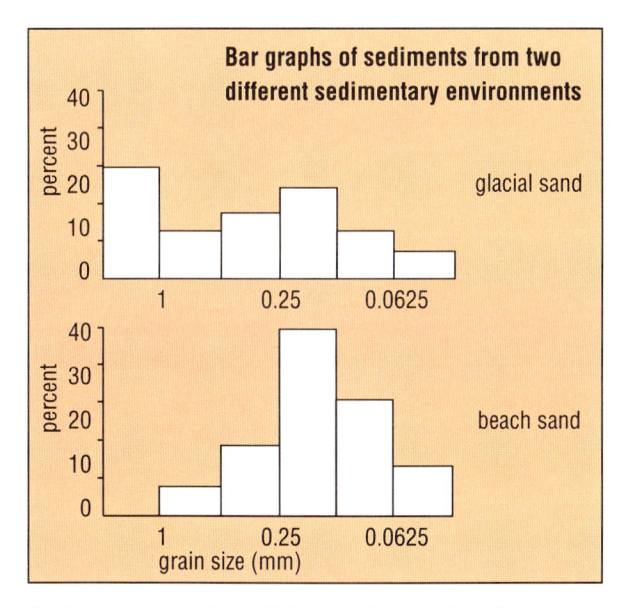

Sediment was collected from a river bed and a desert sand dune. 1 kg of each sample was sieved out. These are the results:

Grain size	Dune Sand	River Sand
Over 2 mm	0 grams	11 grams
1–2 mm	0 grams	35 grams
0.5–1 mm	95 grams	71 grams
0.25–0.5 mm	729 grams	327 grams
0.125–0.25 mm	160 grams	369 grams
0.062–0.125 mm	16 grams	153 grams
0.031–0.062 mm	0 grams	34 grams

3 Plot the results on bar graphs like those above. Which sand is well sorted? Suggest some reasons why the four sands have different size distributions.

Rock formation

Chemicals soaking through piles of sediment play a part in turning them into new rocks, as they cement the grains together.

4 Compare a sand with a sandstone. What are the differences between them? Explain your observations.

Sedimentary rocks made of fragments are given names based on the average size of the fragments in them.

Rocks made of **mud** particles, less than 0.0625 mm across ($\frac{1}{16}$th mm) are **shales** if they have thin layers, or **mudstones** if they do not have layers. **Sandstones** are made of particles with sizes from 0.0625 mm up to 2 mm. Rocks made of pebbles over 2 mm in size are called **conglomerates**.

Some very badly sorted sedimentary rocks can have a range of grain sizes from pebbles to mud. These are often called **greywacke sandstones**.

SECTION FOUR

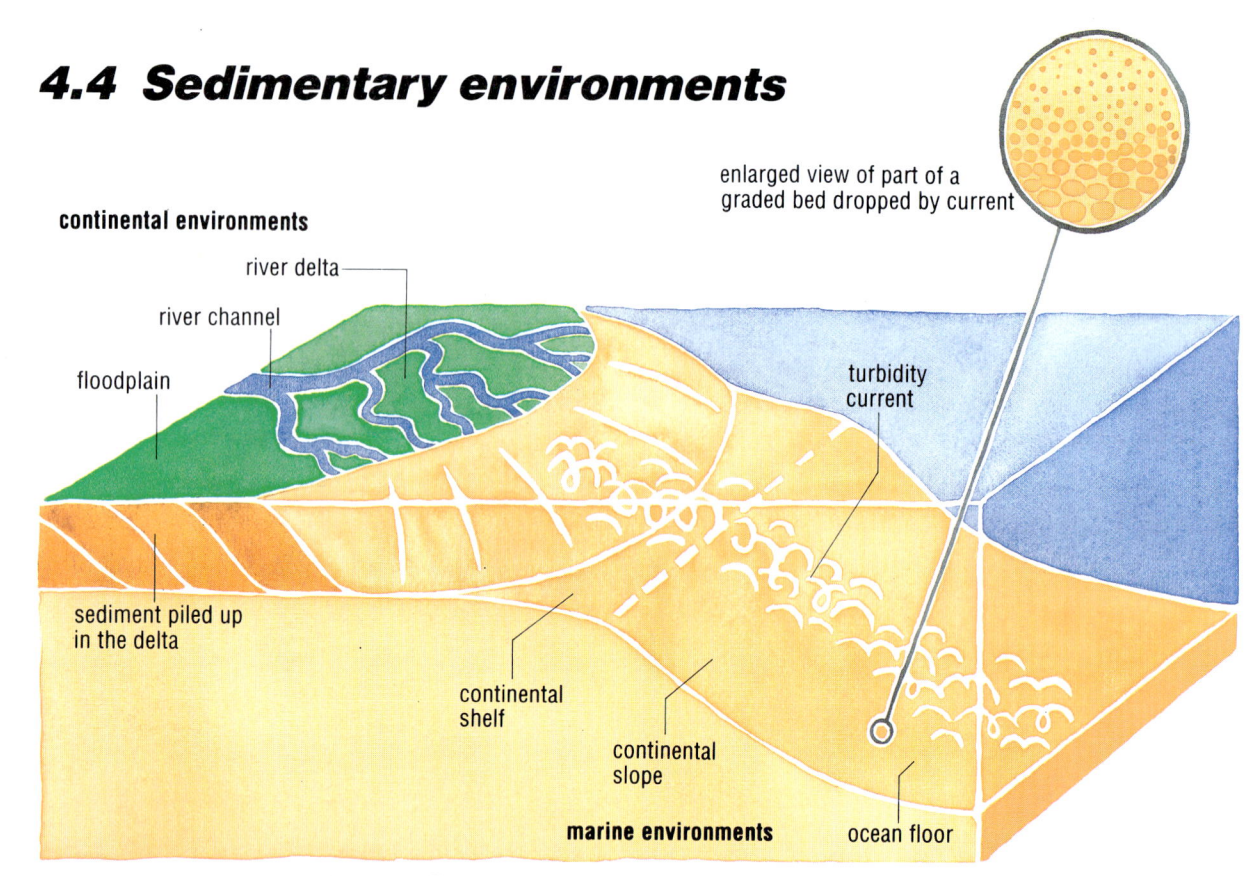

SHAPING THE EARTH

4.4 Sedimentary environments

How some sediments reach the ocean floor

Rivers may deposit sediment in channels and on flood plains. These are examples of **continental environments**.

Sediment may be carried further and out on to the continental shelf. When the river reaches the sea, the water slows and sediment is dropped. It makes flat layers called beds. The continental shelf and the deep sea bed are **marine environments**.

If the sediment builds up above water level at the sea it can form deltas. Delta tops and beaches are above water at low tide but below water at high tide. We call these **intertidal environments**.

1 Why do you think that water slows down when it enters the sea?

As sediment piles up on the continental shelf, it can slip off and form an underwater avalanche. This mixture of water and sediment flows down the slope getting faster, and then rushes across the ocean floor in a **turbidity current.** The larger particles drop first, as the flow slows down. The light mud particles cannot drop until the flow stops. They make layers of **graded bedding**, with bigger particles at the bottom. Greywacke sandstones are often produced in this way.

2 What might start the sediment moving off the continental shelf into deeper water?

Other sedimentary structures include ripples and dunes. **Ripples** form when water moves sediment.

Ripples on a beach

Dunes are large ripples made in faster, deeper flows. Dunes form both underwater and in wind deposits (see page 40). A cross-section of a dune shows layers tilted at angles. This is called **cross bedding**.

Sediment in flat layers has been moving too quickly or too slowly to form ripples or dunes.

3 What is the biggest grain that forms ripples?

Chemical and organic sediments

Evaporites are examples of chemical sediments. They are made when solutions dry up leaving salts behind in layers of crystals.

Seawater is a solution containing many salts:

Salts in seawater

Chemical	Percentage	Order of solubility
Mg and K salts	18.10	1
NaCl	78.04	2
CaSO$_4$	3.48	3
CaCO$_3$	0.33	4

Calcium carbonate, CaCO$_3$, is only just soluble in water, and will form crystals in warm shallow water, when about half of the original water has evaporated.

4 In what kind of climate would evaporites form?

5 If some seawater was evaporated away completely, in what order would the chemicals make crystals on the seabed?

Living things can use chemicals from seawater to make hard parts such as shells or bones. **Corals** and other animals can build up large underwater structures called **reefs** from calcium carbonate. Corals will only live in exactly the right conditions.

6 From the photograph and from your own knowledge, do corals like: warm or cold water? freshwater or seawater? deep or shallow water? clear or murky water? dark or light conditions?

7 Why do animals like corals make hard parts?

8 What do we call rocks mainly made from CaCO$_3$?

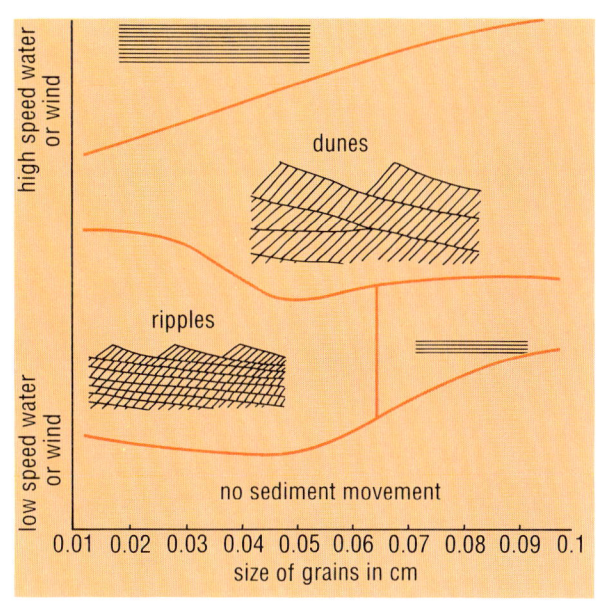

How ripples and dunes form

A coral reef

Chalk is an unusual type of limestone. It is formed by certain one-celled plants called **algae**. They extract the calcium carbonate from seawater to make tiny armour plates. These plates collect on the seabed when the plants die.

4.5 Interpreting sedimentary rocks

Sedimentary rocks cover 75 per cent of the continents. In Britain, the layers of sedimentary rocks contain the evidence for events that shaped our landscape over millions of years.

In Shropshire there is a ridge of limestone called Wenlock Edge. The 30 m thick limestone layer contains solid oval lumps up to 3 m high and up to 12 m across. In between the lumps are flat layers of limestone.

The limestones of Wenlock Edge contain many fossils. These tell us that the rock is of Silurian age, over 400 million years old. The oval lumps are made up of large corals and other fossils. The beds in between are mainly made of fossil shells and a variety of broken fossils.

1 Were these limestones formed on land, in the sea, or between high and low tide?

2 Which of these places best describes the environment where these rocks formed?
river plain   desert   beach   delta
shallow sea   deep sea

3 What could have broken the fossils found in the beds between the lumps? List some ideas.

This sandstone (below) is found in quarries around Mauchline in Strathclyde. It has round grains, all about the same size. It is in thick beds containing curved sloping surfaces. Various evidence dates it as about 270 million years old.

How many types of fossils can you see in this limestone from Wenlock Edge?

4 Which of these places best describes the environment where this sandstone formed?
river plain   desert   beach   delta
shallow sea   deep sea

5 Explain why the following scientific terms could apply to the Mauchline Sandstone:
well sorted   dune bedding.

Sandstone in a quarry at Mauchline

In the Peak District of Derbyshire there is a 325 million-year-old sequence of sandstones and shales called the Mam Tor Beds. They are found near Castleton, and the hill they are named after, Mam Tor, shows them best.

The face of the hill is made of 120 pairs of layers. Each pair has a sandstone layer with a shale layer on top. The sandstone layers have the largest grains near the base and quite often have ripples on top. The shales often have grooves in their top surface where the next sandstone begins.

6 Which of these places best describes the environment where these rocks formed?
*river plain   desert   beach   delta
shallow sea   deep sea*

7 Explain why the following scientific terms could apply to the formation of the Mam Tor Beds:
graded bedding   turbidity currents.

In another part of Derbyshire layers of soft clay are found to contain scratched pebbles and boulders of rocks from far away. Some are igneous rocks from Norway or Western Scotland. The clay often contains gravel, mixed in it or in layers.

8 What evidence suggests that this **boulder clay** was formed by melting ice sheets or glaciers?

Layers in the face of Mam Tor

Mam Tor Beds

Boulder clay found in Derbyshire

4.6 Interpreting a sedimentary sequence

Studying sedimentary rocks on their own can tell us a lot, but a piled-up sequence of sedimentary rocks can often tell us more.

Coalfield areas provide good examples of patterns of layers. These rocks are mostly mudstones, with some sandstones and, of course, coal seams. The coal seams are only a small part of these sets of rocks we call **coal measures**. They are about 300 million years old.

The coal measures can be divided into **cycles**. Each cycle ends with a coal seam.

1 One cycle has been marked on the diagram. How many cycles are there in this sequence?

Here are some extra observations about coal measure rocks.

The black shale layer at the start of each cycle, just above the last coal seam, sometimes contains fossil sea shells.

Sandy shale contains a mixture of sand and mud.

The sandstones sometimes have cross-bedding (see page 43).

The layer under the coal seam in each cycle often contains fossil roots. This layer is often very pale in colour.

The coal seams contain fossils of tree bark and branches.

This diagram shows how we think each part of the coal measure cycle was formed.

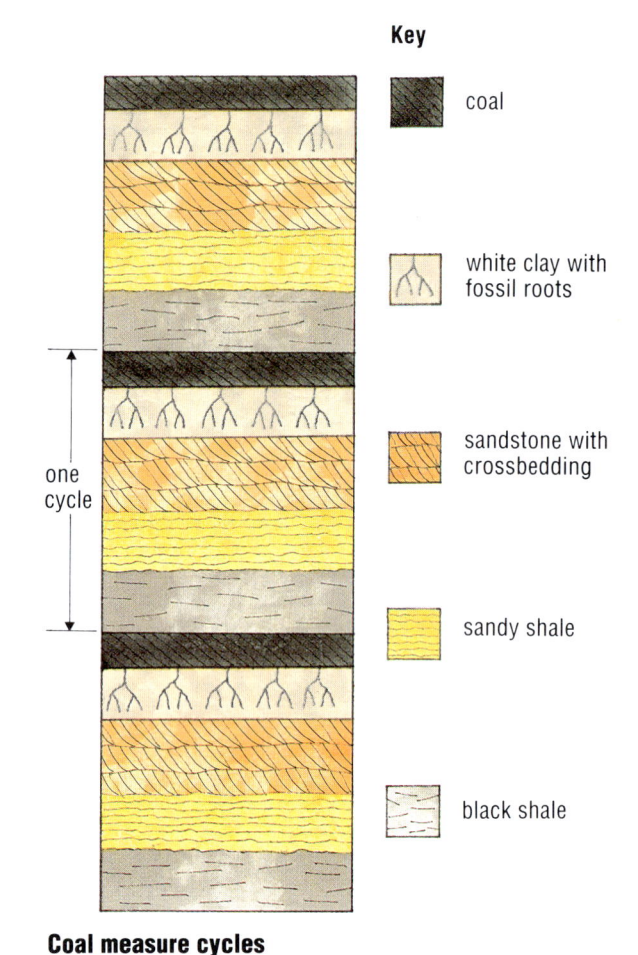

Key
- coal
- white clay with fossil roots
- sandstone with crossbedding
- sandy shale
- black shale

Coal measure cycles

2 Copy the diagram, and fill in the evidence for the explanations of how each part formed.

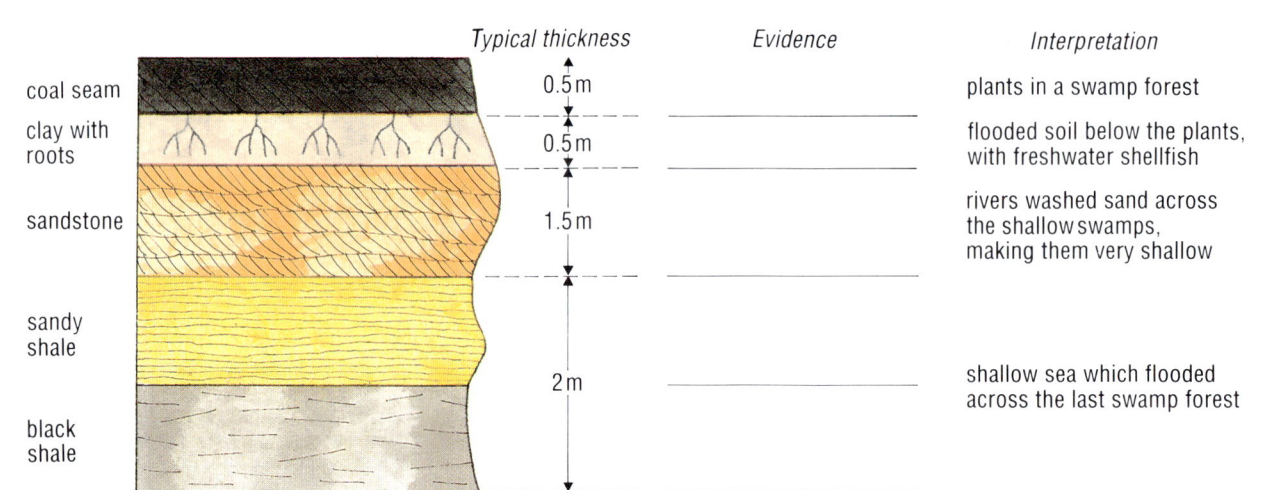

	Typical thickness	Evidence	Interpretation
coal seam	0.5 m		plants in a swamp forest
clay with roots	0.5 m		flooded soil below the plants, with freshwater shellfish
sandstone	1.5 m		rivers washed sand across the shallow swamps, making them very shallow
sandy shale			
black shale	2 m		shallow sea which flooded across the last swamp forest

How a coal measure cycle was formed

Section 4 questions

1 Describe three types of physical weathering.

2 Describe three types of chemical weathering.

3 a) Draw and label a soil profile.
b) Explain how soils forms.
c) Why is there often no soil on steep mountain sides?

4 Explain these discoveries made during experiments on transport of rock fragments:

a) Transportation causes rounding of rock fragments. The rounder the fragment, the further it has been transported.
b) Transportation creates an increasing number of rock fragments.
c) Transportation reduces the average size of the rock fragments.
d) Transportation sorts rock fragments. The more the sediment has been transported, the smaller the range of sizes of particles.

5 Draw a labelled diagram to show how a delta forms.

6 How are the following sedimentary structures formed?

a) graded bedding
b) ripples
c) dunes.

7 a) What chemical has been extracted from seawater by living things to make the material seen in the photograph below?
b) What rock could be formed eventually from this material?

8 A sample of 1 kg of sediment was sieved and the contents of each sieve were weighed.

Grain size	Mass of sediment
Over 2 mm	0 grams
1–2 mm	0 grams
0.5–1 mm	89 grams
0.25–0.5 mm	699 grams
0.125–0.25 mm	170 grams
0.062–0.125 mm	42 grams
0.031–0.062 mm	0 grams

a) Plot a bar graph for this sediment.
b) Is this sediment mainly made of pebbles, sand or mud?
c) Why might it be suggested that the sediment had been windblown for a long time?

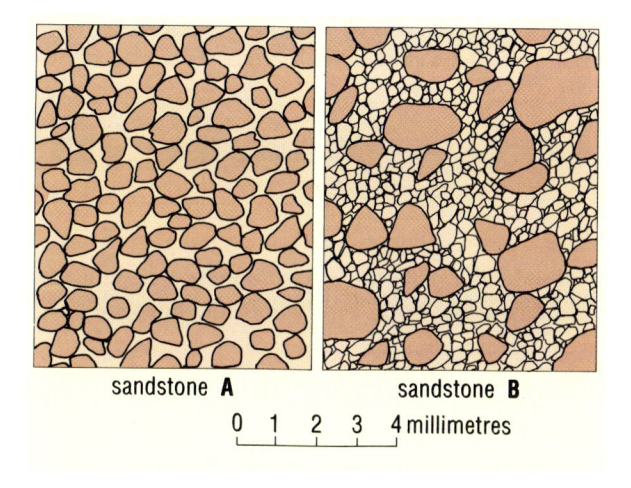

9 These diagrams show microscope views of two sandstones.

a) Which is the best sorted sandstone?
b) Which sandstone has had most energy acting on it during transport?

10 Imagine you are visiting a quarry for sedimentary rocks. Describe how you would tell if the rocks were formed in   **a)** a desert   **b)** a swamp forest   **c)** a glacial area. Give as much detail as possible, and draw labelled diagrams.

11 Find out by library research how caves, stalactites and stalagmites are produced in areas of limestone rock. Produce a report on your findings.

5.1 Volcanic eruptions

The materials below came out of volcanoes. Compare the photographs with specimens. The **lava** was molten material that came out of the volcano and cooled down to crystallize and go solid. The **agglomerate** began as rock fragments blown out of the volcano.

1 A scientist says that gases push materials out of volcanoes. Describe any evidence for her idea in the photographs and rock specimens.

A gas-driven model volcano

Equipment: one fresh bottle of 'fizzy' drink

- Shake the bottle for a few seconds.
- Stand the bottle upright.
- Open the bottle, observing what happens to the liquid.
- Note your observations.
- Suggest how this experiment helps us to understand how volcanoes erupt.

Basalt lava

Agglomerate

These brave scientists below collected gases from Mount Etna. Different volcanoes give out different gas mixtures. Steam, carbon dioxide, nitrogen, sulphur dioxide, hydrogen, carbon monoxide, sulphur and chlorine are the main volcanic gases.

2 List the volcanic gases using chemical formulae as well as chemical names. Here are the formulae:
SO_2, CO_2, H_2, CO, Cl_2, H_2O, S, N_2.

Making a lava flow

Equipment: long glass rod, Bunsen burner, heat-proof mat, goggles

- Using a hot flame, heat the middle of the glass rod until it goes soft.
- Gently pull the ends of the glass rod. Let it sag on the mat.
- Push the soft glass along the mat and look at the patterns produced.
- How does this help to explain the lava surface seen in the photograph?

When Mount St Helens erupted in 1980, it had been **dormant** ('sleeping') for over 100 years. It had not erupted during that time. At first, it threw out small amounts of volcanic ash. Then, suddenly, it blasted gas and ash out sideways, turning forests into wasteland.

Mount St Helens is probably how you expect a volcano to look, but not all volcanoes have a steep cone. Some have a much flatter shape.

Hawaii has volcanoes. Some of them erupt almost constantly, sending out lots of runny lava.

3 One way we can compare the shapes of volcanoes is to measure the average *slope angle*. Use a protractor to measure the slope angle on the pictures of the two volcanoes.

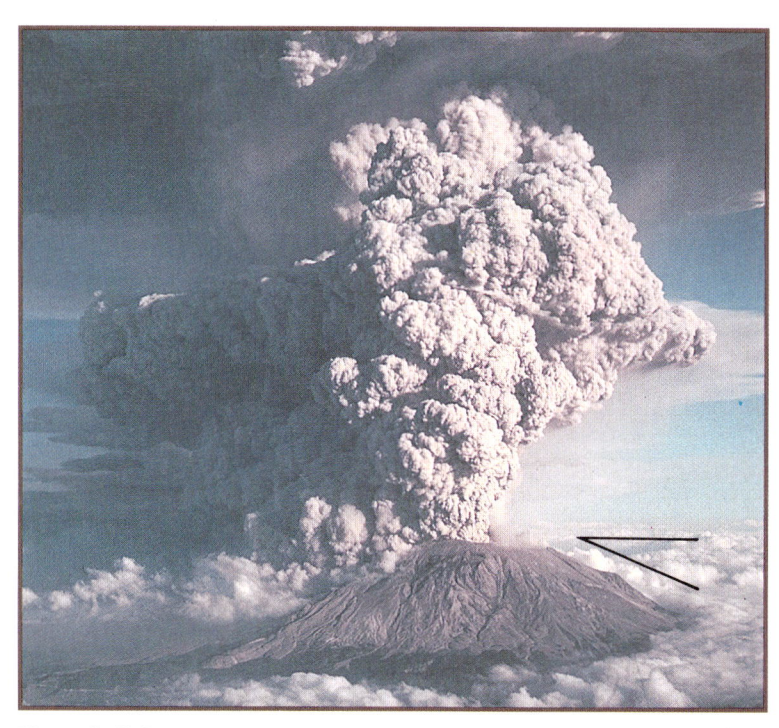

Mount St Helens

A volcano on Hawaii

Volcanoes like Mount St Helens erupt violently after long quiet periods. They throw out ash which piles up around the vent to make a steep cone. They do not erupt very much lava. The lava is sticky because it has a lot of gas and cools quickly.

Other volcanoes, like those on Hawaii, erupt runny lava most of the time. The lava is runny because it has less gas and so heat loss to the air is slower. Lava runs away from the vent to make flattish volcanoes.

4 Write about the two types of volcanoes. What are the differences between them? What are the similarities between them?

Volcanoes like Mount St Helens are called **explosive**, and those like the Hawaiian example **quiet**. Volcanoes of either type which are not active are called dormant.

As the lava cools its colour changes. The hottest melts are **white hot**. As they cool, they become **yellow hot**, **orange hot**, and **red hot**. As they crystallize they become dull red and finally black.

The most common lava is **basalt**. When it is erupted it has a temperature of about 1200°C. It crystallizes to a solid at about 1150°C.

5.2 Igneous rocks

Rocks that used to be molten are found in many parts of Britain.

For example, flat layers of dark rock made of small crystals cover large areas of Antrim. They are about 70 million years old.

1 Where could we find active volcanoes erupting this sort of material?

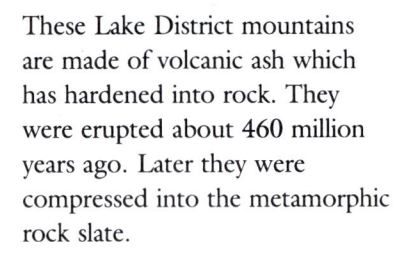

Volcanic rock in Antrim, Northern Ireland

These Lake District mountains are made of volcanic ash which has hardened into rock. They were erupted about 460 million years ago. Later they were compressed into the metamorphic rock slate.

2 Name an active volcano that erupts material like that which formed rocks in the Lake District.

Volcanic rock in the Lake District

The island of Skye has many igneous rocks, formed from material that used to be molten. The different types of molten rock are called **magmas**.

3 These two rocks from Skye probably began as the same magma. What difference can you see between them in the pictures?

Basalt

Gabbro

Investigating grain sizes

Equipment: 100 cm³ beaker, glass tube about 1.5 cm wide and 10 cm long, bung to fit glass tube, stearic acid, wooden rod to just fit inside the tube, sharp knife, hammer, goggles

- Melt the stearic acid in the beaker over a low flame. It melts at just over 93°C.
- Put the bung in one end of the glass tube.
- Pour the melt into the tube.
- Stand the tube upright. When the tube is cool, take out the bung.
- Push the solid from the glass tube with the wooden rod.
- Mark a circle round the solid stearic acid with the knife.
- Put the knife in the slot.
- Tap the knife with the hammer to split the cylinder.
- Study the cut surface with a hand lens.

4 a) How do the sizes of the crystals near the edge compare with the size of the crystals in the middle of the cylinder?

b) Which part of the liquid was cooling most quickly, the edge or the centre?

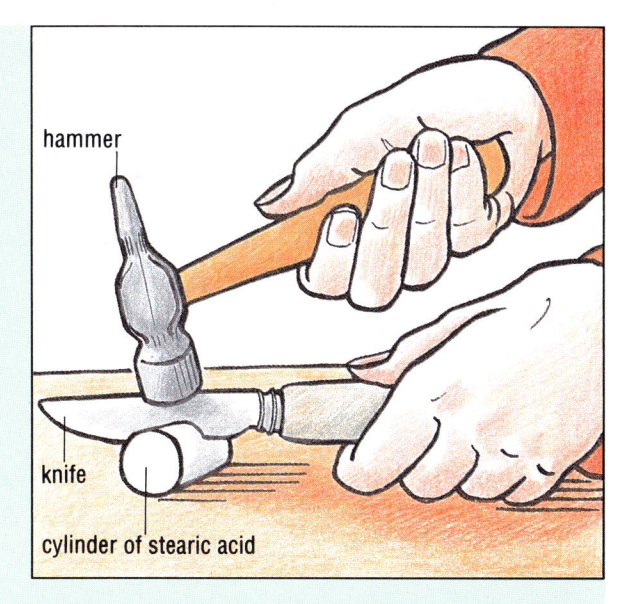

Conclusions might be: slow cooling melts produce smaller crystals than fast ones *or* fast cooling melts produce smaller crystals than slow ones *or* fast or slow cooling makes no difference to the size of the crystals. Choose one of these conclusions.

5 Which rock from Skye cooled most quickly? Which cooled most slowly? Use your experimental result to decide.

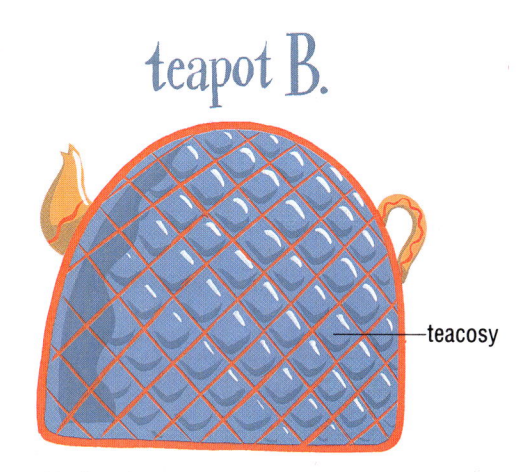

teapot A.

teapot B.

the tea in both pots was at 95 °C at the start

We know that rocks like basalt are lavas. They erupted out on to the Earth's surface. This is why they cooled quickly. The other melts must have lost heat more slowly. We can compare this with how we keep tea hot in a pot.

6 Which teapot will lose heat fastest? Explain your answer. You might find these words useful: *conduction   insulation*.

Molten rock cools more slowly if it is insulated by being under other rocks. When it erupts on the surface of the Earth it cools quickly because it is not insulated.

5.3 More about igneous rocks

The Romans built part of Hadrian's Wall along this ridge in northern England. Features like this are called **sills**. They are layers of igneous rock found sandwiched between layers of sedimentary rock. The igneous rock was squeezed between the layers when it was molten. This sill is called the Whin Sill.

This moorland in Cornwall is made of igneous rock. It was once covered by sediments which have worn away. Several areas like it are linked underground. Large masses of igneous rock like this are called **plutons**.

The pluton is made of **granite**. It has large pale crystals. The Whin Sill is made of **dolerite**. It is a dark rock made of crystals just seen by the naked eye.

The Cornish granite and the Whin Sill dolerite contain different types of mineral crystals.

We can see how that can come about by doing another investigation.

Making 'rocks'

Equipment: test tube, bunsen burner, glass microscope slide, dilute sulphuric acid, potassium nitrate, copper sulphate, glass rod, goggles

- Put one spatula-full of potassium nitrate and one spatula-full of copper sulphate in the test-tube.
- Add an equal volume of acid.
- Stir, and heat gently until you see a clear solution.
- Let the tube cool in the air for a minute, then cool it in water.
- Pour a few drops of the mixture on to the glass slide.

When you have seen the first result, try different proportions of chemicals. You should see that different 'rocks' (mixtures of crystals) will form.

Here are close-up views of the granite from Cornwall and the dolerite from the Whin Sill. Examine specimens of similar rocks.

The different mineral crystals in them tell us that the magma under Cornwall had a different chemical composition to the magma that squeezed in to make the Whin Sill.

The different minerals in rocks melt at different temperatures. The Cornish granite would melt at about 650°C. Granite melts are sticky.

The dolerite from the Whin Sill would melt at about 1200°C. Dolerite is runnier when molten, and has fewer gas bubbles to come out of it.

1 What would be the temperatures (about) of the melts
a) under Hawaii? b) under Mount St Helens (see page 49)?

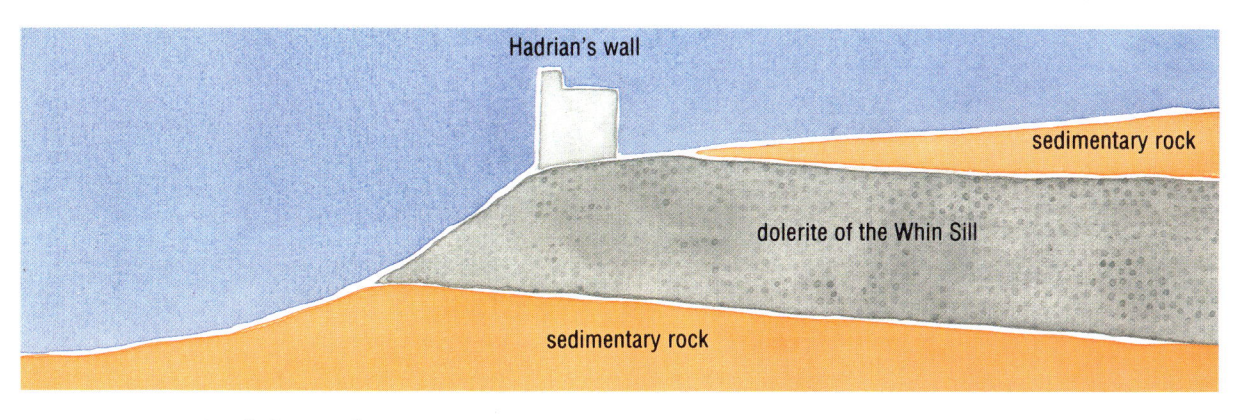

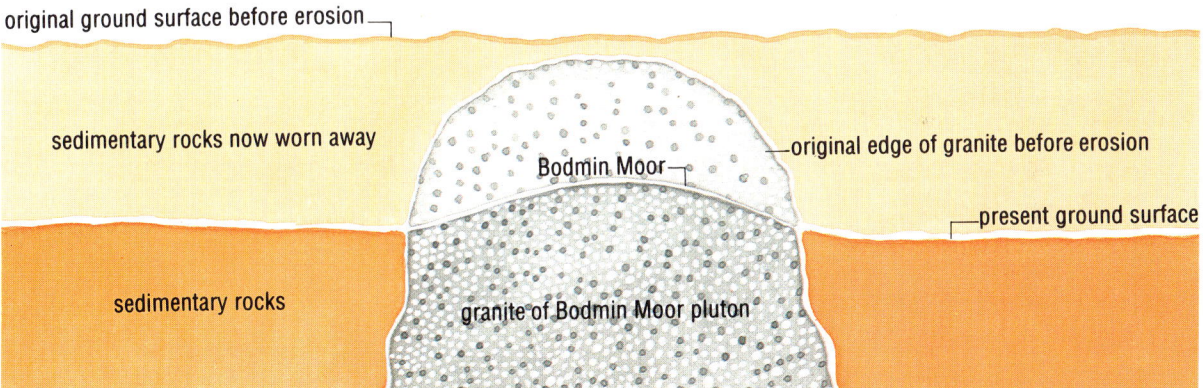

These diagrams show the arrangements of the rocks at the Whin Sill and around the Cornish granite.

2 From the diagrams, explain why the granite has large crystals and the sill has smaller crystals. Why do you think that one would have cooled more quickly than the other?

Igneous rocks have been used for building for thousands of years. They are strong and often attractive.

3 Survey your town for igneous rocks used in buildings.

- Record the crystal sizes.
- If possible take close-up colour photographs of some of them (with a scale in mm included).
- Display your photographs in the order of cooling from fast to slow.
- Try to discover where the rocks were quarried.

5.4 Zones of volcanoes and earthquakes

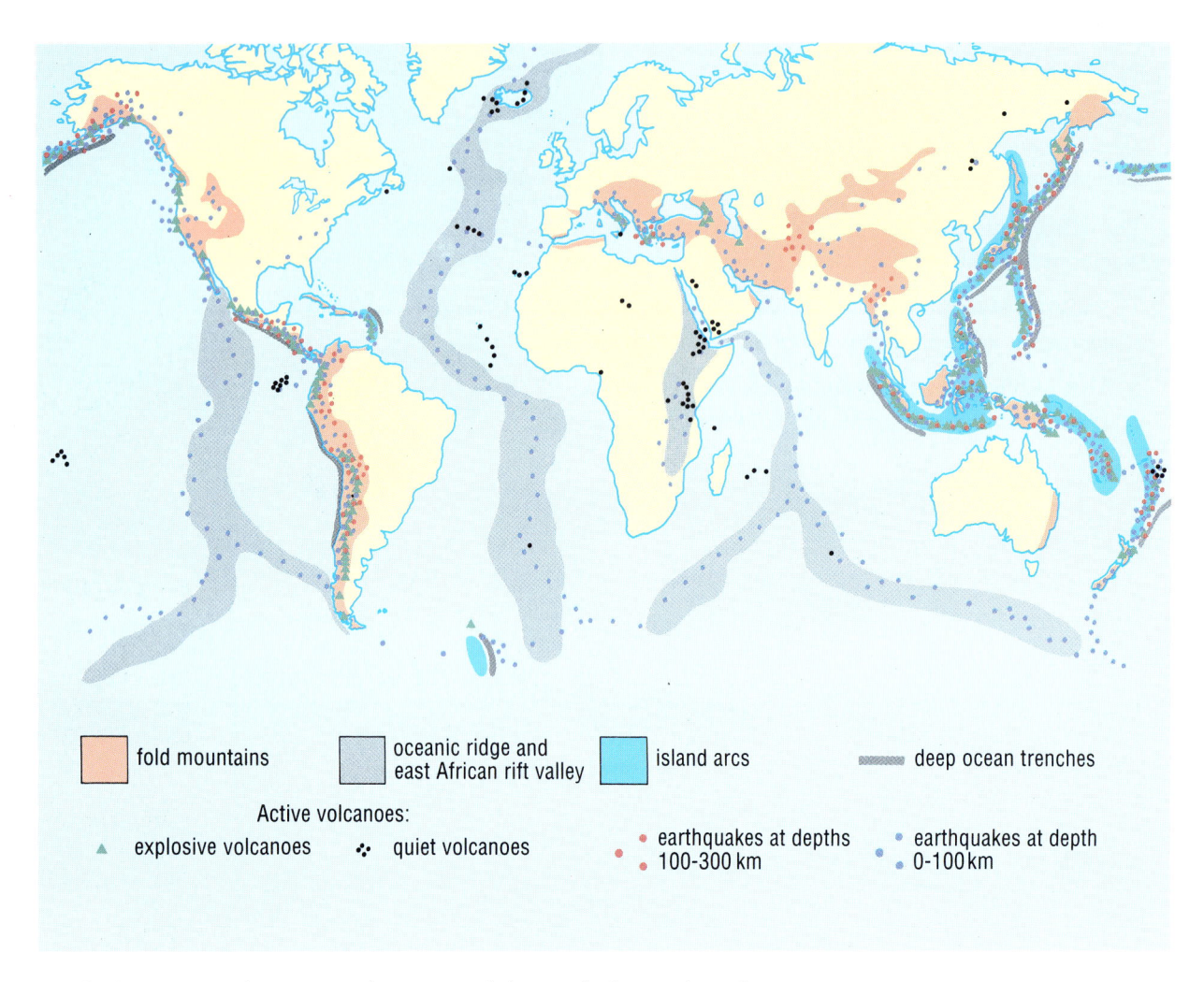

Legend:
- fold mountains
- oceanic ridge and east African rift valley
- island arcs
- deep ocean trenches

Active volcanoes:
- ▲ explosive volcanoes
- ∴ quiet volcanoes
- • earthquakes at depths 100-300 km
- • earthquakes at depth 0-100 km

We find igneous rocks in most places around the Earth, but *active* volcanoes are not found everywhere.

There are about 500 active volcanoes at present, and this map shows where they are found. Some are under the oceans, and some are on the continents. Some are of the explosive type that erupt mostly ash, others are of the quieter type that erupt mostly basalt lava.

The map also shows the location of the main **earthquake zones.** Notice that there are some patterns connecting volcanoes and earthquakes.

1 Describe any pattern you see in the location of volcanoes.

2 Name any places where you know that volcanoes have erupted and find them on the map.

3 Name any places where you know that earthquakes have happened and find them on the map.

4 Describe the types of volcanoes and earthquakes along a) ocean ridges b) island arcs.

Earthquakes happen when large natural forces affect rocks so that they break and move. A break in a rock is called a **fault**. The breaking rocks release energy into the Earth, which shakes.

Once rock has broken and moved, it can move again if new forces build up around it. Some faults move many times if there is enough energy to build up forces around them. Earthquake zones are usually places where there are many faults, called **fault zones**.

5 This building has been damaged by an earthquake. Describe how the different building materials have been affected.

You can make a tiny earthquake by slowly bending a stick of blackboard chalk. If you listen in total silence you will hear the energy being released as the chalk breaks.

6 What kind of energy does the chalk contain *before* it breaks?

7 What kind of energy does the chalk release when it breaks?

The effects of earthquakes depend on how easily the rocks move when energy builds up. There is always friction between rock surfaces. Rough and jagged surfaces produce more friction than smooth ones. More energy needs to build up to move rough surfaces against each other, so more energy is released once they start to move. This creates a more severe earthquake.

Some scientists have suggested that we could reduce the damage from earthquakes by lubricating the rock surfaces. They drilled down to a fault and pumped in water. This reduced the friction and there was a minor earthquake. When the water was pumped away from the fault, the rocks were stopped from moving for a long time, but when they did move they caused a severe earthquake.

8 Make a list of advantages and disadvantages of trying to control earthquakes.

Forces and rock movements

Equipment: block of rock fitted with a hook, forcemeter

- Put the block on a longer flat rock and gently pull on the hook with a force meter.
- Measure the force needed for the top block to move just a little.

You can try this experiment with different sized rock blocks and with different surfaces between the rocks – rough or polished.

The rock cannot move at once because you need to overcome the friction between the surfaces.

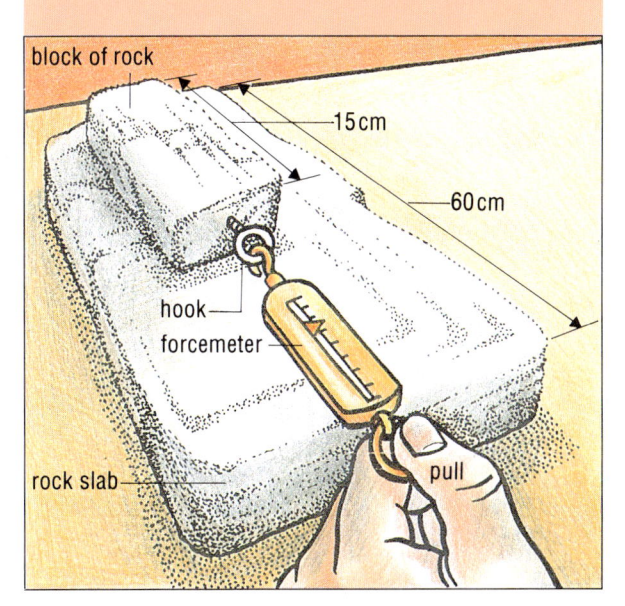

5.5 The effects of earthquakes

The Mercalli Scale of Earthquake Effects

Mercalli, an Italian scientist, studied how ordinary people described what had happened to them during earthquakes. He divided their experiences and behaviour into 12 levels of *intensity*, and in 1902 produced this scale:

Level	Description
1	Only felt by very few people. Birds and animals uneasy. Hanging objects may swing.
2	Felt by some people mainly upstairs in buildings.
3	Noticed by quite a few people but they may not realise that it is an earthquake. Vibrations like passing lorries.
4	Many people notice; walls may creak, cars may rock.
5	Nearly every notices it. Cracked plaster in walls sometimes. Some fragile objects may fall and break.
6	Everyone notices. Books may fall off shelves, people may run out of buildings. Chimneys may be damaged.
7	Everyone runs out of buildings. It is difficult to stand up. Some damage to buildings, more in poorly designed ones.
8	Slight damage even to well designed buildings. Serious damage to some buildings. Some walls and tall structures may fall.
9	Ground cracks, major damage to reservoirs and underground pipes. General panic.
10	Most buildings destroyed. Rails bend slightly. Landslides. Serious ground cracking.
11	Rails bend badly, bridges fall, gaps in ground.
12	Total damage. Waves on ground surface. Objects thrown up in the air.

1 Look at these photographs of earthquake damage. What Mercalli numbers would you give to what you see in each?

Earthquake damage in Sicily

Earthquake damage on Santorini, Greece

Earthquakes are quite rare in Britain. When they do happen they are small compared to the earthquakes in major earthquake zones. In 1990, on 2nd April at about 2.45 p.m., people suddenly noticed the ground shaking. It was one of the strongest earthquakes in Britain of the twentieth century.

In **Shrewsbury** some old chimneys were damaged and some of the bricks from these chimneys fell into the streets.

In **Bridlington** the effect was like a passing heavy lorry.

In **Oxford** there were some reports of cars rocking.

In **Saltash** some people who were upstairs felt the earthquake slightly.

2 What Mercalli numbers would you give to these four descriptions?

Collecting information from many people around the country produced Mercalli numbers for these towns.

Map of the British Isles showing major faults (Great Glen fault, Highland Boundary fault, Minch fault, Moine thrust fault, Southern Upland fault, Pennine/Craven fault, Welsh Borderland fault, Lizard-Start thrust fault) and Mercalli numbers for towns:

- Ayr 2
- Coldstream 2
- Carlisle 3
- Belfast 2
- Peel 3
- Carnforth 4
- Bridlington
- Colwyn Bay 5
- Dublin 2
- Holyhead 4
- Liverpool
- Shrewsbury
- Newtown 6
- Grantham 4
- Aylsham 2
- Aberdovey 5
- Walsall 5
- Newquay 4
- Ludlow 6
- St David's Head 3
- Hereford 5
- Cambridge 3
- Oxford
- Bristol 4
- Farnham 3
- Sidmouth 3
- Saltash

Base map for data on earthquake 2 April 1990

- Trace the outline of this map.
- Plot the numbers only on your copy.
- Add numbers for Bridlington, Shrewsbury, Oxford and Saltash using the information above.
- Join the dots marking towns with the same Mercalli numbers to make rough circles. These are known as **isoseismals**. The lines must not cross.

3 Where do you think the earthquake happened? This is called the **focus**.

4 If your home is on the map, mark it. What Mercalli number describes how people in your home would have experienced this earthquake?

5 Some of the major faults that cross the British Isles are marked on the outline map. Which fault is most likely to have moved to cause the earthquake of 2nd April 1990?

6 Produce a newspaper front page for 3rd April 1990 to report how different parts of Britain experienced this earthquake. Include eyewitness accounts from at least five different places.

5.6 Seismic waves

The 1990 Shropshire earthquake happened 15 km underground, but was felt by people in many parts of the British Isles. Much stronger earthquakes happen around the world, and although they may not be felt by people in Britain they can be detected by special equipment.

Seismic waves are the energy waves sent through the rocks of the Earth by earthquakes. They spread like waves on a pond when a stone is dropped in. The instruments that pick up seismic waves are **seismometers**. When they are linked to recording systems they make a **seismograph**. The record of the waves is a **seismogram**. People who study earthquakes are called **seismologists**.

A seismic observatory

1 Copy this flow diagram for a seismic recording station and add the correct labels to the three boxes.

There is an international network of seismographs which monitor movements all over the Earth.

add ... GRAM, ... GRAPH, ... METER to complete the labels.

Detector → Recording System → Output

SEISMO ...   SEISMO .....   SEISMO ...

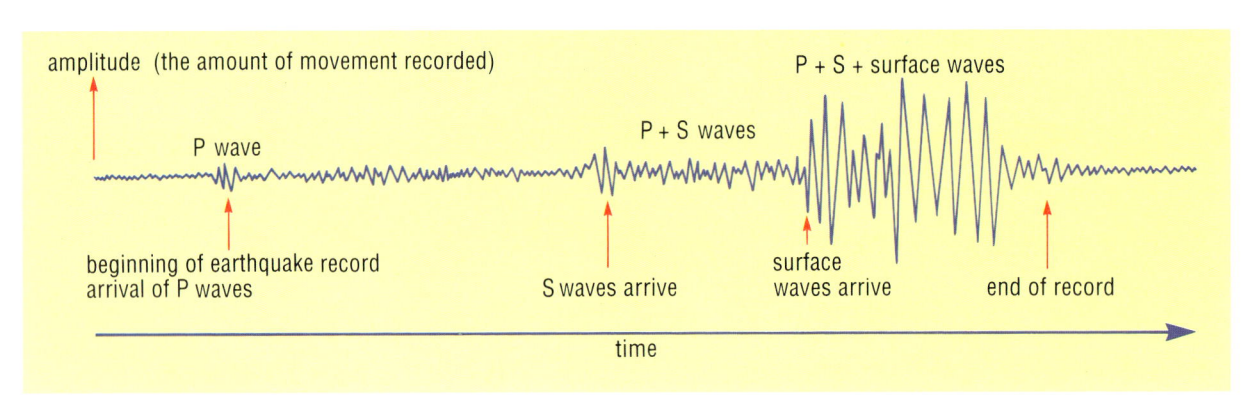

A seismogram (earthquake record)

This is a typical seismogram record from one earthquake. The waves must have started from the site of the earthquake, the **focus**, all together, but, like runners in a marathon, the waves do not reach the seismometer together.

The first arrivals are **primary** waves, or **P-waves**.

Next come **secondary** waves, **S-waves**.

2 Which travel fastest, the P-waves or the S-waves? Explain how you know.

P-waves and S-waves have travelled *through* the Earth, but the final group of waves travel the long way, around the curved surface of the Earth. They are the **surface waves.**

3 From the *amplitude* of the seismogram waves, decide which waves carry the most seismic energy.

direction of travel of waves ⟶   direction in which rock particles move (vibrate) ⇔

Primary or P-wave ⟶

Love wave ⟶

undisturbed rock

Secondary or S-wave ⟶

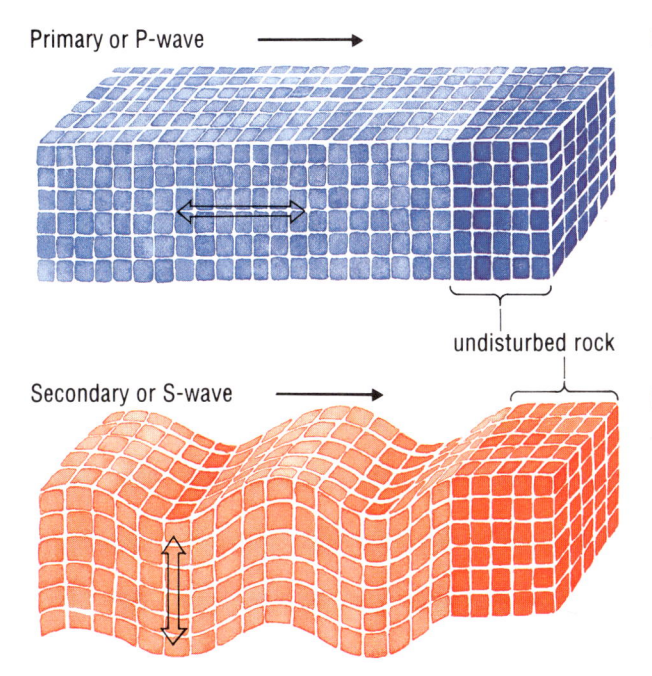

Rayleigh wave ⟶

undisturbed rock

Seismic waves that travel through the Earth

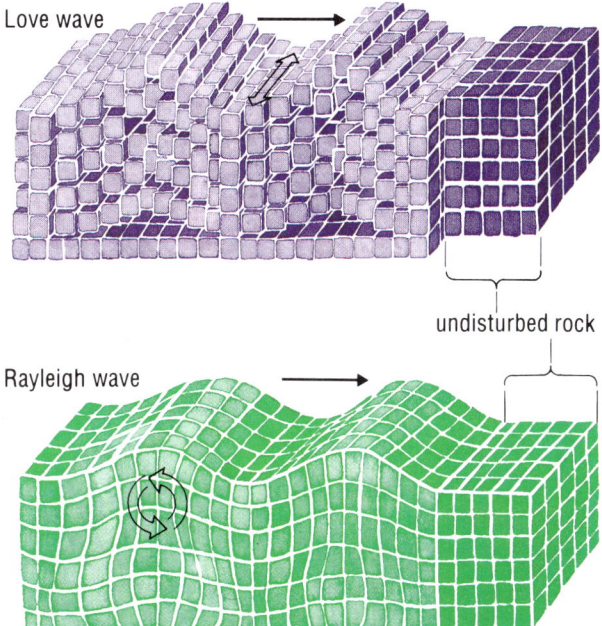

Seismic waves that travel across the surface of the Earth

Like all waves, seismic waves are either **longitudinal** or **transverse**.

Longitudinal waves have particles vibrating in the *same direction* as the wave travels. Transverse waves have particles vibrating *at right angles* to the direction the wave travels.

4 Study the diagrams of the way P-waves and S-waves move.

a) Which one is a longitudinal wave?
b) Which one is a transverse wave?

To help us remember which seismic wave is a longitudinal wave, we can think of longitudinal waves as **P***ush-pull waves* and we can think of transverse waves as **S***haking waves*.

Use a Slinky to make a P-wave, an S-wave and then both together.

5 Study the diagrams of the ways the two different surface waves move.

a) Which one of them is a transverse wave?
b) How does the other surface wave travel?

There is another important difference between P-waves and S-waves. S-waves cannot go through liquid material. Get some volunteers to be 'atoms' in a rock. Use them to model seismic waves.

Waves through rocks

- Line up six people to be 'atoms' in a rock.
- Rocks are usually solid. Link the 'atoms' by putting their hands loosely on the shoulders of the next 'atom'.
- Gently push and pull the last 'atom' to send a P-wave along the row.
- Gently shake the last 'atom' from side to side to send an S-wave along the row.
- Now 'melt' the rock by asking the 'atoms' to drop their arms to their sides.
- Gently shake the last 'atom' from side to side and send an S-wave along the row.
- Gently push and pull the last 'atom' to send a P-wave along the row.

6 In what ways does this model show that the inside of the Earth is mostly solid?

5.7 Faults and folds

Earthquakes happen when rocks move along fault lines (see page 55).

We know that Britain is not in a major earthquake zone. The many large fault zones running through the rocks of Britain provide evidence suggesting that in the distant past, British rocks were affected by major earthquakes.

1 a) Look at the movement shown by the rocks in the photograph.
b) Which side appears to have moved up?
c) Has this fault been caused by forces pushing the rocks together (**compression**) or by them being pulled apart (**tension**)?

A fault through layers of sedimentary rocks

Some British fault zones are very large, running for many kilometres across the country and continuing deep into the earth.

Some of our main landscape features are caused by fault zones. For example, the Midland Valley of Scotland is a block of fairly soft rocks that has dropped down between two fault zones. The rocks to the north are the hard metamorphic rocks of the *Highlands*. To the south are the hard sandstones of the *Southern Uplands*.

2 Look at the diagram and decide which fault is the **Highland Boundary Fault** and which fault is the **Southern Uplands Fault**.

Faults are formed when large forces build up quickly in rocks. The rocks behave in a *brittle* way and break. If the force builds up very slowly and continues for a long time the rock may bend instead. This is how **folds** are formed. Folds are evidence that rocks can behave in a **plastic** way. They show that the rocks have been **compressed.**

Upfolds are called **anticlines**. Downfolds are called **synclines.**

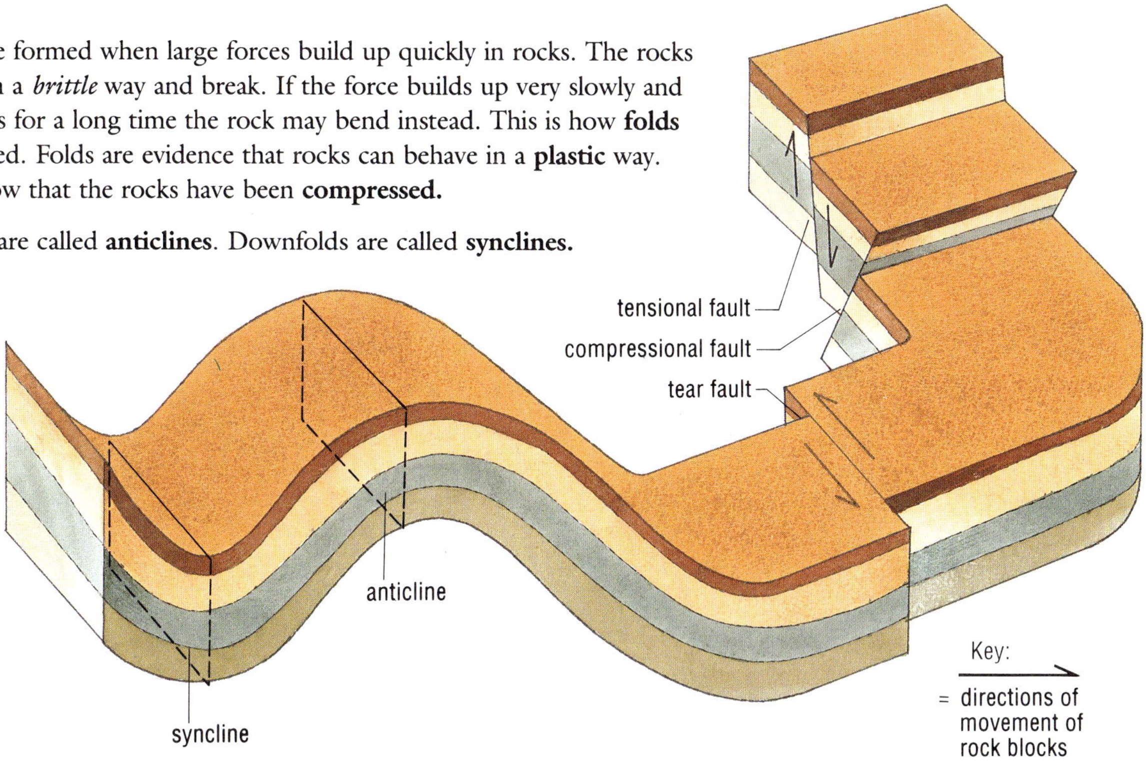

tensional fault
compressional fault
tear fault

anticline

syncline

Key:
→ = directions of movement of rock blocks

Compression in folds

- Measure the original length of one layer in this set of sedimentary rocks (follow the folds with cotton or string and then measure the length used). This is **M1**.
- Compare it with the actual width of the photograph. This is **M2**.
- Divide M2 by M1. This gives a **compression ratio**. It indicates how much the rocks have been forced to fold.

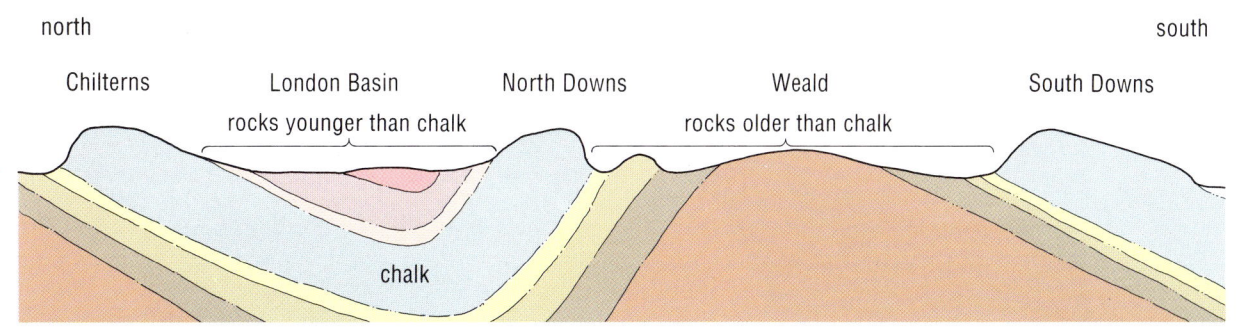

north — Chilterns — London Basin — North Downs — Weald — South Downs — south

rocks younger than chalk

rocks older than chalk

chalk

Folded rocks in South-East England

Some very large folds make major landscape features. The south of England is made of a set of sedimentary layers which have folded up and been eroded.

3 a) Copy the diagram and dot in the layers above the landscape as they would have been before erosion.

b) Find and label the *syncline* and *anticline* in the diagram.

5.8 Metamorphic rocks

These rocks are not just folded. From their layering, they appear to be sedimentary rocks, but in fact they are **metamorphic rocks.**

The word *metamorphic* means *changed in shape* and so we need to know: what have they been changed *from* and what have they been changed *by*?

Most metamorphic rocks began as sedimentary rocks, and especially as the very common clay-type rocks such as *shale*.

1 Examine these metamorphic rocks: **schist**, **slate** and **gneiss**. Compare them with a shale.
a) Which of the three metamorphic rocks is most like the shale?
b) Which is least like the shale?

Metamorphic rocks near Oban, Scotland

The process which changed shale into a metamorphic rock is similar to the way in which we make pottery.

2 How does soft pottery clay become a plate?

Metamorphic rocks are made if heat, pressure or both heat and pressure affect other rocks. When we look at metamorphic rocks, the banding looks like sedimentary layers. In fact, whereas in sedimentary rocks *fragments* are *layered*, in metamorphic rocks *crystals* are *lined up*. This is called **cleavage** and is caused by huge pressure building up in the rock during severe folding.

Slate splits parallel to the flat crystals, but we can only see them with a microscope as its crystals are very small.

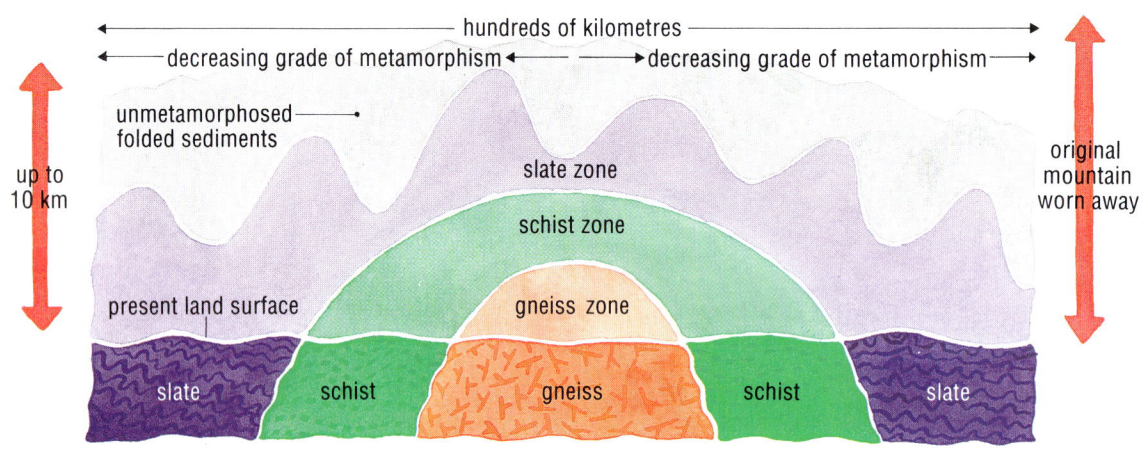

A fold mountain belt

Slate, schist and gneiss are often found in areas of fold mountains, for example the Scottish Highlands. These mountains are the eroded remains of a mountain chain that was once as high as the highest mountains today, such as the Himalayas and the Alps.

3 How does the position of the three metamorphic rocks in the diagram correspond to their similarity to shale? The most altered is termed the **highest grade** of metamorphic rock.

Metamorphic rocks that are made inside fold mountains by both heat and pressure are called **regional metamorphic rocks**.

This graph describes regional metamorphism.

4 Fill in a copy of this chart to show the conditions needed to make the three typical regional metamorphic rocks.

Rock Type	Temperature °C	Pressure millibars
Slate		
Schist		
Gneiss		

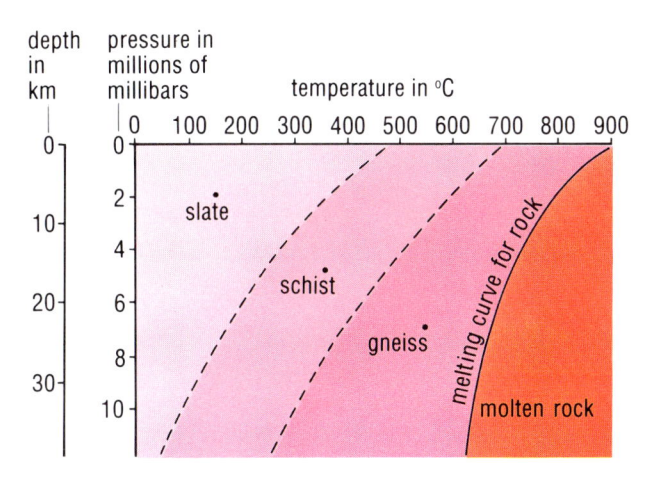

The conditions responsible for regional metamorphism

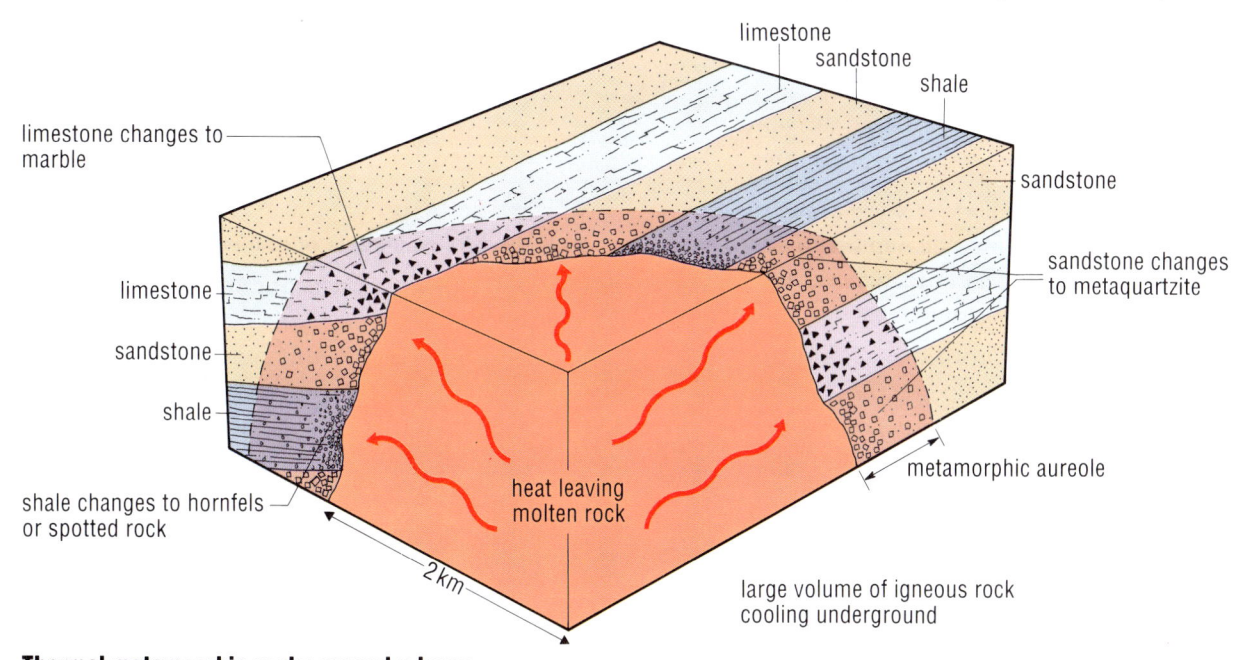

Thermal metamorphic rocks around a large granite pluton

Metamorphic rocks can also be caused by heat alone. The heat usually comes from an igneous rock that is cooling down underground. This type of change is called **thermal metamorphism**.

One example is the dolerite of the very thick Whin Sill (pages 52 and 53). Above and below the sill are limestone layers which have been changed by heat into a crumbly form of **marble** where they touch the igneous rock. This is called a **baked margin**.

The bigger the source of heat, the larger the effects will be. The area of metamorphic rocks around a large igneous mass is called the **metamorphic aureole.**

Thermal metamorphism does not change shale to slate, schist or gneiss. Instead, it changes shale to **spotted rocks** and **hornfels**.

As we have seen, clay-type rocks make a wide range of metamorphic rocks. Other original rocks make different metamorphic rocks.

Compare hand specimens of marble and limestone; compare hand specimens of metaquartzite and sandstone.

5 Which of each pair is the metamorphic rock?

Section 5 questions

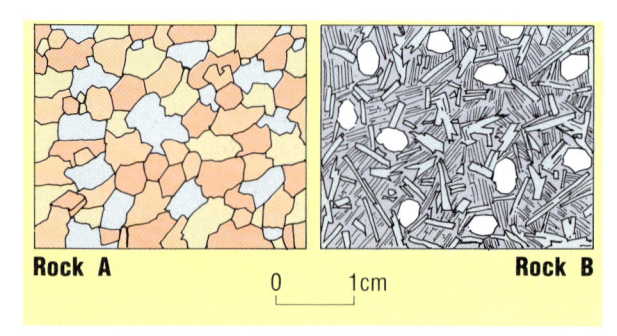

Rock A **Rock B**
0 1cm

1 a) Which of these two igneous rocks cooled most quickly?
b) What caused the round bubbles in rock B?
c) Which of the two is most likely to have solidified underground? Give your reasons.

2 Volcanoes erupting a granite-type melt tend to be more violent than volcanoes erupting a basalt-type melt. Why is this?

3 Explain the differences between the words; *seismometer   seismograph   seismogram.*

4 Here are some reports received about an earthquake. Give a Mercalli number to each report, and list the letter codes of the reports in order, starting with the place nearest the focus.

a) Some parked cars rocked.
b) It was difficult to stand up.
c) Vibrations like a large lorry going by.
d) A few people felt it, but hardly anyone on the ground floors.
e) Quite a few people ran outside. The librarian had to reshelve a lot of books.

5 This graph shows the time gap between P-wave arrival and S-wave arrival at places at increasing distances from the focus of an earthquake.

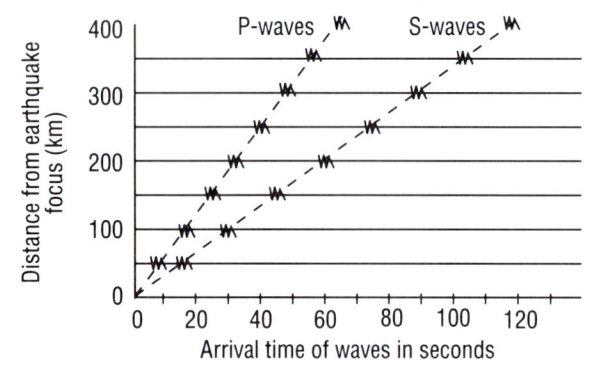

Seismograms at different distances from earthquake

a) Why do P-waves arrive before S-waves?
b) How long does it take P-waves to travel 200 km?
c) From your answer to part **b)**, find the speed of P-waves.
d) How long does it take S-waves to travel 200 km?
e) From your answer to part **d)**, find the speed of S-waves.
f) A seismogram record shows that P-waves from an earthquake arrived at the monitoring station 32 seconds before the S-wave arrived. How far is the station from the focus of the earthquake?

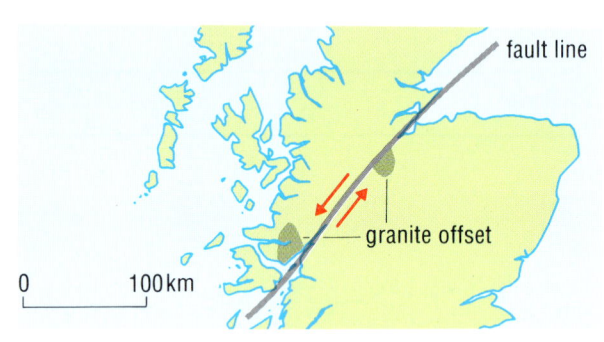

6 This map of part of Scotland shows how a major fault has broken an area of granite.

a) Measure the displacement of the fault using the scale.
b) What kind of fault is this: tensional, compressional or tear?

7 Draw diagrams to show how the landscape of:

a) The Midland Valley of Scotland
b) The South east of England

have been produced by earth movements. Which area shows mainly the *brittle* behaviour of rocks? Which area shows mainly the *plastic* behaviour of rocks?

8 Put these metamorphic rocks in order according to their grade of metamorphism: schist, slate, gneiss.

9 Write out corrected versions of these statements, by changing the **bold** word:
a) Regional metamorphism only affects small surface areas.
b) Thermal metamorphism is caused by heat and pressure.
c) Hornfels is formed by metamorphism of limestone.
d) The roots of fold mountain chains are mainly made of **thermal metamorphic** rocks.

Summary: The Rock Cycle

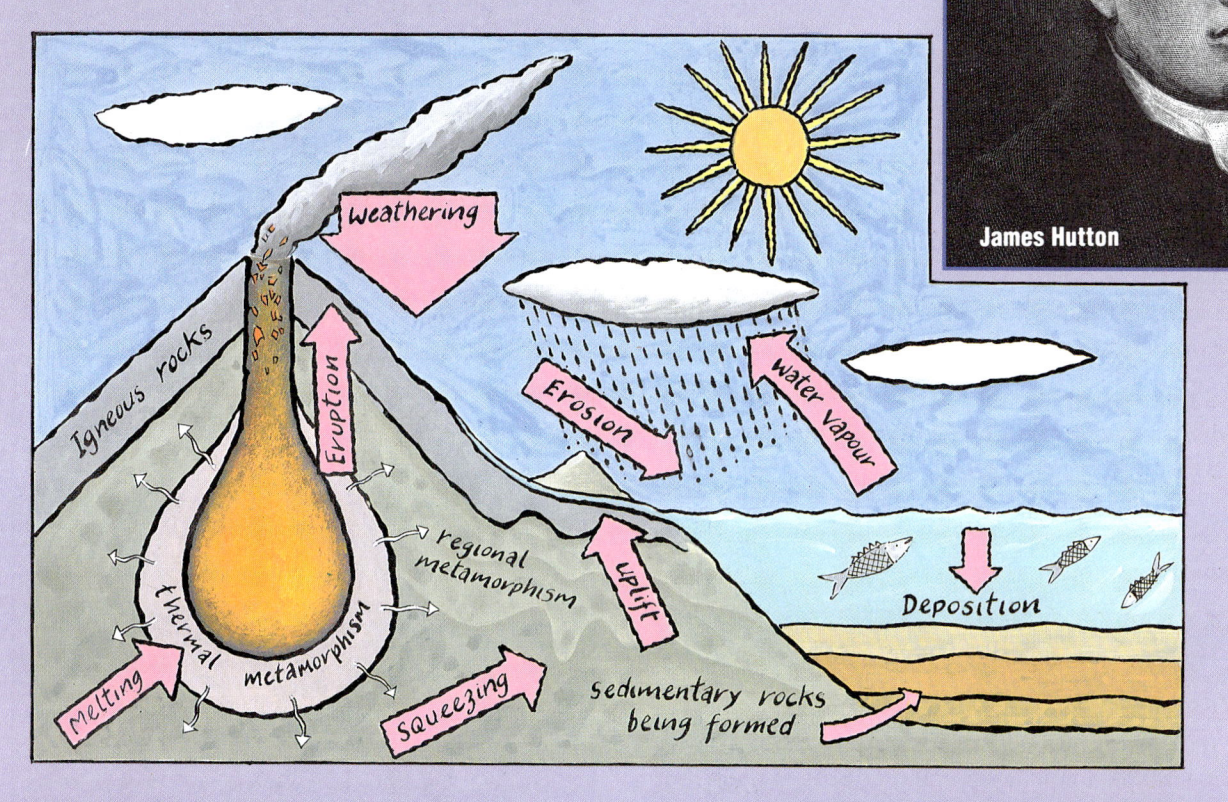

James Hutton

The rocks on the Earth's surface are made of material that has been **recycled** by the natural processes of the Earth. The atoms in any rock were once in many other rocks.

Some processes happen on the surface of the Earth. The energy driving **surface processes** comes from the Sun and from gravity. The Sun produces the air movement we call weather and also drives the water cycle.

Some processes happen inside the Earth. The energy driving **internal processes** comes from heat given out by **radioactive decay** of certain atoms.

The materials making the outer layers of the Earth are slowly moving around the **rock cycle**.

1 Use the diagram of the rock cycle to answer these questions:

a) How do sedimentary rocks turn into metamorphic rocks?

b) How do igneous rocks turn into sedimentary rocks?

c) How do metamorphic rocks turn into igneous rocks?

The Scot **James Hutton**, who lived from 1726 to 1797, put together the idea of the Rock Cycle. He wrote a book called *The Theory of the Earth* in which he pointed out that the processes that made rocks in the past are still making new rocks.

Hutton's idea that natural processes have always been working in more or less the same way is known as **Uniformitarianism**. It may seem obvious today, but in Hutton's time many people thought that the Earth had been created all in a few days and that nothing had changed since the Creation.

2 What would the Earth be like if there were no surface processes?

3 What would the Earth be like if there were no internal processes?

The processes of the rock cycle help to concentrate economically important Earth materials such as gold and oil. Earth scientists are involved in finding these concentrations and helping to extract them.

THE EARTH – USED AND ABUSED

SECTION SIX

6.1 The Earth-shapers

When this footprint was made, the walker lived on a planet affected only by natural processes. Whoever she or he was, the walker could not know that distant descendants would be earth-shapers.

The footprint is in volcanic ash, nearly 3.5 million years old. It is from Laetoli, in the African Rift Valley. The walker was someone like 'Lucy', the oldest named person. Her bones were found further north in the same rift valley.

'Lucy' was named while her bones were being cleaned and assembled at an expedition camp. The workers were listening to a tape of the Beatles' album 'Sergeant Pepper' and the track 'Lucy in the sky with diamonds' suggested a name for this distant ancestor of ours.

1 Compare Lucy and the modern human skeleton. How are they different? How are they similar?

For most of human history, as one variety of upright ape slowly evolved into another variety, people lived in a simple way. They found food around them, but over the generations they were constantly challenged by changing climates. When food got scarce they adapted by digging with sticks and bone fragments, the first tools.

2 How would digging tools help our ancestors to find more food?

Eventually they began to use fragments of rock as tools as well. Then they found that one rock could chip another rock. This made a better shaped tool for the job.

3 Compare these stone tools. Match the correct caption to the correct tool.

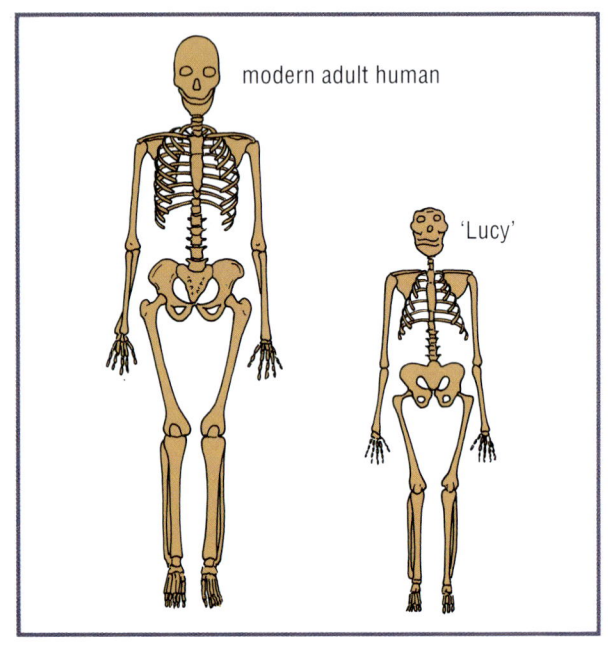

For perhaps two million years, walkers like 'Lucy' used stones, bones, wood, skins and other natural materials to live as well as they could. They developed speech about 1 million years ago. Only 10,000 years ago they started farming.

4 List three reasons why speech was an advantage for early humans?

Hide scraper (4400 BC)   **Axe head (3000 BC)**   **Spearhead (10000 BC)**

Then about 6000 years ago someone discovered that one kind of rock did something strange when it became hot in a campfire. A new hard, shiny material came out of it. We now call this **copper**. Rocks or minerals from which we can extract metals are called **ores**.

The discovery of the first metal was a turning point for humans. It began the rapid change from a world that made people adapt, to a world shaped by people to suit themselves. Writing was invented soon after this.

5 How did writing help change the world?

Other metals began to be discovered in other rocks. Nearly 3000 years ago **iron** was discovered to be one of the hardest metals. It has been at the centre of industry ever since. As more energy was produced from **fuels** such as charcoal, coal and oil, it became easier to get more metals from their **ores**.

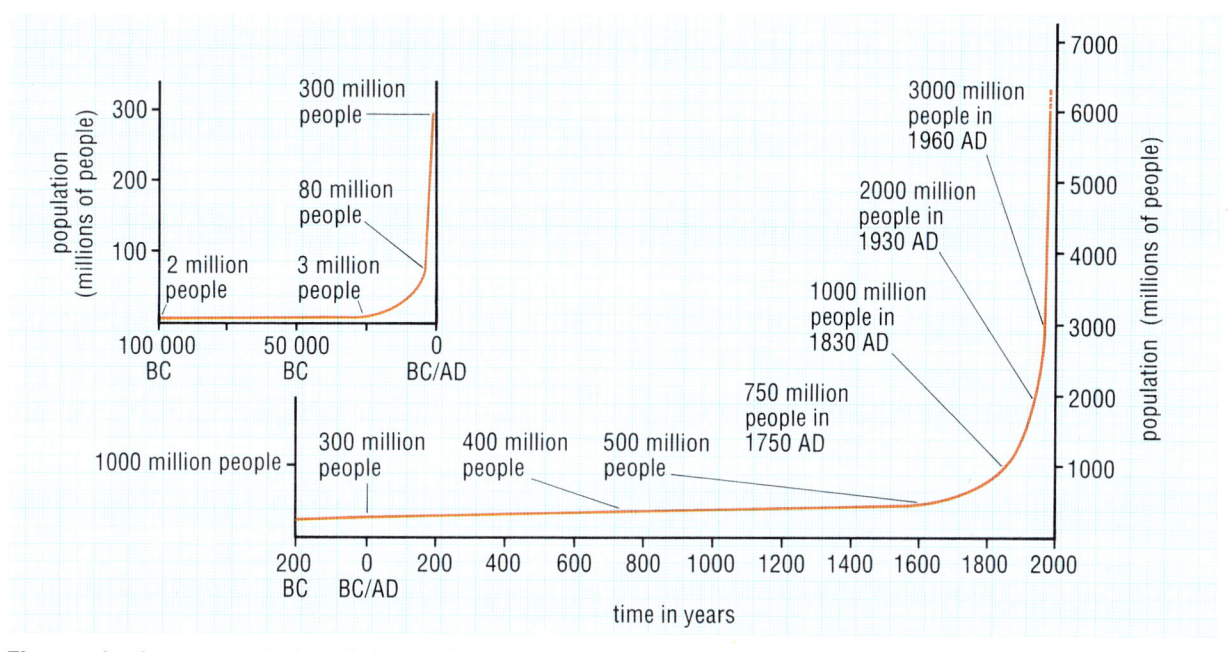

The growing human population of the Earth

At present it takes about 30 years for the world population to double. We want more and more things made from materials from the Earth. We use more and more energy. We make more and more waste.

6 a) In what year will there be twice as many people as there are now?
b) How old will you be then?

We find human activity has affected every continent and every ocean. Now we are even changing the mixture of gases in the air.

Our brainpower has brought us from a bare foot print in the volcanic ash of the African Rift Valley to this bootprint on another planet. Where will it take us next?

Bootprint on the moon

6.2 Building materials

People have made homes and other buildings out of earth materials for at least 10,000 years. Many houses are still made of **mudbrick**.

Clay is taken from the bed of a river or a lake shore. The clay is shaped into blocks and dried in the sun. Runny mud is used as **mortar** to stick the bricks together.

Mudbrick buildings start to fall apart after about 20 years, so they are knocked down and new buildings are made with new mudbricks.

Town sites slowly grew on the rubble of old buildings, to make an artificial hill or **tell**. Some tells are over 10 m high, and thousands of years of building and rebuilding must have happened on the site. A cutting through a tell gives a slice of history.

Tel Lachish in Israel

Roman villa in Pompeii, Italy, with stone walls, concrete columns, and a brick door arch

A house made of mudbricks

Strong **cement** mortar can be made from limestone and clay heated together. **Concrete** is made by mixing cement with sand or gravel in various mixtures. The Romans used concrete in foundations and for domes over 2000 years ago. They sometimes added volcanic ashes to the mixture.

1 Why is concrete a popular building material?

Rocks have been cut into building stones for thousands of years. Choosing the rock depends on what is available and what it is for. Some rocks cut easily into neat blocks along the bedding layers. Others have to be cut with special saws. There is still a big demand for building stones for decorative purposes, for gravestones and for the restoration of old buildings. Cheaper manufactured alternatives are normally used for the main structure of buildings.

2 List the questions an architect would think about before choosing a building stone.

In many climates, like Britain, mudbrick would weather away quickly. **Fired bricks** last a lot longer. They are clay bricks heated in **kilns** at about 1000°C. In effect, fired bricks are artificial metamorphic rocks. In Britain, fired brick did not come into general use until the sixteenth century.

3 Are fired bricks most like regional metamorphic rocks or thermal metamorphic rocks?

4 Suggest why some fired bricks look very different from other fired bricks.

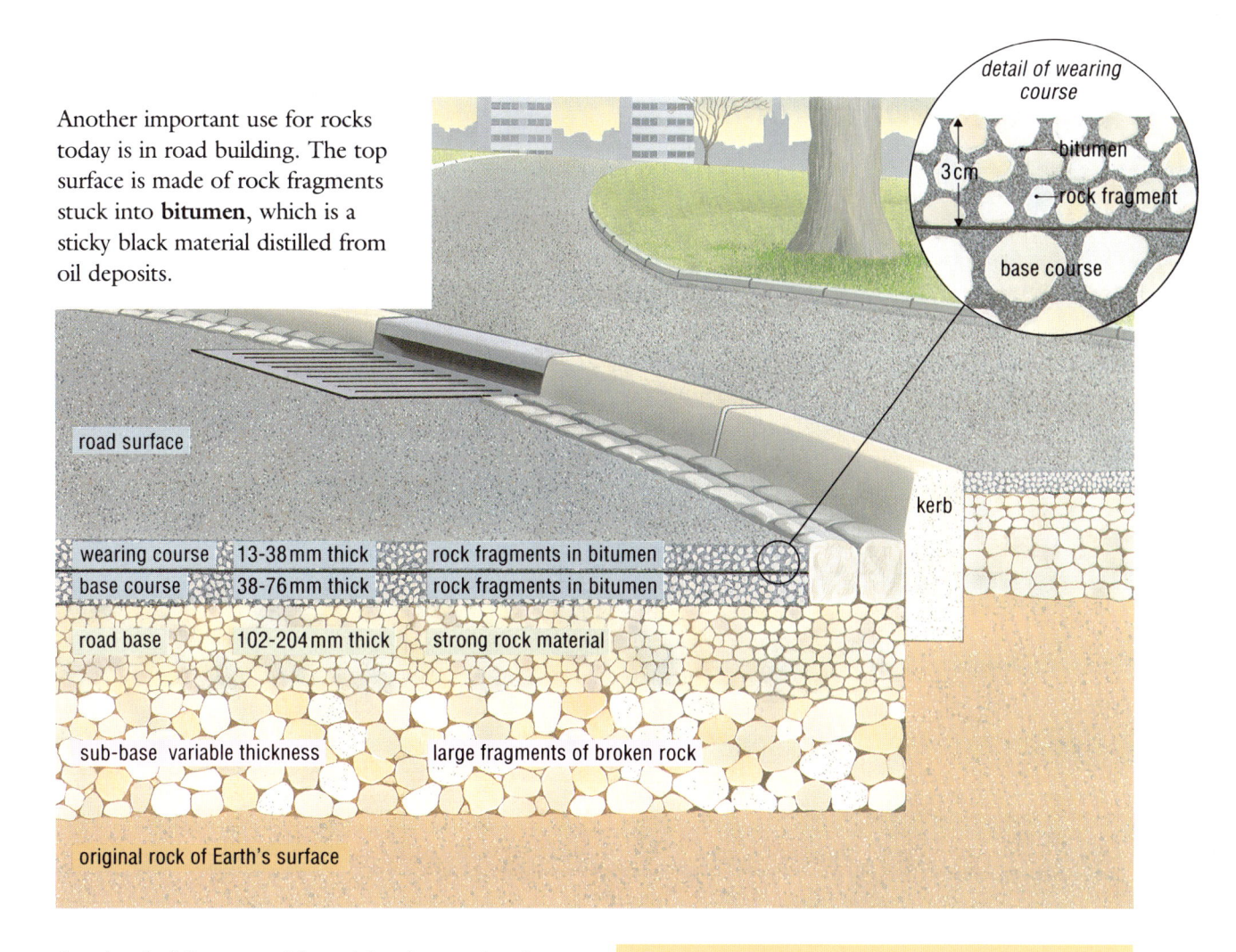

Another important use for rocks today is in road building. The top surface is made of rock fragments stuck into **bitumen**, which is a sticky black material distilled from oil deposits.

Another building material used for thousands of years is **plaster** made from the mineral **gypsum**, (calcium sulphate). The gypsum powder is heated to drive out water from its crystal structure. When it is remixed with water it must be used fairly quickly before it sets.

5 List some reasons why we usually plaster walls.

Crushed stone, sand and gravel are used in very large amounts. They are known as **aggregates**. Aggregates are needed for roadbuilding and to make concrete. Large amounts of limestone are also needed for making concrete. These materials are dug from **quarries**.

Quarries can be very big and many are not attractive. Plans to open new quarries are often opposed by some local people. Other local people may welcome the new jobs and money that quarries bring into an area.

6 Write two letters to your local paper, one from a person *in favour* of a new quarry and one from a person *against* it, giving your reasons.

Ideas for investigating building materials

a) How do different building materials cope with different weathering processes?
b) If you were a contractor, how would you choose a roadstone?
c) What are the strongest concretes? (mixtures of cement with sand and/or gravel in different proportions)
d) Compare the advantages and disadvantages of natural slate and artificial tiles in roofing.
e) What affects the setting time of plaster?

● Make sure you carry out fair tests.
● Produce detailed and clear reports.

7 Find out if any earth materials are extracted in your local area, and if so what types. How many jobs are created by this form of industry, and what are the values of the products compared to the costs involved in extracting them?

6.3 Extracting coal

Coal is a valuable source of low-cost energy. It can be mined by the **deep mining** method using shafts, or by the **opencast** method using quarrying to reach the coal seams.

During opencasting, the soils are taken off first and stored around the edge of the site. These **soildumps** hide the pit, and help to cut the noise from the site. The contractors put the soil back after the site is refilled.

The layers of coal measure rocks above the coal seams are known as **overburden**. They are dug out in slices by large shovels. Dump trucks carry the overburden to storage in the **overburden mound** or to the **compaction benches**. (see **D** below).

The overburden mound can usually be seen from the surrounding area. It is shaped to make it appear more like a natural hill. Grass is planted on the slopes to improve its appearance. The mound is used up when the hole is refilled.

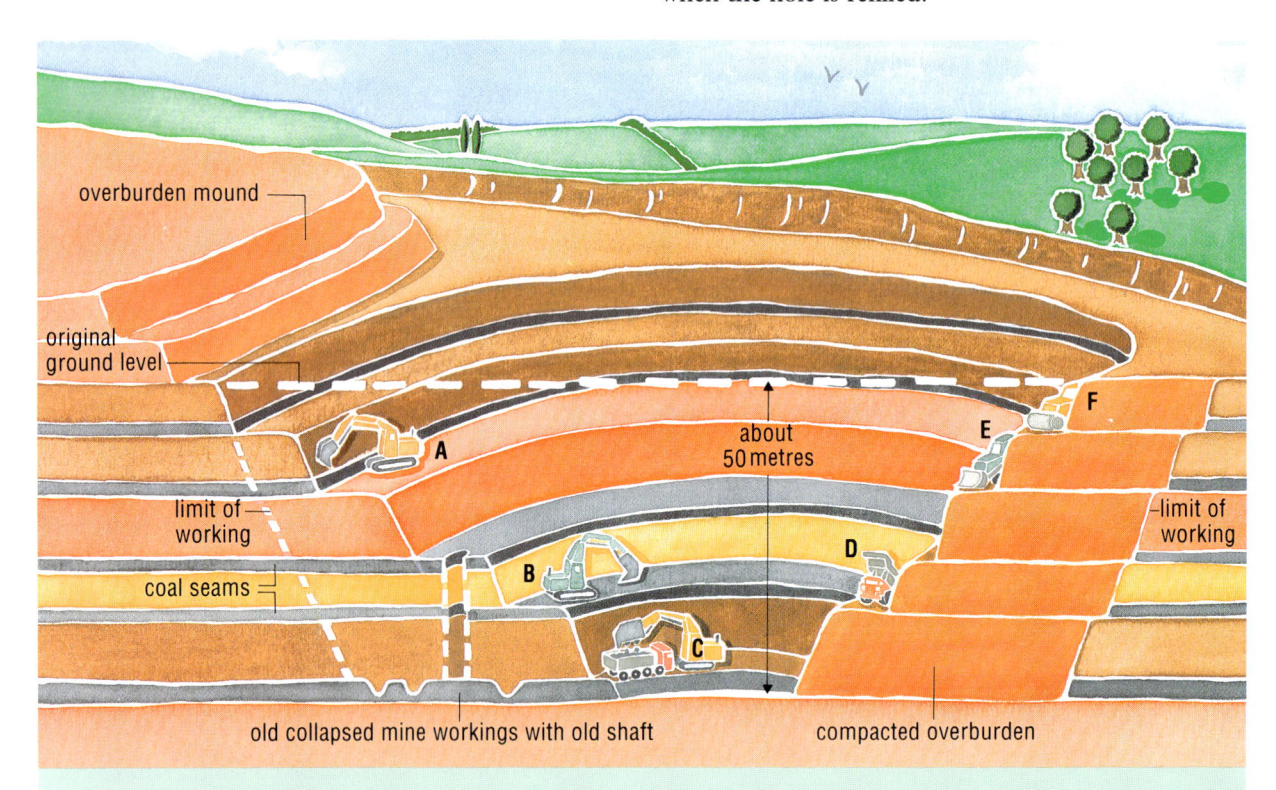

The main processes of opencast mining

In the picture, the new excavations are on the left, and the right side is being refilled.

A Layers of overburden are being cut away. This will be taken to the overburden mound or to the compaction benches (see **D**) by dump trucks.

B The top of a coal seam is **cleaned** by scraping and sweeping. Anything which cannot be used as fuel is removed before the coal is cut.

C The coal seam is lifted and loaded on to a truck. It will be taken to ground level for crushing, and taken away by customer's lorries.

D Overburden may be dumped on a compaction bench. This part of the site has had the coal seams removed and is now being filled in.

E A bulldozer spreads the dumped overburden to make a layer on the compaction bench.

F The overburden is compacted. Here a vibrating roller pushes the overburden down to squeeze the rock fragments together. The whole site will be finished off this way. The original soil will be put back on top.

Lots of water is found in opencasting operations. Diesel pumps are used to pump it out. The coal has to be dry because wet coal will not burn well. The water is not clean and cannot be piped straight off the site. It is pumped into **lagoons** where the dirt can settle out. When it is clean the water is channelled off. It is tested to avoid pollution.

Opencast coal mining is an industrial activity which can affect the environment. Sites are designed to reduce that impact. **Wheel wash machines** clean the wheels of all lorries leaving the site, to keep mud off local roads.

People often think opencast mines must be dusty. To stop dust, **water bowsers** spray water on to site roads. This damps the surface and prevents dust from flying about.

To restore the land, overburden is moved back into the hole. Special machines compact the filling. This breaks down the material into small pieces and squeezes out pockets of air.

As layers of filling build up, technicians test the work to ensure that the restored land is stable for re-use. The soils are put back last.

Wheel wash unit

Water bowser with pressure spray

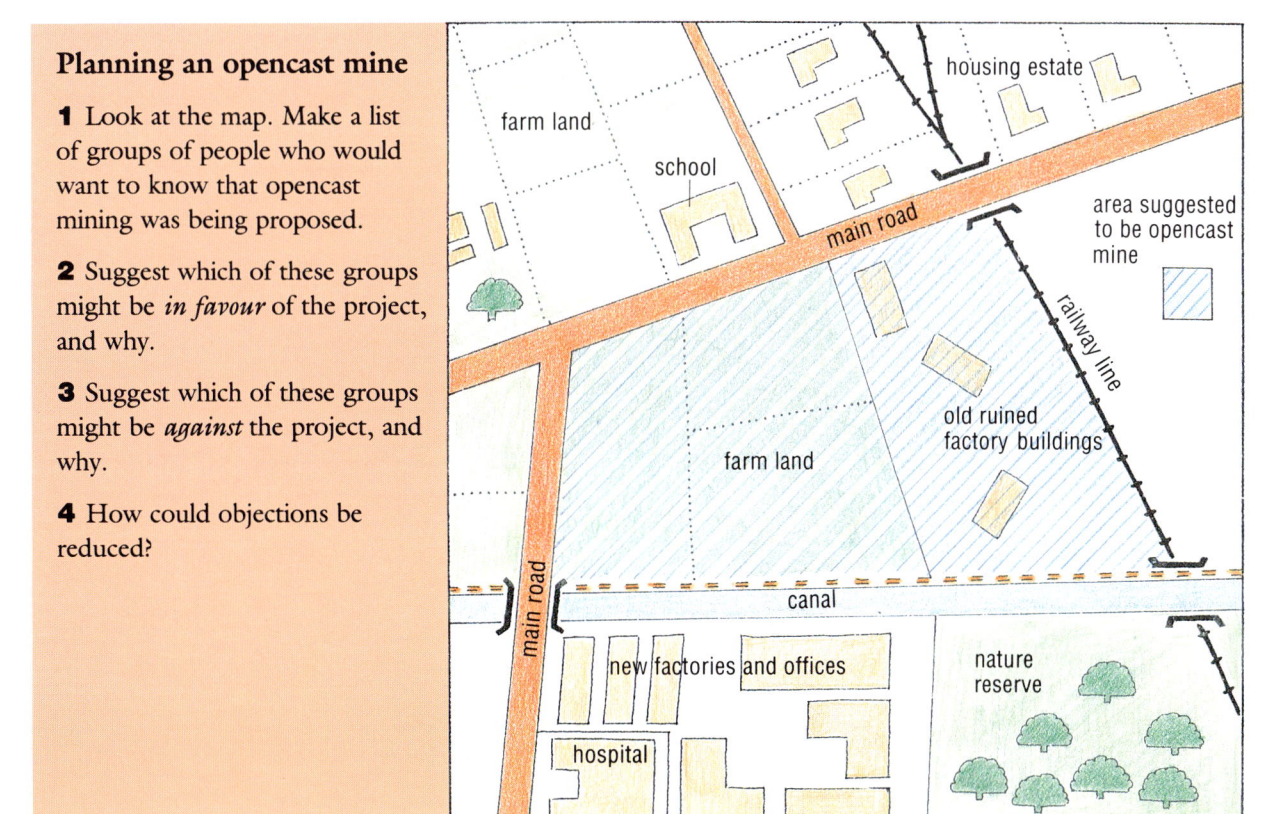

Planning an opencast mine

1 Look at the map. Make a list of groups of people who would want to know that opencast mining was being proposed.

2 Suggest which of these groups might be *in favour* of the project, and why.

3 Suggest which of these groups might be *against* the project, and why.

4 How could objections be reduced?

6.4 Oil and gas

Like coal, oil and natural gas are **fossil fuels**, formed from ancient living things. The animals and plants that produced oil and gas lived in seas, not swamps like the coal measures (see page 46).

Probably most oil and gas comes from **algae**, simple plants. When they died, fossil fuel deposits were only formed if a certain sequence of events happened. (In brackets, you will see how each step could stop the process. Then no oil or gas could be found at that place.) The whole process may take millions of years.

First the dead algae were quickly covered by fine mud on the seabed. The mud kept oxygen and predators away from them. (The remains could be eaten or the decaying material could wash away.)

As the mud squashed them down and they were warmed up by heat from inside the Earth, **bacteria** rotted the soft parts to make oil and gas. The mud is the **source rock** for the oil and gas. (If the temperature was below 60°C the oil or gas would not form, and if it was over 160°C the algae remains would break up without forming oil and gas.)

The drops of oil and gas then moved upwards, collecting in rocks with pore spaces, such as sandstones, replacing the water that would normally be there. Rocks that can hold oil and gas in this way are called **reservoir rocks**. (If there was no suitable reservoir rock, the oil and gas might stay thinly spread in the source rock.)

The oil and gas kept moving up until they came to a less porous rock layer, which stopped them. This is the **cap rock**. (If there was nothing around the reservoir rocks, the oil and gas would leak away.)

The rock layers were then affected by earth movements shaping the layers to make a **trap** which kept the oil and gas in the porous rock. Sometimes natural shapes in the rock layers can act as traps.

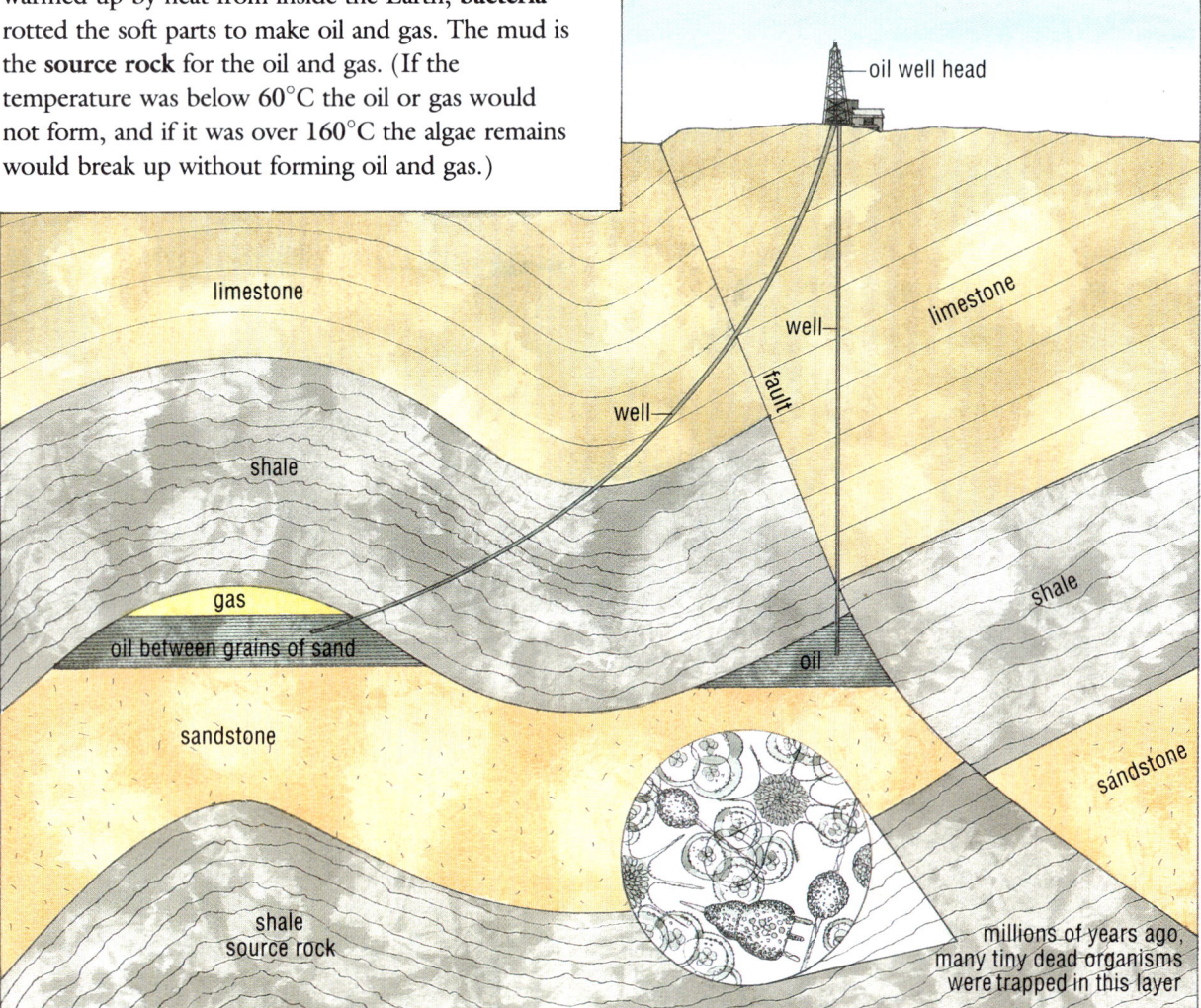

Some examples of oil and gas traps

Reservoir rocks and cap rocks

- Devise an investigation to discover which rocks make the best *reservoir* and *cap* rocks.
- You might find the following apparatus and materials useful, but use your own ideas as well: cooking oil; electronic balance; measuring cylinder; beakers; water; stopwatch; Plasticine; salt water; tap water.
- You might find it particularly interesting to investigate the following rocks, but add others if you wish: sandstones (try different types); shale; rock salt; limestones (try different types); igneous rocks (try different types).

Finding oil traps

Companies looking for oil and gas use various scientific methods. **Drilling** a borehole is the last step, as it is expensive. Long before a drilling rig appears, other methods will be used to decide if drilling is worth trying.

If possible, geological maps (showing the layout of rocks on the ground) and air photographs of the areas are made first. If the area is underwater or heavily forested, this may not help much.

Seismic surveys reveal the arrangement of the rock layers without drilling. Seismologists make artificial earthquakes using explosives, compressed air or by vibrating heavy weights.

Seismic waves travel into the Earth but bounce back from the rock layers. The waves are picked up by seismometers and then a computer draws a picture of the rock layers. It needs a skilled scientist to work out what the picture means.

Oil company scientists working on the results of a seismic survey

When a spot is chosen, drilling starts and the drillhole is washed through with a fluid to cool the bit and to bring up the rock fragments. These are examined to check what layers are being drilled at different depths.

The drilling fluid, called **drilling mud**, has to be a heavy mixture to balance any high pressures found in the hole. It usually includes barium sulphate, a very dense compound found as the mineral barite.

When some layers need more careful study, they are **cored** using a hollow drilling bit. As the borehole might go into a reservoir rock, rigs have special equipment to balance any pressure found underground. When oil or gas are found they do not rush out of the hole. They are detected by a rise in the pressure in the hole and stopped from escaping by the weight of the drilling mud.

Oil drilling rig

SECTION SIX

THE EARTH – USED AND ABUSED

6.5 Ores, metals and chemicals

For over two million years our ancestors used wood, stone, bones and animal skin. Then perhaps 6000 years ago the metal **copper** was discovered, probably by accident (see page 67). Copper has several ores, one of which is the green mineral **malachite**.

This discovery changed history, for copper could be shaped into new tools such as thin blades and fine needles. These could not be made from stone or wood.

Getting metals from ores needs *energy* to break the metal atoms out of the **chemical compound**. Our ancestors did not know the science of chemical reactions, but they discovered a technology: the extraction of metals by heating. Later, when the science was understood, electrical extraction was also developed.

Extracting copper from an ore

Equipment: malachite, reaction tube, Bunsen burner, clamp stand, bung and tubing

- Put some malachite powder in a reaction tube and clamp it as shown.
- Heat the tube over a Bunsen flame. Observe and note any changes.
- When no more changes happen, put a bung in the top of the reaction tube with a connection to the gas supply.
- Heat the tube again with gas flowing through. Burn off excess gas at the side hole.
- Observe and note any changes.

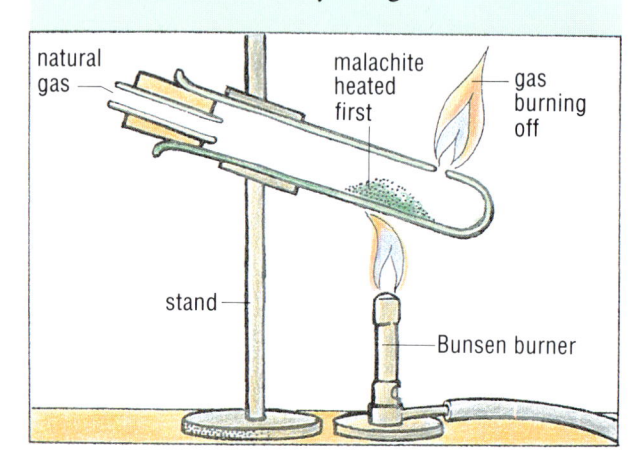

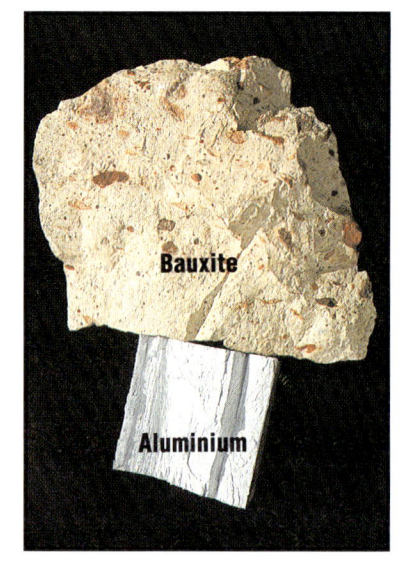

Metal	Rock or mineral ore	Metal first extracted	Extraction method
Magnesium	Magnesite	1808	Electrical
Aluminium	Bauxite	1825	Electrical
Zinc	Zinc blende	0 AD	Heating
Iron	Haematite	1200 BC	Heating
Tin	Cassiterite	2500 BC	Heating
Copper	Chalcopyrite	3500 BC	Heating

As people were able to use more energy, they extracted metals that were more tightly combined in their ores. The most **reactive** metals need large amounts of electrical energy to extract them.

Calchopyrite — Copper

Bauxite — Aluminium

Haematite — Iron

Metal ore deposits

Metal ores are found in a variety of places. Here are three examples of the way ores can be formed. There are many other ways as well.

Some ores are found in **veins** produced when hot solutions found their way along cracks and faults in rocks. The solutions often come from the melts that form igneous rocks and from the groundwater in the surrounding rocks. The ores of Southwest England were formed like this.

Some ores are formed when rocks weather. This concentrates the metal atoms into a weathering product. *Bauxite* is formed in this way.

Some ores are concentrated in river beds when the heavy grains settle after being eroded from thin veins upstream. These are **placer deposits**. Cassiterite placers are found in Malaysia; placer gold is found in many parts of the world.

As metal atoms are found in most rocks, the important point about an ore body is that it is a *concentration* of the metallic minerals.

Ores and metals

- Examine ore minerals. Examples are haematite; bauxite; galena; cassiterite; chalcopyrite.
- Devise a key to help an exploration team identify these ore minerals. (You should not expect the team to have laboratory equipment with them.)

Test drilling for salt in Cheshire

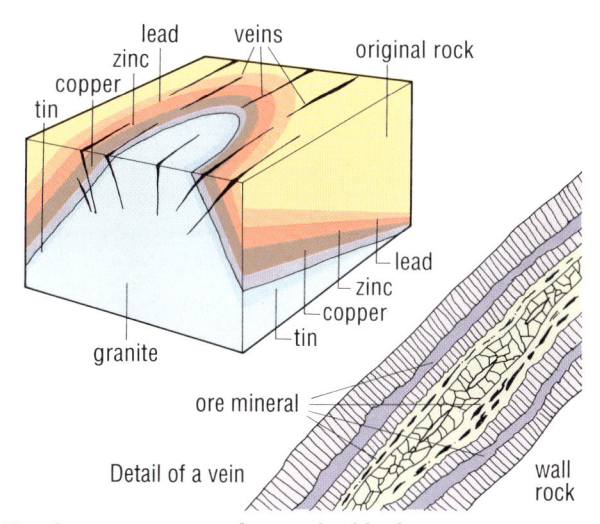

Metal ore zones around a granite block

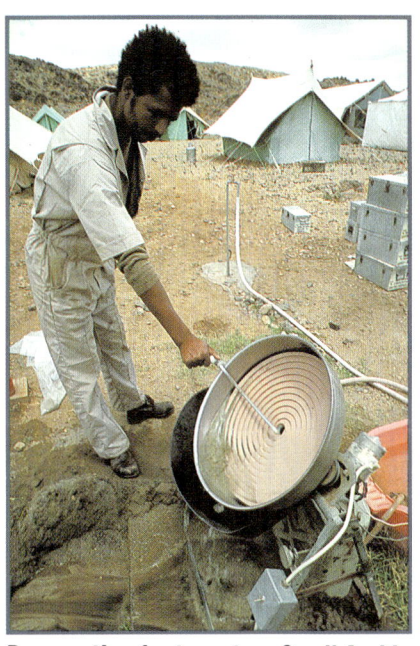

Prospecting for tungsten, Saudi Arabia

Minerals as a source of important chemicals

Many rocks and minerals provide important chemicals for industry. **Rock salt** is the most obvious example. It has always been important in food. Roman soldiers were even paid part of their wages as salt, their *salarium*. The word *salary* derives from this. Now one main use of salt is as a road de-icer in winter. It is also our source of **sodium** and **chlorine**.

Layers of salt were formed in Britain long ago by the evaporation of an ancient sea (see page 43). It is either mined as rock salt, or dissolved underground and the solution, **brine**, is pumped up to the surface and evaporated.

6.6 Some pollution problems

As more people have used the Earth's materials the composition of the atmosphere has changed. Our activities make gases not normally found in air. The biggest source of this **air pollution** is the burning of fossil fuels.

Burning coal was used to heat most homes in British towns until the 1950s. **Smoke**, particles from the fires, went up chimneys and hung in the air. Also, one natural chemical in coal is **iron sulphide**. It is only there in small amounts, but burning coal makes **sulphur dioxide**.

The air in cities in Britain became very polluted. People breathing in smoke and sulphur dioxide could become very ill.

1 What groups of people might be most affected?

Then in December 1952, in London, the weather was cold and very damp. With the air pollution this damp air made a **smog**. During one week, over 2000 people died because of smog. The Government decided to clean up the air, and in 1956 the **Clean Air Act** was passed to cut down coal burning in cities. This created **Smokeless Zones**. Air quality has improved since.

Testing for solid particle pollution

- Dry and weigh some filter papers.
- Put them outside at chosen sites for a week.
- Bring them in and dry them carefully.
- Weigh them again.
- Is there any link between the amount of pollution and the places you chose to test?

In Los Angeles, California, different problems are caused by car exhaust fumes. The main gases involved are **carbon monoxide**, **hydrocarbons** and **nitrogen oxides**. Los Angeles is in a bowl between hills and this sometimes traps dense air. The heat and ultraviolet light cause chemical reactions in the gases and make **photochemical smog**.

2 Why are photochemical smogs rare in Britain?

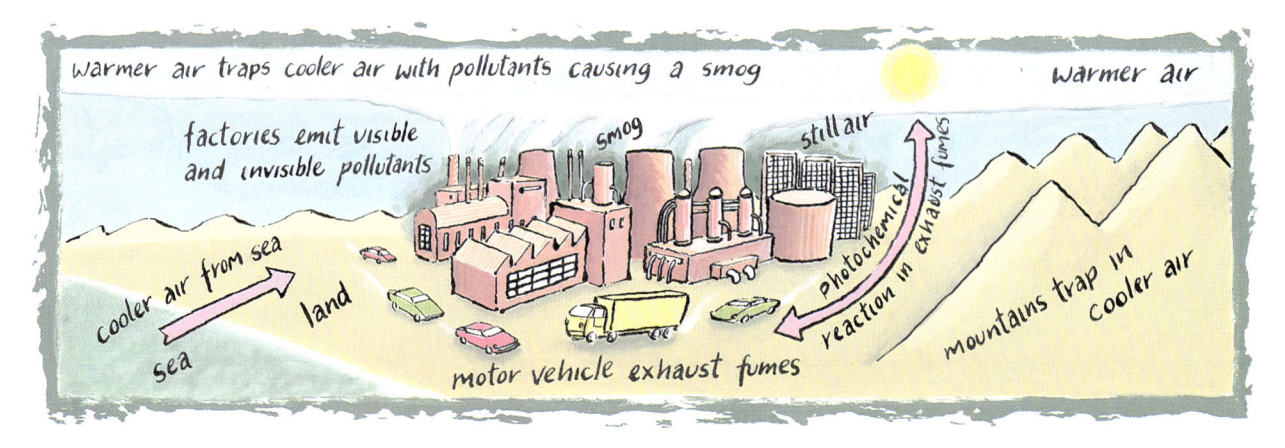

Much of the solar energy reaching the Earth is converted to heat energy. This then radiates away, and would all escape into space if the gases of the atmosphere were not there to stop it. These gases reflect back much of the heat, acting like the glass in a greenhouse. The Earth would be a much colder place without them. However, manufacturing processes and burning fossil fuels are producing more of the gases which give this **Greenhouse Effect**, such as carbon dioxide, methane, and nitrogen oxide. As a result, the Earth is warming up.

Some scientists expect the Greenhouse Effect to warm the Earth by 2°C before 2100 AD. Sea levels rise as the ocean water expands. The polar ice caps may thicken at first, as more water evaporates from seas and falls as snow. Later the ice caps may start to melt and become thinner, and the seas rise more, covering low-lying land.

The Greenhouse Effect may change climates all over the Earth. Some experts think that 10 per cent of the world's people may become refugees. If we do not cut production of greenhouse gases the world could change dramatically.

Another problem is the thinning of the **ozone layer**. The ozone layer cuts down the amount of **ultraviolet light** from the sun reaching the Earth. Ozone, O_3, easily breaks down to oxygen, O_2, when certain gases rise from the Earth. Thin ozone allows extra ultraviolet to reach the Earth's surface. This could cause more people to get skin cancer, and might affect many other living things.

Spraying an oil slick with chemicals

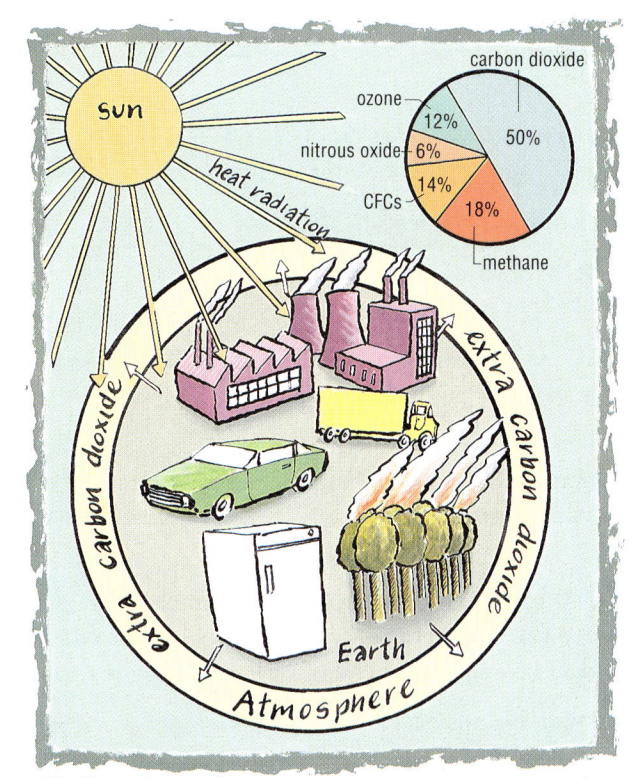

The Greenhouse Gases

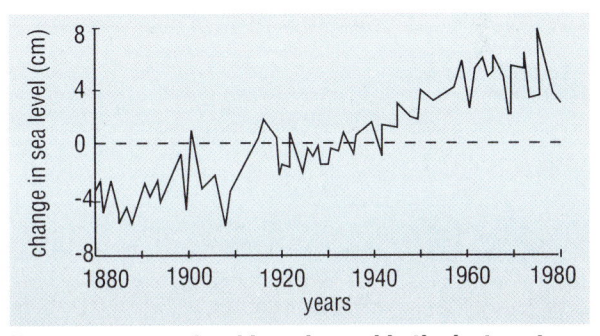

How average sea level has changed in the last century

Pollution of the seas

Large quantities of oil are sometimes spilt on the oceans when tankers are wrecked. The oil is difficult to clean up. Even the chemicals used to break up the oil can cause damage to plants and animals.

Oil pollution at sea

- Half-fill a test-tube with water.
- Put some drops of cooking oil into the tube.
- Shake the tube and observe what happens.
- Add some drops of washing-up liquid.
- Shake the tube again, and observe.
- Expand this experiment into an investigation to devise better ways of clearing up oil.

6.7 Our throwaway world

Humans have always produced waste. Today we make far more rubbish than our ancestors.

1 Suggest reasons why this is so.

2 What kinds of wastes are produced by:
a) shops b) farms c) servicing garages?

Wastes can be solids, liquids or gases. Waste disposal is an important industrial activity.

Some solid waste can be **recycled** and some can be burned, but burial in **landfill sites** is essential for some materials.

Landfilling is similar to filling and compaction at an opencast coal site. Instead of overburden, waste is compacted into the quarry. Soil is rolled on to the layer of waste at the end of each day to act as a seal.

Domestic dustbins are the main source of waste for landfill sites. In recent years many people have begun to take some materials to recycling centres such as bottle, can or paper banks. Also, people often use some wastes as composting material for gardens.

3 Try to classify the different kinds of rubbish put into your dustbin at home.

Problems can be caused by bad landfill sites. Liquid waste might leak into the surrounding rocks if they are porous. Then it could find its way into underground water.

4 Why is it worrying if liquid waste gets into underground water?

Another problem is that rotting organic material can make methane gas. This is the same as natural gas. It can collect in spaces in the landfill site.

5 Why could methane gas be dangerous if the landfill site was built on later?

With special equipment the methane can be piped off and used in small power stations to make electricity.

6 Compare these two landfill sites. What are good and bad design points for landfill sites?

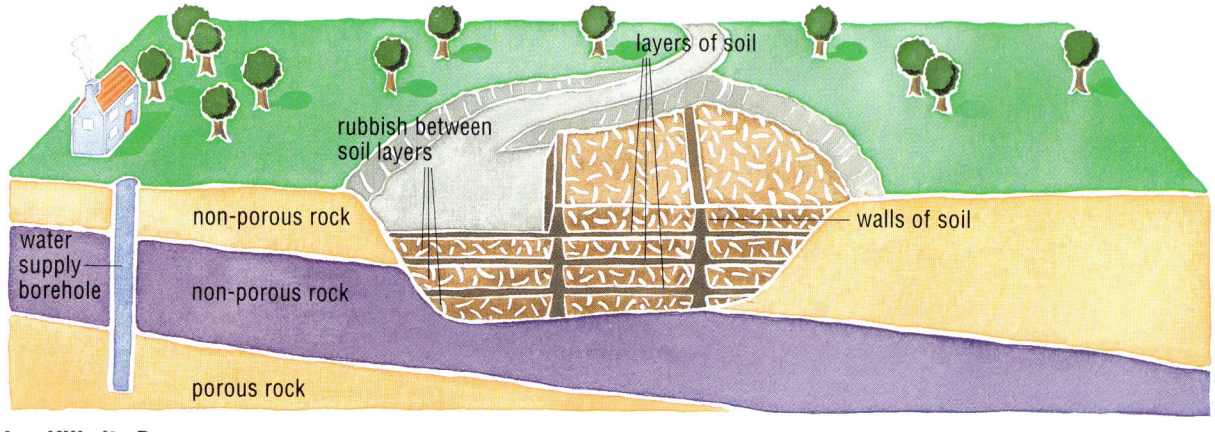

Landfill site A

Landfill site B

Using an old quarry as a landfill site can be very profitable. In 1985 a quarry owner could earn £10 to dispose of a cubic metre of rubbish in the Midlands, and £56 per cubic metre in London.

7 Why is landfill very expensive in London?

8 What would be the 1985 value of an old quarry 10 m deep and roughly 2000 m² in area

a) in London?
b) in the Midlands?

Special wastes need special arrangements. Liquid chemical wastes from industry and radioactive wastes from nuclear power stations are a problem.

9 Why would landfill be a bad way to dispose of chemical and radioactive wastes?

Discuss with your group these possible ways of disposing of chemical and radioactive wastes.

10 What are the good points about each suggestion?

11 What are the bad points about each suggestion?

a) Putting them down old deep mine shafts.
b) Putting them in old salt mines.
c) Launching them into space.
d) Pumping them into abandoned oil fields.
e) Pumping them into the sea.
f) Dumping them on the seabed.
g) Putting them into ocean trenches.

Section 6 questions

1 Explain why mudbrick is a reasonably good building material in some climates, but not in others.

2 What are the a) advantages b) disadvantages of fired brick compared to building stone?

3 a) Draw a labelled diagram to show the structure of a typical road.
b) Suggest why the road is made of various layers.

4 Describe and illustrate the processes involved in working an opencast coal site.

5 Explain why sedimentary rock layers do not always contain oil or gas.

6 Draw a diagram to show why faults and folds are important in the formation of many oilfields.

7 Explain the difference between the technical terms *source rock*, *reservoir rock*, *caprock* used in the oil industry.

8 Describe how new oilfields are discovered.

9 Draw a timechart to scale to show the dates of discovery of some important metals.

10 Draw diagrams to show why the Greenhouse Effect causes the earth to become warmer.

The next questions require you to research information from books in a library or from computer-held databases.

11 List the building materials in your school or home. Find out:

a) The raw materials needed for each material. Chart your findings.
b) Where have those materials come from? Record your findings on outline maps of Britain, Europe or the world.

12 Describe and illustrate the processes involved in working a deep coal mine.

13 On outline maps of Britain, Europe or the world show the location of coal deposits, oil fields and gas fields that are currently of economic value.

14 Find the chemical formulae of metal ores and construct chemical equations to show how metals can be extracted from them.

15 Make posters on the modern methods used to extract the following metals from their ores:

a) copper   b) aluminium   c) iron.

16 Report on the allegation that *acid rain* is produced by burning coal in power stations, and that it causes damage to the environment.

17 Prepare a 5 minute television script on the Greenhouse Effect and on damage to the ozone layer. Aim for scientific accuracy but also aim to be understood by the ordinary viewer.

7.1 Our round world

From the coast, this would be the view of a ship sailing out towards a lighthouse.

From the ship, the view is rather different.

1 Explain these two different sets of pictures.

View from the dockside

View from the ship

About 2600 years ago, Pharaoh Neco sent a ship's crew from Egypt with orders to sail through the Red Sea and south along the coast of Africa. The midday Sun was ahead of them.

They sailed west round the Cape of Good Hope and then northwards again around West Africa to the Straits of Gibralter. Sailing east again they came back to Egypt after two years.

They brought back many stories, but one thing was hard to believe. They said that when they were passing the southern part of Africa, the Sun was to their north. No-one believed them.

2 Can you explain their observation?

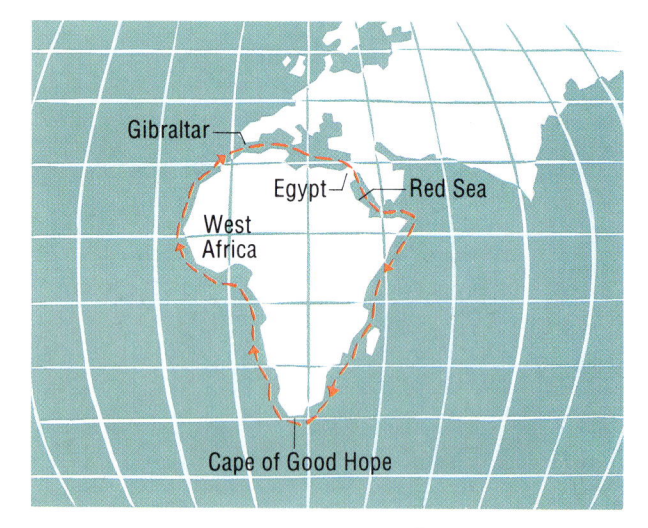

Sailing round Africa

By the time of the Greek thinker Pythagoras, 2500 years ago, it seems that most people accepted that the Earth was a round ball. The puzzle was: how *big* is the Earth? Over 2000 years ago, a Greek called Eratosthenes tried to measure the Earth. He lived in Egypt.

Eratosthenes noticed that on Midsummer Day, at midday, the Sun was directly overhead in southern Egypt. 800 km further north at Alexandria on the same day, it was not overhead. It was 7.2° south from vertical.

Eratosthenes knew that a whole circle was 360°

$$\frac{7.2°}{360°} = \frac{1}{50}$$

He concluded that 800 km was therefore $\frac{1}{50}$ of the Earth's circumference.

3 Calculate the Earth's circumference.

Eratosthenes also knew:
Diameter of circle = Circumference ÷ π

Since π is 3.14, we cay say:
Earth's diameter = Answer to Question 3 ÷ 3.14

4 What is the diameter of the Earth using Eratosthenes' method?

As it happens this is almost exactly the diameter of the Earth as measured by modern scientists: 12,750 km. Of course Eratosthenes did not use kilometres. His units have been converted.

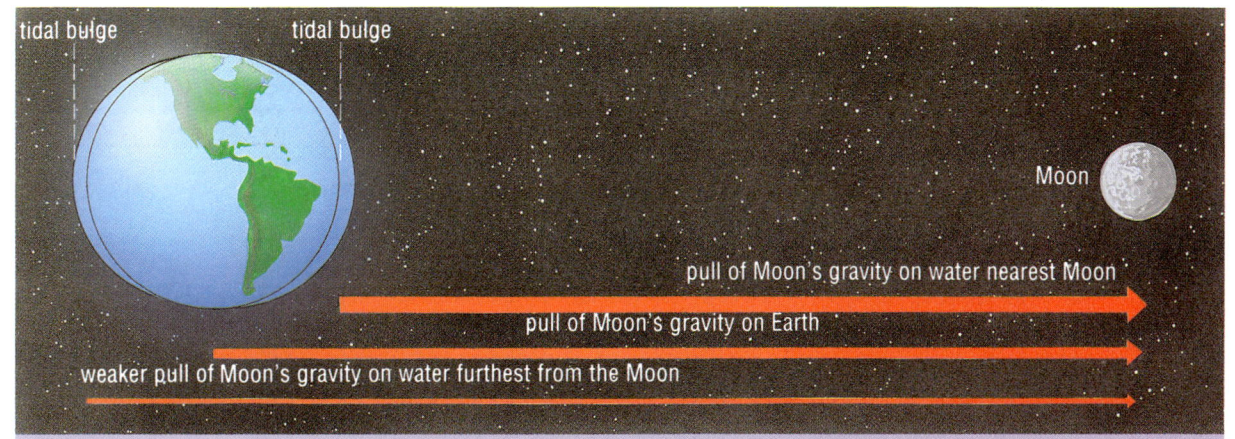

At the same time as Eratosthenes was working, another Greek, Aristarchus of Samos, suggested that the Earth travelled round the Sun. He was mainly ignored for over 1500 years.

If people had believed Aristarchus, the force of **gravity** might have been understood long before Sir Isaac Newton described it in the seventeenth century.

Newton worked out that the movement of the Earth round the Sun can be explained if all objects produce a *force of gravity* which pulls on all other objects. Gravity holds the Earth in its orbit around the Sun. He was the first to explain why oceans have **tides**.

Newton showed that the gravity of the Moon pulls water into **tidal bulges**. As the Earth turns these affect different places.

High tides on the side of the Earth *facing* the Moon are easy to explain by the Moon's gravity pulling the sea. The high tide on the other side of the Earth is more difficult to explain.

The water on the far side of the Earth is pulled by the Moon's gravity *less* than the Earth itself is pulled.

Newton's theory of gravity was also the key to understanding many things seen in the sky at night.

7.2 Patterns in the sky

For thousands of years people have looked at the sky at night. The stars appeared to make patterns which they interpreted as animals, people or objects. Anyone watching the sky for a few hours – perhaps shepherds guarding a flock of sheep – would see that the pattern of stars appears to move around one special star.

Imagine a black umbrella with bright spots painted on the inside. If you turn the umbrella *anticlockwise* around its handle the spots move around one point in the middle. This is how the stars appear to move around the Pole star, **Polaris**.

Really, the sky is still and the Earth is turning under it. Imagine keeping the umbrella still, but turning *yourself* clockwise.

The star patterns imagined by people long ago are still used by scientists to make star maps. The patterns are called **constellations**.

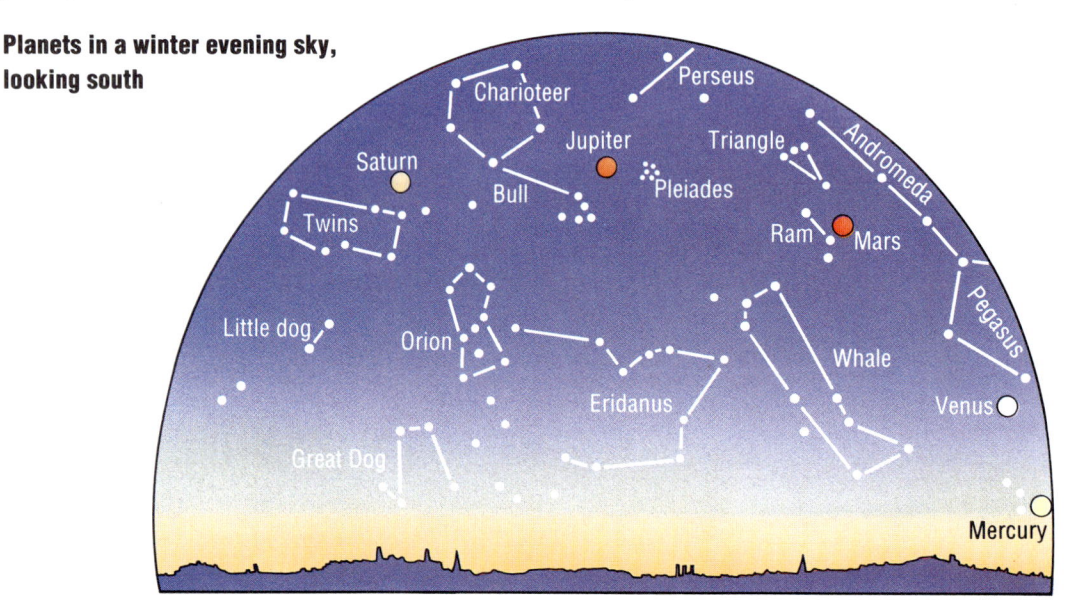

Planets in a winter evening sky, looking south

People noticed that five lights in the sky moved about. During one night they seemed just like **fixed stars** but after a few weeks they had moved to different positions. These moving lights glow steadily – they do not twinkle like the stars. They became known as **planets** from a Greek word meaning *wanderer*. Some cultures named them after various gods and goddesses.

1 Try to match these names to the descriptions of planets **a)** to **e)**:

Jupiter, the 'king god'; Mars, the god of war; Venus, goddess of love; Saturn, the old father of Jupiter, who walks very slowly; Mercury, the speedy messenger of the gods.

a) This planet moves quite quickly, but is seen only just before sunrise or just after sunset.
b) This planet is also near the Sun in the sky, but is the brightest planet.
c) This planet is red, so it reminded people of blood.
d) This planet is a golden orange, perhaps rather royal, they thought.
e) This planet moves very slowly.

Long ago people thought the stars were all the same distance from Earth, like the umbrella spots. This is how the discovery was made which changed this opinion.

The distance between all the stars looks fixed, but by looking at them carefully, and then again six months later, scientists see that some stars appear to have moved a little. This is because the stars are now being seen from the other side of the Earth's orbit around the Sun, and an effect called **parallax** is operating.

Looking from the window of a moving car, the trees and buildings close to you appear to 'move past' much more quickly than those further away. The nearer trees and buildings appear to move more than the further ones. The apparent movement is called parallax, and this can be used to calculate the distance to the stars from the Earth. The car's journey is the same as the Earth's orbit between different sides of the Sun.

Parallax measurements show that even the nearest other star, *Proxima Centauri*, is 42.75 million million kilometers away. We can write this as 4.275×10^{13} km.

2 Light rays travel at 300,000 km/second. How long does it take for light to reach us from Proxima Centauri? Show how you work it out. These units are called **light years**.

Proxima Centauri is 4.5 light years away. For comparison, the Moon is about *1.5 light seconds* away. The Sun is about *8 light minutes* away from Earth, or 144 million kilometres.

On very clear nights away from city lights we can see a faint ragged band of light across the sky. The !Kung people of Southern Africa call this *The Backbone of the Night*. It is made of millions of stars that are so far off that we cannot detect parallax. We call it the **Milky Way**.

The Milky Way is an edge-on view of a great disc of stars. The Milky Way goes all round our sky, so we are inside the disc. It is thinner in one direction, thicker in the other, so we are not even at the centre of the disc. The Milky Way is our view of our **galaxy**.

Even further away are other galaxies made up of vast numbers of stars. The **Andromeda Galaxy** is over 2 million light years away. Our Milky Way Galaxy would look like this from outside.

Millions of these galaxies are seen further and further away in space. They make up the **Universe** which is perhaps 20,000 million light years across.

Milky Way

Andromeda Galaxy

7.3 Evidence from the sky

People all over the world have been charting the sky for hundreds of years. **Hypatia of Alexandria** made instruments called **astrolabes** to measure the positions of objects in the sky. She lived in the fourth century, and worked at the great Library of Alexandria, in Egypt. She was murdered by early Christians for studying the stars.

This is an **observatory** built for Jai Singh II, Maharaja of Jaipur, in the eighteenth century. His five observatories were built for a project to improve the Indian calendar.

The Delhi Observatory

1 Why does accurate measurement of movements in the sky help make an accurate calendar?

Telescopes magnify images of things in the sky. The first lens-based telescope was made by **Hans Lippershey** of Holland in the early seventeenth century. Later that century the English scientist **Sir Isaac Newton** made telescopes with curved mirrors.

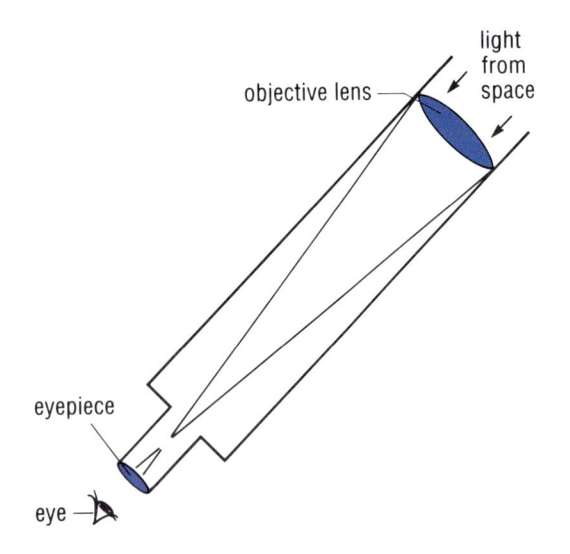

A lens-based (refracting) telescope

Telescopes made it possible to see things that could not be seen before. In 1610, the Italian **Galileo Galilei** saw small objects moving around Jupiter. They are like our Moon, orbiting the planet.

New planets beyond Saturn were found by telescopes. In 1781, **William** and **Caroline Herschel** found the first. It was named **Uranus**. Then, in 1846, **Neptune** was found by **Johann Galle**, when he studied part of the sky suggested by mathematician **Urbain Leverrier**. It was the first planet predicted by calculations. The most recent discovery was in 1930, when **Clyde Tombaugh** found **Pluto**.

> Solid evidence from space hits the Earth all the time. Lumps of material fall into the atmosphere from space. Mostly the lumps are tiny grains. A few are rocks with masses of several tonnes.
>
> When lumps of space material enter the atmosphere they are travelling at very high speed. They flash across the sky and most burn to dust. They are seen as flashing streaks called **meteors**.

About 100,000 tonnes of space material arrives on Earth each year. When the lumps survive to hit the earth they are called **meteorites**. Most are very small, but if the lumps are big they may make **craters**. We only see the most recent craters, due to weathering and erosion.

Investigating the formation of impact craters

Equipment: sand, gravel, metre rule, electronic balance.

- Spread sand in a tray.
- Weigh an individual grain of gravel on an electronic balance.
- Drop the grain of gravel on to the sand from 1 m.
- Investigate how the diameter of a crater relates to: mass of gravel; height of drop; depth of sand; wet or dry sand.
- Change one variable at a time, and draw up tables and graphs to display your results.
- What conclusions can you make?

Meteorites are classified as **iron**, **stone** or **stony-iron** meteorites. Stones are the most common and are mostly made of rock rather like volcanic basalt but with bigger crystals. Meteorites are the oldest rocks so far dated at about 4600 million years old.

Meteorites are hard to find. A few thousand have been collected around the world. Since research began in 1969 many have been found on the ice in Antarctica, where they are seen most easily.

Meteor crater in Arizona, which has a diameter of 800 metres

The Antarctic meteorites include 30 iron meteorites, 12 stony-irons and 558 stones.

2 Draw a chart to show the percentage of each meteorite type in the Antarctic collection.

Some very unusual meteorites have been found in Antarctica. Six are made of rock which matches moonrock.

3 How could rocks have travelled from the Moon to the Earth?

Even more amazing are two meteorites made of rock which scientists think came from Mars. They must have travelled in a similar way.

Iron meteorite (Arizona, USA)    **Stony-iron meteorite (Chile)**    **Stony meteorite (Barwell)**

7.4 Space technology

Nearly 300 years ago, Sir Isaac Newton described this thought experiment: Imagine a gun on a high tower. Fire the gun, and the cannon ball falls to Earth some distance away. With more explosive in the gun, the cannon ball flies further. The Earth is curved, so the cannon ball flies round the curve. It is pulled to Earth by gravity.

Now imagine lots more explosive in the gun. The cannon ball falls, but the Earth curves away below it. The cannon ball 'falls' round the Earth and comes back to the tower.

1 Newton knew that this was a thought experiment, or theory. Why could it not be tried?

Objects in orbit are *not* outside the effect of gravity. They are **free-falling** under the influence of gravity.

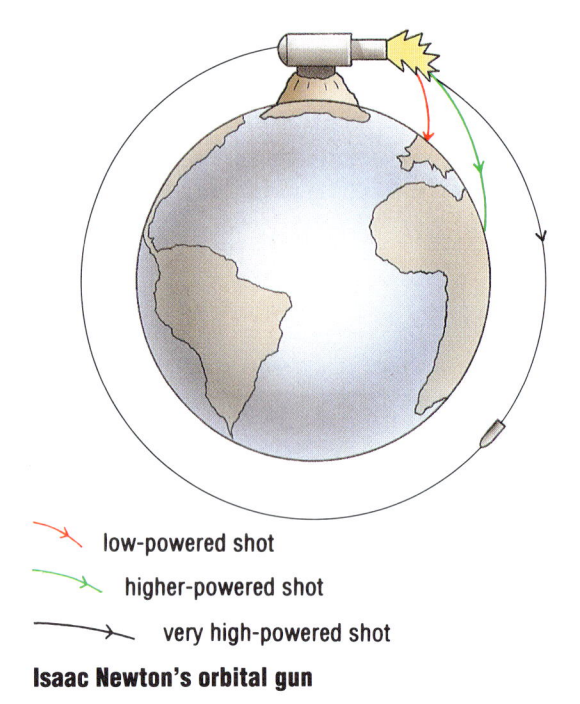

→ low-powered shot
→ higher-powered shot
→ very high-powered shot

Isaac Newton's orbital gun

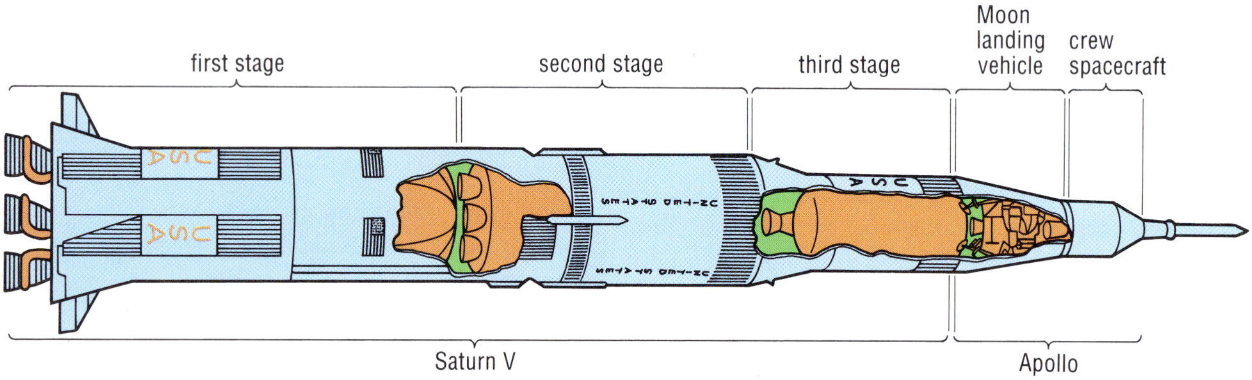

The Saturn V multistage rocket system used to send the Apollo missions to the Moon

Newton's discovery was vital to the development of space travel, but suitable machines were also needed. Rockets propelled by gunpowder were invented in China, many centuries ago. **Konstantin Tsiolkovsky** worked out many of the ideas needed to use them for space travel during the nineteenth century. He suggested using one rocket to lift another. The first rocket would drop away. The second would fire when it was already high up and going very fast. **Multistage rockets** are still the basis of space transport systems.

2 What are the advantages of multistaging?

A big increase in power was possible by using **liquid fuels**. This was first tried by **Robert Goddard**. His ideas were taken up by German scientists. They made rockets for Adolf Hitler's armies. Most modern space technology is directly based on the German developments.

During the Cold War period after 1945, new rockets were built to carry nuclear warheads. These rockets were found to be powerful enough to put **artificial satellites** into orbit around Earth. There are many uses for these satellites. They can be used to photograph the Earth for military reasons, to observe the weather or to help find ores and fossil fuels.

3 Imagine you are a rocket engineer in 1950, before any satellites had been put in orbit. Write a report to your government explaining the value of satellite technology.

One special satellite orbit was suggested by **Arthur Clarke** in 1945. Clarke pointed out that satellites just above the atmosphere would make one orbit in 90 minutes, but satellites further away take longer to make one orbit.

Clarke showed that in an orbit 36,000 km from the Earth, a satellite takes exactly 24 hours to orbit the Earth. It appears to stay over one point, as the Earth turns under it. This is called a **geostationary satellite**.

Clarke suggested using a satellite in this orbit to carry radio messages around the world. This is exactly how **communication satellites** now work. Unfortunately Arthur Clarke did not patent his idea, so he does not get paid for the use of the Clarke Orbit.

4 Why are some weather satellites in the Clarke orbit, and others much nearer the Earth?

Space technology has lifted telescopes above the atmosphere, giving clearer pictures of the Universe. Also, space vehicles have studied nearly every object in our solar system.

Some spaceprobes are now far out in space, beginning journeys to the stars. They carry plaques and sound recordings about us, their builders. Perhaps one day some other beings will find them and so learn about us.

The Voyager space probe being tested before launch in 1977

Despite some tragic accidents, regular flights of the American Space Shuttle and the constant crewing of the Russian *Mir* space station have made space flight seem routine. However, there was nothing routine about the exploration of the Moon by the astronauts of the Apollo missions from 1968 to 1972.

5 Describe and explain some of the design differences between a crewed spacecraft and an automatic spacecraft.

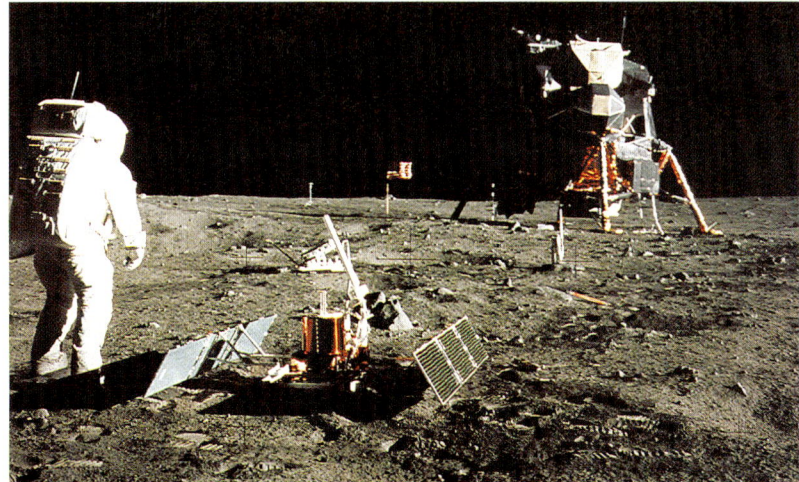

Apollo 11 astronauts, Neil Armstrong and Edwin Aldrin, conducting experiments on the Moon

7.5 Our neighbour in space

The **Moon** has always been important to humans. Its light made it possible to extend hunting time into the night. It changed shape in a way which marked out time; we still use a month as an important part of our calendar. A month is (roughly) the time from one New Moon to the next. It takes about 28 days from New Moon to New Moon.

1 How many days after New Moon would you see the phases shown? Some are already marked.

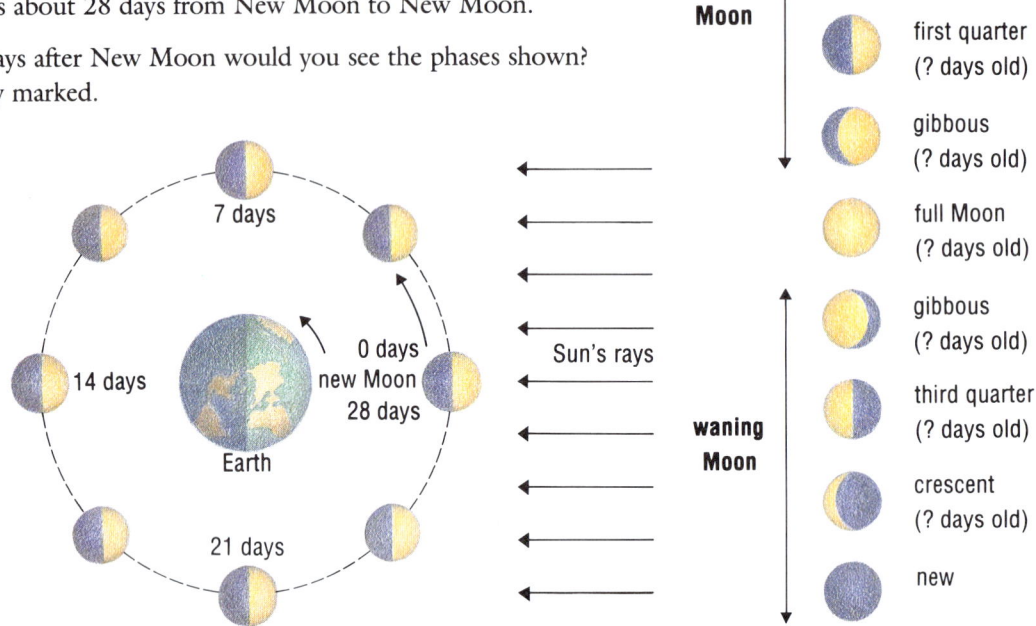

The orbit of the Moon and the phases we see

waxing Moon:
- new (0 days)
- crescent (4 days old)
- first quarter (? days old)
- gibbous (? days old)

- full Moon (? days old)

waning Moon:
- gibbous (? days old)
- third quarter (? days old)
- crescent (? days old)
- new

The Moon keeps one face towards the Earth. Nothing was known about the far side until 1959, when it was photographed by a Russian spaceprobe.

The Moon has light and dark parts. Scientists used to think the dark areas were seas.

The **Seas** are really fairly flat areas of basalt. They are about 3500 million years old. The **Highlands** are about 4200 million years old, and are made of a rock called **anorthosite**.

Diameter: 3476 km
Mass: 7.35×10^{22} kg (0.012 Earths)
Temperature: 120 K to 393 K
(−153°C to 120°C)
Atmosphere: None
Coloured dots show where spacecraft landed

THE NEARSIDE OF THE MOON
- Sea of Showers
- Sea of Serenity
- Sea of Tranquility
- Ocean of Storms

2 Examine specimens of basalt and anorthosite. List their differences and similarities. Measure the density of anorthosite. From your discoveries, list differences and similarities between the main rocks of the Moon and the Earth.

The rings on the Moon are **craters**. Some scientists thought the craters were volcanoes. Others said they were caused by the impact of large meteorites. Impact was later found to be the main crater-forming process.

Do Seas or Highlands have most craters?

- Cut a 1 cm square hole in a card.
- Put the card over the Sea of Showers on the Moon map opposite.
- Count and note the number of craters you see in your 1 cm square.
- Move to another Sea, and count again.
- Do this for six Seas and six Highland areas.
- Work out an average for the number of craters in a 1 cm square for Seas and Highlands.

The main layers of the Moon's surface

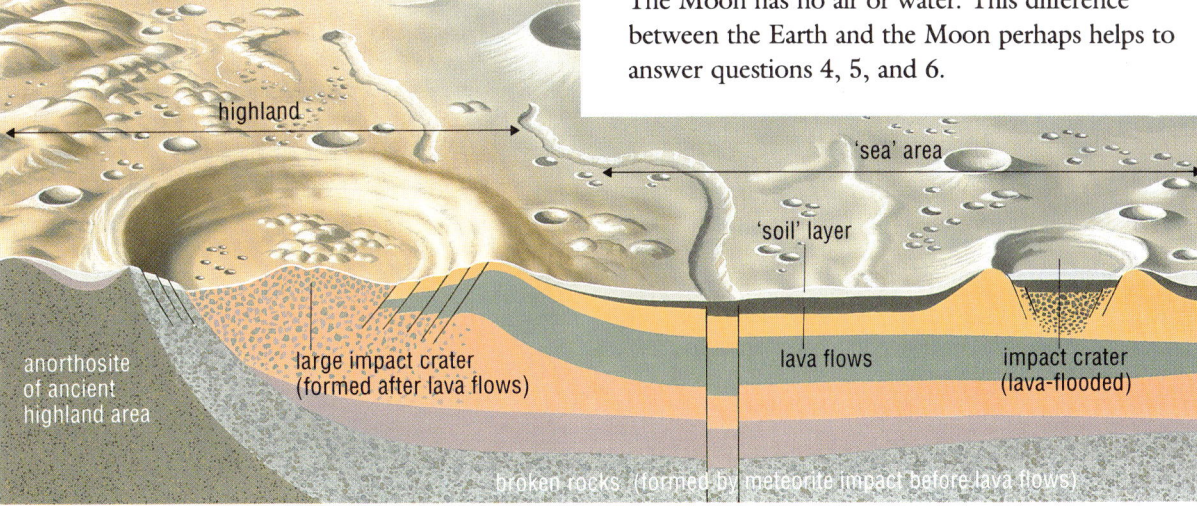

The objects that hit the Moon to make the craters must have been smashed in the impact.

3 Here are two ideas to explain the lack of many craters on the Seas:

a) More meteorites landed on the Highlands.
b) The meteorites landed all over the Moon, but then basalt lava came out and covered the craters on the lower areas. Since then very few big objects have fallen on the Moon.

Which of these ideas is most likely, and why?

4 Suggest why Moon craters have not worn away.

We think the Moon has looked the same for a very long time. Long ago, giant meteorites probably fell on Earth as well as on the Moon.

5 Why do we find very little evidence of these giant meteorites that fell on the Earth?

The Moon's soil is not like soil on Earth. The soil is a layer of tiny rock fragments and glass beads. The glass beads were made when impacts by meteorites melted the moonrock and threw tiny drops across the Moon's surface.

6 List some reasons why the Moon's soil is so different to our soils.

The Moon has no air or water. This difference between the Earth and the Moon perhaps helps to answer questions 4, 5, and 6.

The Moon travels around the Earth at an average distance of 382,000 km. It moves at just about 1 km/s in its orbit. It is held in this circular path by the gravitational pull between the Earth and the Moon.

Forces and orbits

- Tie a rubber bung on to 50 cm of string.
- Swing the bung around your head.
- What do you feel on your hand?

The Moon's pull on the Earth is an equal force to the Earth's pull on the Moon.

7.6 The inner planets

Apart from the Sun and the Moon, Venus is the brightest object in the sky. It comes nearer Earth than any other planets, apart from our own Moon, yet it has always been a place of mystery.

Venus is almost the same size as Earth. Through a telescope it appears as a white disc or crescent, with no features. It is covered by cloud. For a long time, people thought they were like our clouds, made of water droplets. In the last fifty years scientists have found Venus to be a very unpleasant place.

Carbon dioxide makes up 97 per cent of the atmosphere. The remaining 3 per cent includes sulphuric acid. Venus suffers from an extreme greenhouse effect.

Spaceprobes have dropped into Venus' atmosphere to measure the temperatures and pressures. They do not last long at the surface.

1 Plot these results on two graphs.

Height in km above Venus' surface	Temperature in °C	Pressure (Atmospheres)
125	230	No data
100	180	No data
75	200	0.005
50	340	1
25	550	16
0	750	90

2 What properties do materials need if they are used to build a Venus probe?

In 1990 the *Magellan* spaceprobe began producing a detailed map of Venus from orbit around the planet. The map used radar, not ordinary photography.

3 Why is radar needed to map Venus?

The nearest planet to the Sun is Mercury, in many ways a larger version of our own Moon.

4 How does the landscape of Mercury appear to have been formed?

5 Does Mercury show evidence of having air or water? Give evidence for your answer.

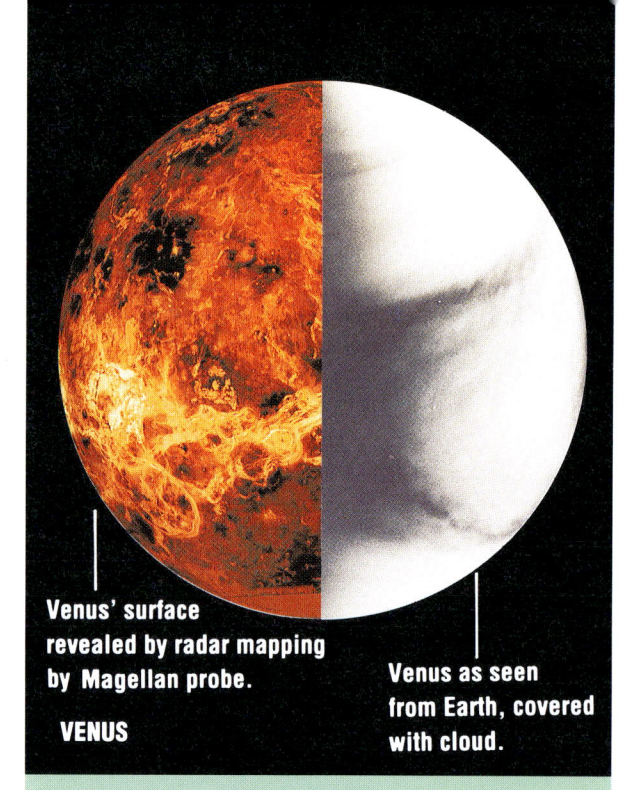

Venus' surface revealed by radar mapping by Magellan probe.

Venus as seen from Earth, covered with cloud.

VENUS

Diameter: 12,104 km
Mass: 4.8689 x 10^{23} kg (0.8 Earths)
Temperature: 737 K (464°C)
Atmosphere: 97% CO_2. 0.1% H_2O vapour. Traces of CO, HCl, HF

MERCURY

Diameter: 4,878 km
Mass: 3.3022 x 10^{23} kg (0.06 Earths)
Temperature: 90 K to 600 K (approx. 380°C on day side)
Atmosphere: None

People have thought Mars is inhabited. Through telescopes, some said they could see 'canals' on Mars. When spaceprobes studied Mars, it was clear that this was an optical illusion.

Mars has a thin atmosphere. The surface pressure is about 0.007 atmospheres. Even so, there are strong winds at times, and the dusty surface is blown about to make sandstorms.

Mars has features that may be evidence of processes like those on Earth.

6 Study the photograph. It shows evidence of *volcanoes*, *canyons*, and *craters*. Match the letters to the features.

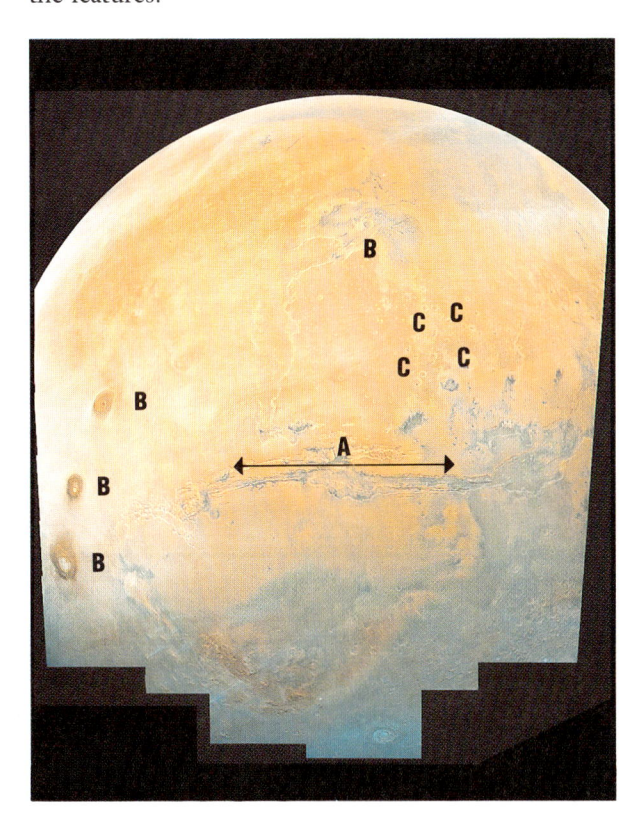

One Martian volcano is the largest known on any planet. **Olympus Mons** is 25 km high, 600 km in diameter, with a 65 km diameter crater. It is made of basalt lavas.

Mariner Valley is 2500 km long, up to 5 km deep and from 100 to 200 km wide. Scientists are still wondering if Martian canyons were carved by water alone, or by giant flows of mud.

The problem of life on Mars was investigated by the Viking probes which landed in 1976. They sampled the soil and tested for signs of life. The results seem to be negative.

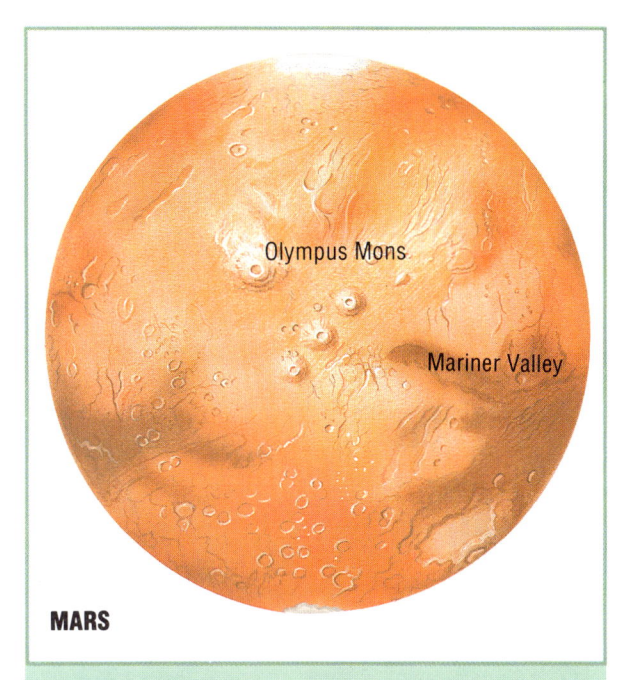

MARS

Diameter: 6775 km
Mass: 6.45 x 10²³ kg (0.108 Earths)
Temperature: 150 K to 299 K (-123°C to 26°C)
Atmosphere: 95% CO_2, 3% N_2.
Traces of H_2O, Ar, O_2

Is there life on Mars?

Design an investigation to test soil for life. What evidence will you look for?

When you have designed your experiment, you need some samples to test:

- Take a rich soil, a poor soil, and some sand.
- Choose two and heat them in an oven for several hours to sterilize them.
- Label your three samples for another group. Only you know which has not been sterilized.
- Now test samples supplied by another group.

You should be able to evaluate your experiment and improve it. You could even think about how results could be sent by radio to Earth.

7.7 The gas giants and their moons

The **Voyager** mission explored more worlds than any other journey of discovery. Two spaceprobes launched in 1977 explored the outer solar system. We can only touch on some *Voyager* discoveries. Between them, *Voyager 1* and *2* visited Jupiter, Saturn, Uranus, and Neptune. These planets are the gas giants as their atmospheres are an important feature.

Diameter: 142,800 km
Mass: 1.899×10^{27} kg (318 Earths)
Temperature: 150 K (approx.) (−120°C)
Atmosphere: 90% H_2, 4.5% He
Traces of Methane, Ammonia

Jupiter

In 1610, Galileo discovered four moons orbiting Jupiter. One, **Io**, was red. As *Voyager 1* passed Io in 1979, **Linda Morabito** at Voyager Control used a computer to improve one picture. She saw a bright plume above Io. She had found the first active volcano beyond Earth.

Io is affected by the enormous gravity field of Jupiter. Its force squeezes Io as it orbits, producing tidal bulges 100 m high. This generates heat, melting material and creating volcanoes.

A volcano erupting on Io

1 Io is a small world with a small gravity field.

Material erupted from Io's volcanoes travels up at speeds around 1 km/s. On Earth, material erupted from volcanoes moves up at about 50 m/s. Explain this difference.

The features seen on Jupiter are weather systems in the top of its deep atmosphere. The **Great Red Spot** is rotating anticlockwise. It appears to be a storm that has raged for centuries. The Earth would fit inside it.

2 Bright flashes are sometimes observed in the clouds of Jupiter. What could they be?

Saturn

Saturn's **rings** may be only 10 m thick. They are made of millions of fragments about 10 cm across; the remains of moons broken up by tidal forces.

Saturn's largest moon is **Titan**. Bigger than Mercury, it has a dense atmosphere. At its surface the pressure is 1.6 atmospheres.

Titan's atmosphere is mainly nitrogen, but mixed with methane and ethane. With a temperature of −178°C these chemicals form pools. Layers of haze cover Titan because the chemicals make a **photochemical smog**.

After studying Saturn, *Voyager 1* set off out of the Solar System at an angle into deep space. *Voyager 2* continued the misson.

Uranus

From Earth, telescopes had found five moons around **Uranus**, and nine thin rings. *Voyager 2* found ten new moons and at least two new rings. Very little light is available this far from the Sun. *Voyager 2* had to be sent new computer programs by radio link to enable it to take clear pictures.

The atmosphere is mainly helium and hydrogen but the blue-green colour of Uranus is caused by methane in its upper atmosphere. Winds at speeds of 360 km/hour are common on Uranus.

3 Explain how the rings could have been formed.

SATURN and some of its moons

Diameter: 120,000 km
Mass: 5.684×10^{26} kg (95 Earths)
Temperature: 140 K (-133°C)
Atmosphere: 94% H_2. 6% He

Neptune

Working with less than half the light available at Uranus, *Voyager 2* sped past **Neptune** in 1989. Again, methane causes the colour. Neptune has rings and its own family of moons.

Triton, the largest moon of Neptune, has a similar atmosphere to Titan. *Voyager 2* found evidence of 'volcanoes', possibly driven by liquid nitrogen, erupting from the surface of Triton.

4 a) What gases might we find on Triton?
b) Why is the atmosphere of Triton hazy?

The four giant planets may have similar features, but each one had something new for *Voyager*.

Diameter: 50,538 km
Mass: 1.028×10^{23} kg (17 Earths)
Temperature: 50 K (-223°C)
Atmosphere: 85% H_2. 13% He. 2% methane CH_4

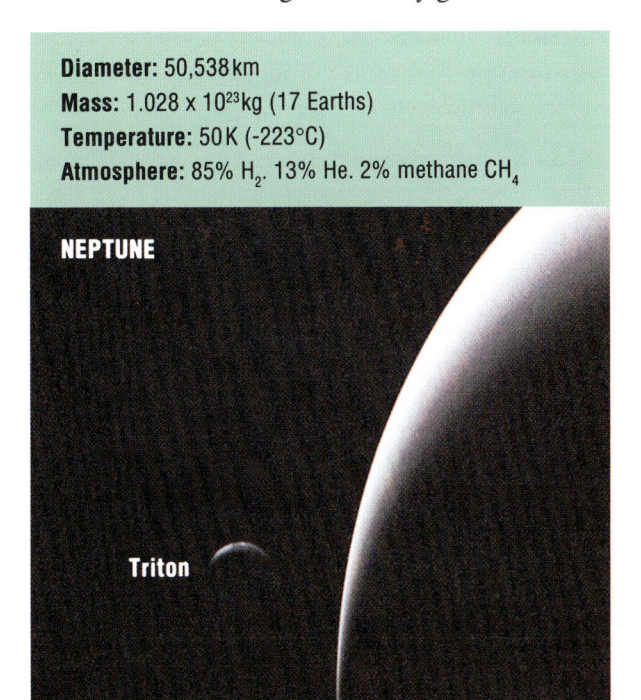

NEPTUNE

Triton

URANUS

Diameter: 51,118 km
Mass: 8.722×10^{22} kg (15 Earths)
Temperature: 50 K (-223°C)
Atmosphere: H_2, H_2O. ammonia. methane

7.8 The solar system

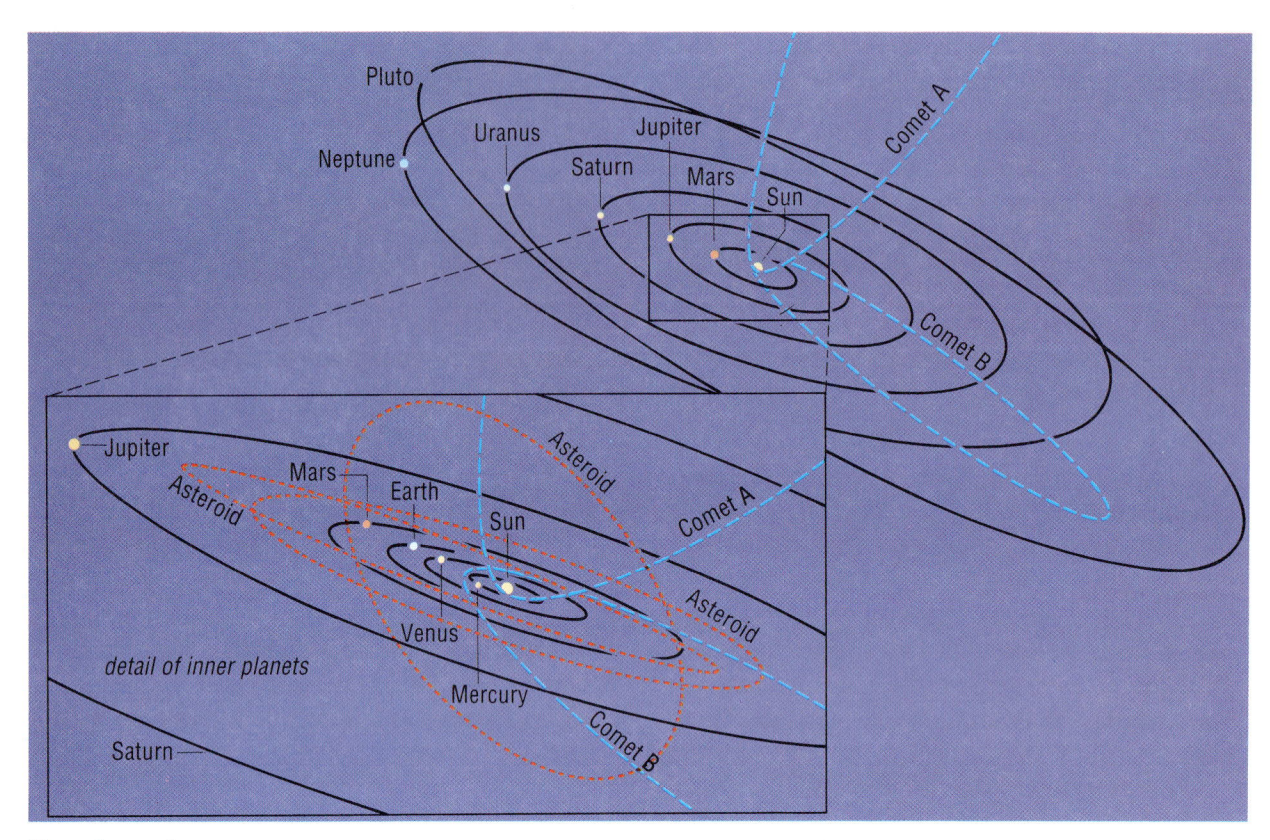

The solar system

The Solar System includes many objects apart from the Sun, the inner planets, the gas giants and the various moons.

Between Mars and Jupiter are hundreds of small objects, the **asteroids**. Some stray further in or out. Mars has two small moons, which may well be asteroids caught by Mars' gravity. Crashing asteroids are responsible for some of the impact craters on moons and planets.

Most meteorites seem to have been part of asteroids that broke up. The iron meteorites came from the centres of these objects, and the stony meteorites from their outer parts.

In even less regular orbits are the **comets**. They are lumps of 'dirty ice' which start off far away, well beyond Neptune and Pluto. Some are pulled in by the gravity of the outer planets. If they travel near the Sun they warm up and give off long tails of gases. Comets, as well as asteroids and meteorites, may be involved in making craters on moons and planets.

Planets and distance from the Sun

Planet	Distance from Sun (km × 10⁶)	Main gases in atmosphere
Mercury	58	
Venus	108	
Earth	150	
Mars	228	
Jupiter	779	
Saturn	1427	
Uranus	2870	
Neptune	4497	
Pluto	5900 (average)	none?

1 Copy the table and fill in the main gases found in the atmosphere of the planets.

2 a) Which planet gets most heat from the Sun?
b) Which planet gets least heat from the Sun?

3 Suggest why the chemicals found on a planet depend on its distance from the Sun.

The origin of the planets

Scientists believe that small objects in orbit around the Sun pulled in other small objects which crashed into them. They grew bigger in this way, sweeping up most of the material in the system. The worlds with no atmosphere, like our Moon, still show the large craters made in the later stages of this process.

How the Sun and Planets formed

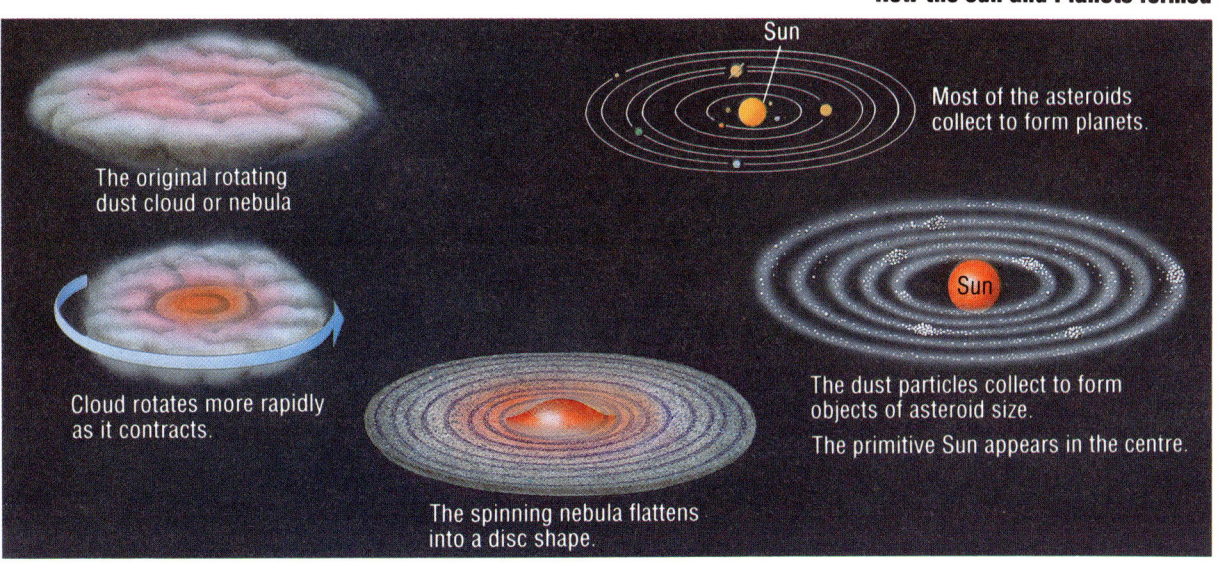

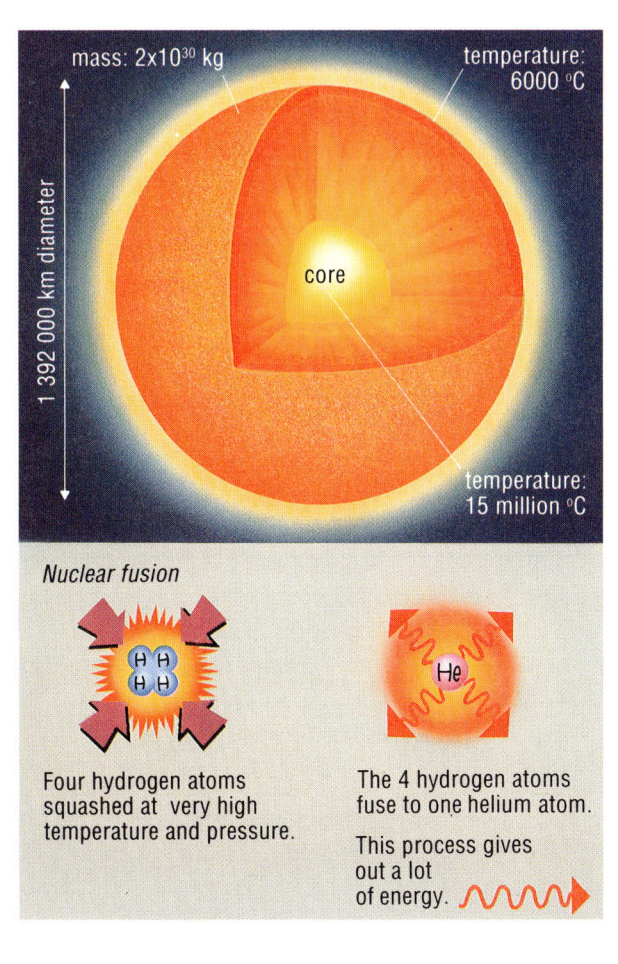

The original rotating dust cloud or nebula

Cloud rotates more rapidly as it contracts.

The spinning nebula flattens into a disc shape.

Most of the asteroids collect to form planets.

The dust particles collect to form objects of asteroid size.
The primitive Sun appears in the centre.

mass: 2×10^{30} kg
temperature: 6000 °C
1 392 000 km diameter
core
temperature: 15 million °C

Nuclear fusion

Four hydrogen atoms squashed at very high temperature and pressure.

The 4 hydrogen atoms fuse to one helium atom. This process gives out a lot of energy.

The Sun

The Sun itself is a star. Other stars may also have planets. The Sun was formed where most of the small particles that collected to make our solar system happened to gather. It became big enough to collect most of the hydrogen gas in this part of space. It also became big enough to force all the other smaller objects to orbit around it.

Inside the Sun the inner gases became squashed under more and more gas. The pressure and temperature became high enough to push hydrogen atoms together to make helium atoms. This process produces a huge amount of energy. It is called **nuclear fusion**.

4 Which object in our Solar System has the strongest gravity field?

So far we think that the Sun has used up about half of its hydrogen. The mathematics of nuclear fusion suggests that it has been 'switched on' for about five billion years, and could last another five billion years.

5 a) How many hydrogen atoms are needed to make a helium atom?
b) What kinds of energy are made by the Sun?

7.9 Stars and galaxies

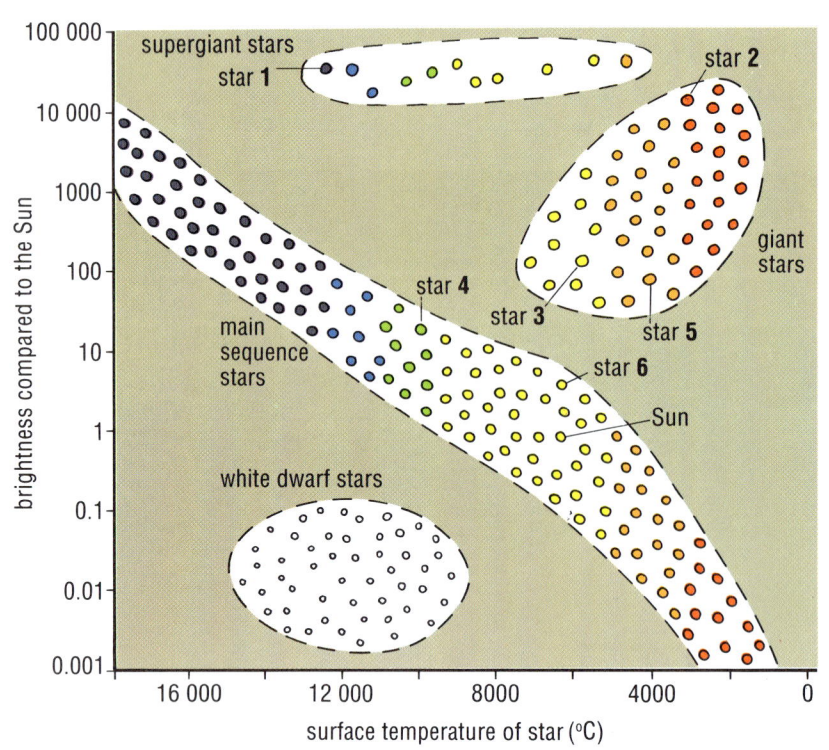

The Hertzsprung-Russell Diagram

If you look at the stars, they seem all the same. Look more closely, and some are brighter than others. Some have different colours: red, yellow, white, even pale blue.

Early in the twentieth century, two astronomers quite separately discovered that there are various types of stars. **Ejnar Hertzsprung** and **Henry Russell** showed that the colours, which are caused by different temperatures, and the true brightness of the stars could be plotted to make the **Hertzsprung–Russell diagram**. The brightness and temperature of stars changes over time, and these changes are described as the life cycle of a star.

1 There are many bright stars in the sky around the constellation (star group) **Orion**. Match the numbered stars on the Hertzsprung–Russell diagram with these stars.

Star	Temperature in °C	Brightness compared to Sun
Sirius	10 000	25
Capella	6000	150
Rigel	12 000	40 000
Procyon	6500	8
Betelgeux	3500	17 000
Aldeberan	4500	90

Not all stars give out a steady glow. Some show changes in brightness. They are called **variable stars**.

In 1912 **Henrietta Leavitt** found that special stars called **Cepheids** change brightness in a regular way.

This discovery by Henrietta Leavitt was the key to measuring the distance to nearby galaxies. By timing the periods of Cepheids in a galaxy, it is possible to find their true brightness and so the distance of the galaxy can be worked out.

Some galaxies are over 10 000 million light years away. Light that left them over 6000 million years before Earth formed is arriving now.

7.10 Back to the Big Bang

Looking into space is looking back in time. The Sun is 8 light minutes away. The Andromeda Galaxy is 2,000,000 light years away. Telescopes show us galaxies far off in space. We see them as they were long ago.

The galaxies are rushing apart with energy they gained at the beginning of time – the **Big Bang**. It is thought that in a fraction of a second, the matter of the universe appeared as a tiny dot and exploded apart. We do not know where the matter came from. The Universe is still expanding, perhaps 20,000 million years later.

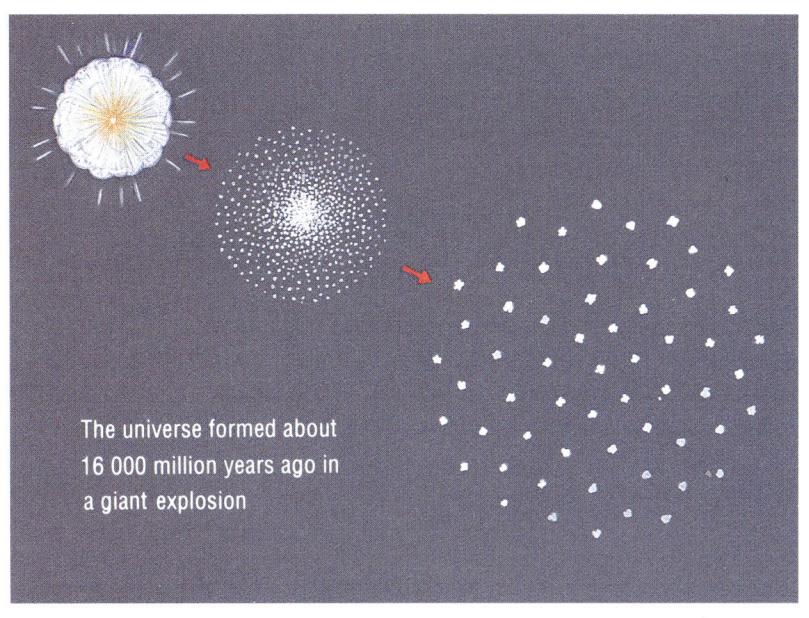

The universe formed about 16 000 million years ago in a giant explosion

The Big Bang

Modelling the expanding universe

- Blow up a balloon a little.
- Using a marker pen, put dots all over it.
- Put one dot in another colour. This is our galaxy, the Milky Way.
- Blow the balloon gently to its full size.

1 What do you observe?

The whole universe is expanding, and surrounding galaxies are moving away from us. The mathematics of the Big Bang is a challenge to the best minds of our time. Events in the first microseconds of time fixed the future development of the universe.

Probably very few people could work out the calculations needed to understand the very early universe. Some of the most important work on these problems has been done by **Professor Stephen Hawking**.

Hawking has pushed back the limits of our understanding in spite of almost total physical disability caused by a disease of the nervous system. Using state-of-the-art technology, including a voice synthesiser, Hawking's lectures and books have changed our understanding of the universe.

Professor Stephen Hawking

Section 7 questions

1 Which of the following observations help us to prove that the Earth is round?

a) The Sun crosses the sky from east to west.
b) Even from the highest mountain we cannot see every part of the world.
c) When sailing ships approach from the sea, we see the tips of their masts first.
d) The Moon is sometimes seen during the day.

2 a) Explain how Eratosthenes measured the size of the Earth.
b) Suggest ways he could have measured the distance across Egypt when the only ways of travelling were by foot or by horse.

3 a) If Venus had oceans, would you predict tides to happen in the oceans? Explain your answer.
b) Why does Venus *not* have oceans?

4 The stars are always in the sky. Why do we not see stars during daytime, even if the sky is very clear?

5 These diagrams show the constellation **Taurus** on two nights a month apart.

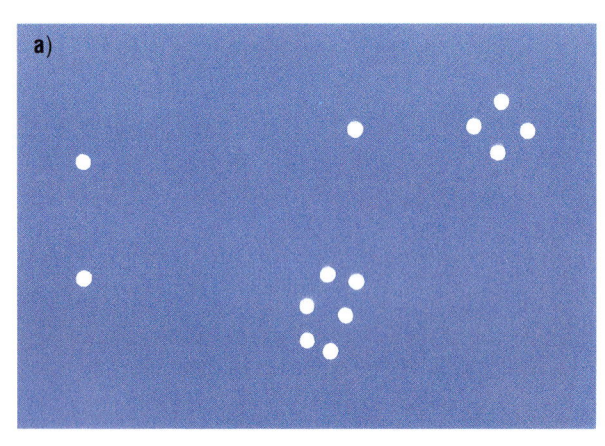

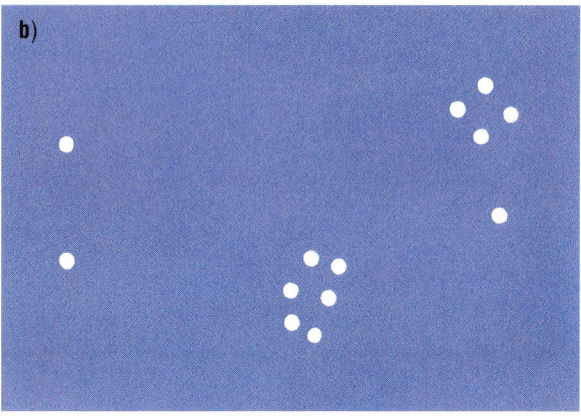

a) What evidence is there that one of the objects is a planet?
b) Why would the planet not always be among the stars of Taurus?

6 The brightest star in the sky is **Sirius**, 8.7 light years away. How far is that in kilometres?

7 a) Why do you think meteorites often show signs of having been heated very strongly just before they landed?
b) Why is Antarctica a good place to find meteorites?
c) Describe and account for the three main types of meteorite.

8 Explain how satellites can be used for:
a) weather forecasting   **b)** television transmission
c) spying.

9 Explain why a telescope is a time machine.

10 Explain why we need to measure distances to far-off galaxies as part of our attempt to find the age of the Universe.

11 Some observations of galaxies suggest that they are not moving as fast as they were in the past. What force could be slowing them down?

12 Design a package of information about humanity that could be fixed to a deep space vehicle that might be found by people on a planet of another star.

13 Write a postcard to your friends, describing your visit to study the Moon on the school field trip for 2048 AD.

14 You are Captain Krok, in charge of the first tourist trip around the planets of the Solar System. Produce a leaflet to encourage people to book tickets.

15 Why is an understanding of the force of gravity the key to explaining the Universe? Give examples.

16 Describe some of the contributions made to science by: **a)** Hypatia of Alexandria   **b)** Galileo Galilei   **c)** William and Caroline Herschel   **d)** Henrietta Leavitt   **e)** Stephen Hawking. You should use library books and databases to compile your answers.

Summary: The scale of the Universe

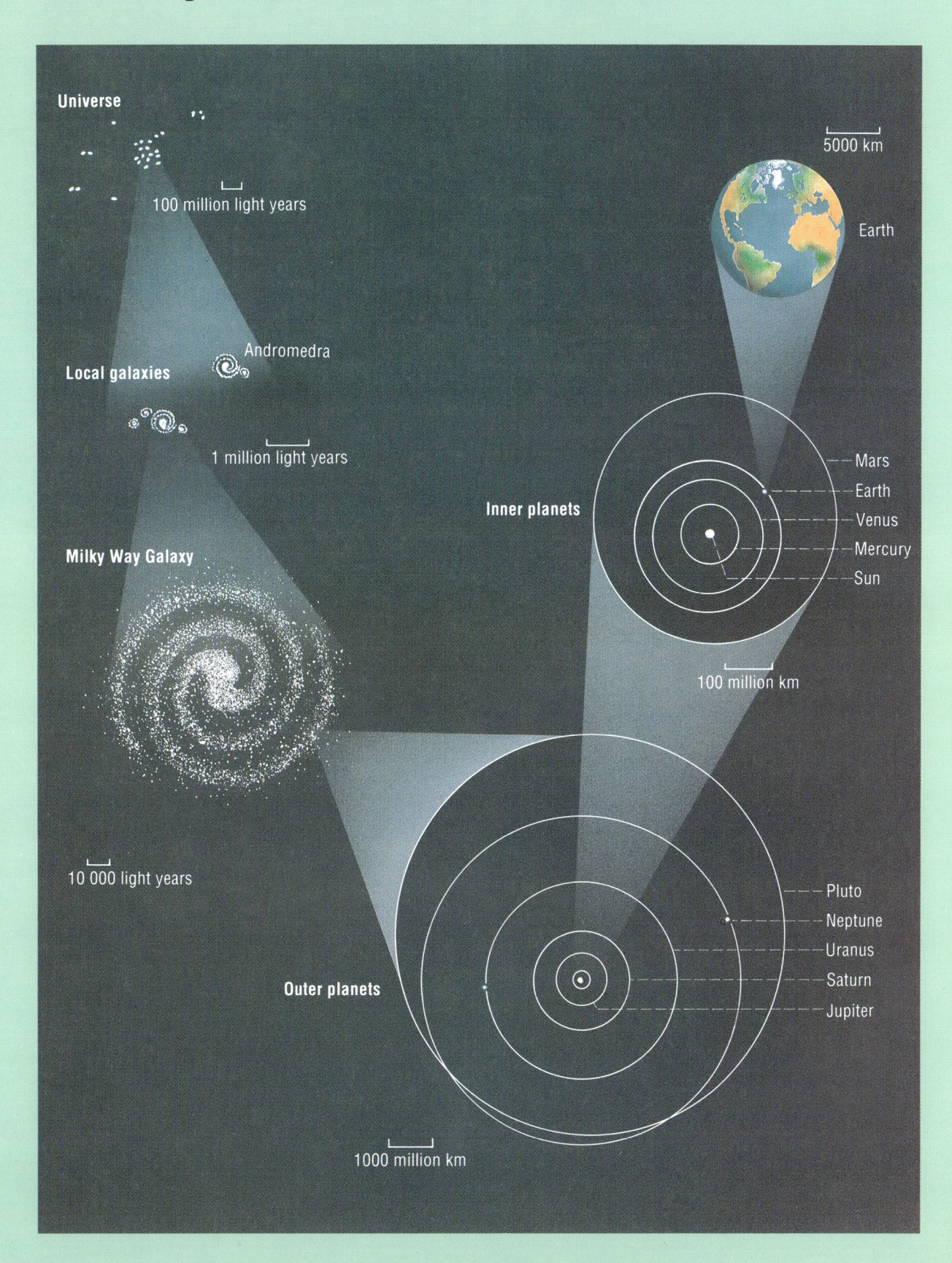

Universe
100 million light years

Local galaxies
Andromedra
1 million light years

Milky Way Galaxy
10 000 light years

Outer planets
- Pluto
- Neptune
- Uranus
- Saturn
- Jupiter

1000 million km

Inner planets
- Mars
- Earth
- Venus
- Mercury
- Sun

100 million km

Earth
5000 km

99

8.1 Continental drift and sea-floor spreading

Early in the seventeenth century, **Francis Bacon** noted that the newly-mapped American coasts looked as though they could fit into the coasts of Europe and Africa, like pieces of a giant jigsaw.

As rocks and fossils were mapped on both sides of the Atlantic, more evidence appeared to suggest that the continents had once been joined up. There was also evidence that land areas had drifted through different climatic zones.

In Britain, rocks of Carboniferous age, over 300 million years old, appeared to have formed in tropical swamps near the equator (see page 46). One hundred million years later Britain was covered by deserts, suggesting that it was in a similar position to the Sahara today (see page 44).

1 Trace the diagram below, cut out the continents, and fit them together as a jigsaw.

In 1915 **Alfred Wegener** suggested that all the continents had once been joined, but had split apart and moved around the world.

This theory of **continental drift** suggested that millions of years ago there could have been a giant supercontinent which Wegener named **Pangaea**. When ocean floors were explored after 1945, new evidence appeared about ocean crust and ocean ridges. This helped to explain why the super-continent may have broken up.

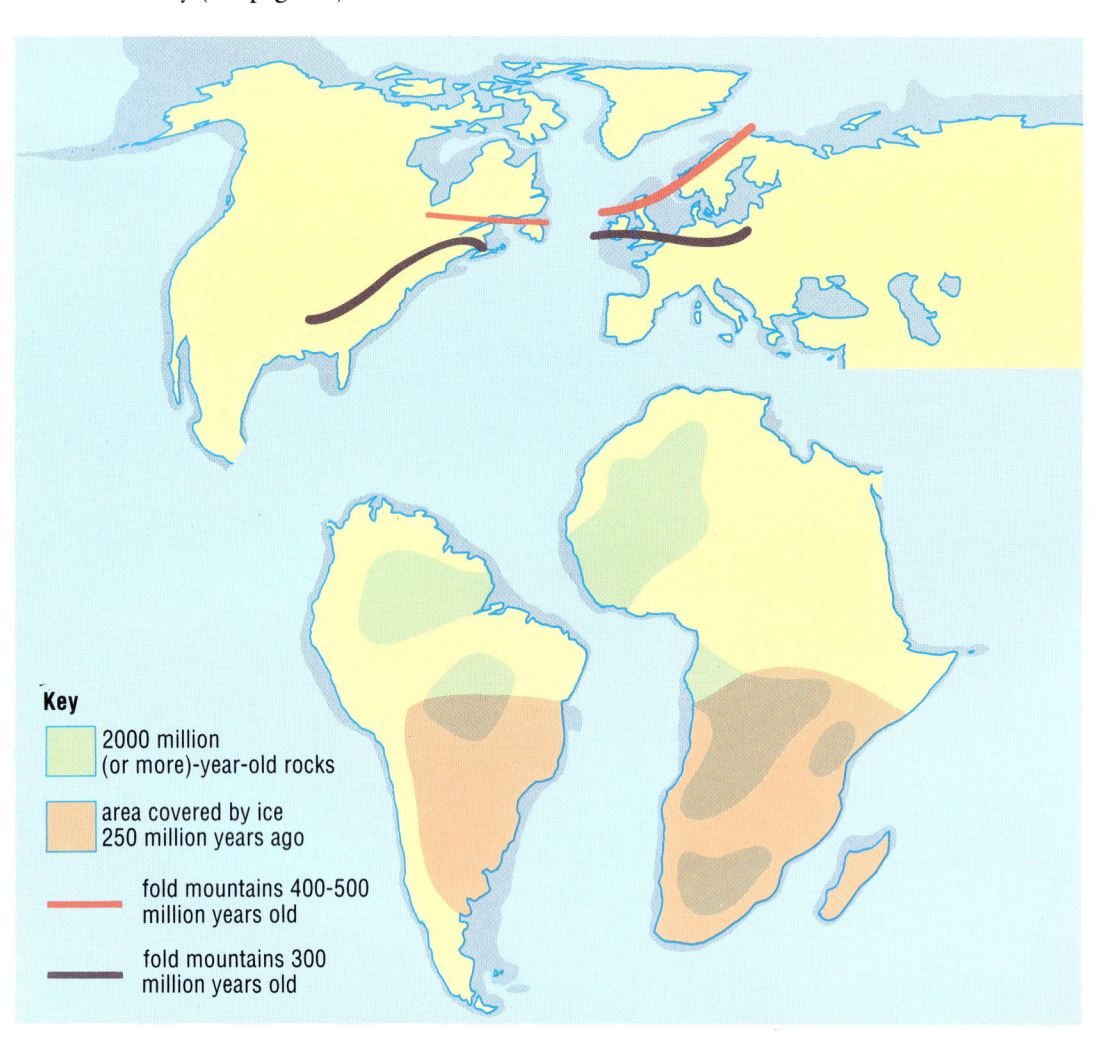

Key
- 2000 million (or more)-year-old rocks
- area covered by ice 250 million years ago
- fold mountains 400-500 million years old
- fold mountains 300 million years old

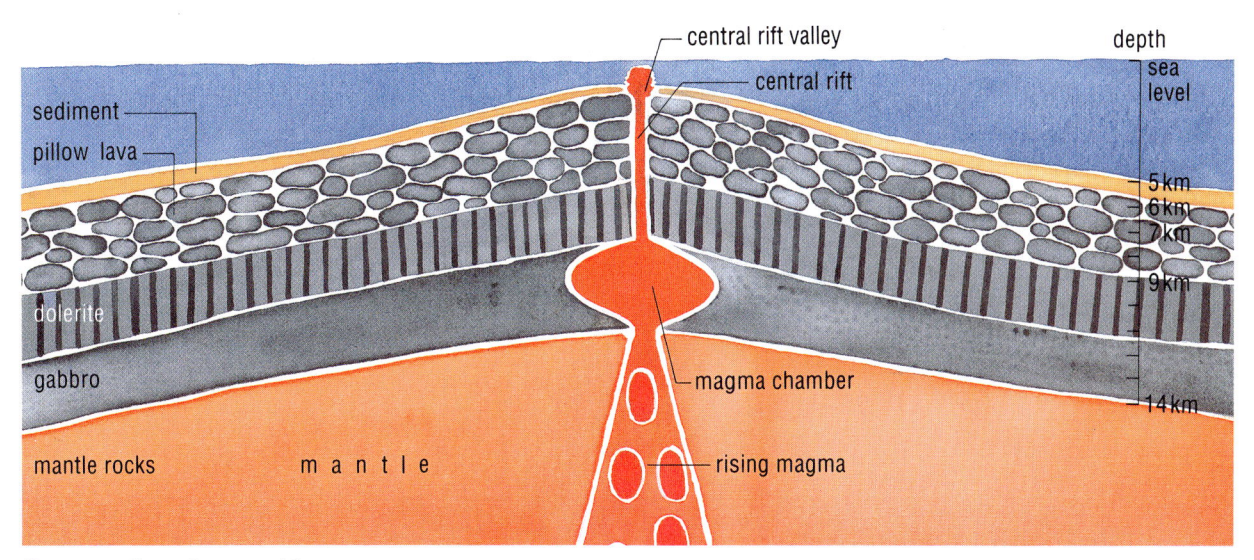

Cross-section of ocean ridge

Mid-ocean ridges and oceanic crust

Scientists studying the sediment that collects on the sea floor noticed that on ocean ridges the layer of sediment is far thinner than in ocean basins. Further observations showed that the ocean floor at ridges is made of new rock being formed by volcanic activity. This is sometimes called **sea-floor spreading**. The lavas are pushed out of vents rather like toothpaste if you give the tube a series of jerky squeezes. The rocks are basalt lavas, called **pillow lavas** because of their rounded shape.

2 Why is the sediment layer on the ocean floor thicker further away from the ocean ridge?

Beneath the basalt pillow lavas are rocks formed from magma which solidifies before reaching the surface. **Dykes** made from **dolerite** lie immediately below the lavas, and below these is a rock called **gabbro**.

3 Pillow lavas have smaller crystals than the rocks lying beneath them. Write a possible explanation for this.

Road cutting exposing pillow lava in Yugoslavia. These originally formed underwater.

8.2 Shrinking oceans and colliding continents

If extra ocean floor is being produced at ridges, and nothing else is happening, it is hard to explain why the Earth is not getting bigger. However, in the 1950s **Hugo Benioff** discovered a region of earthquake activity which ran at an angle down through the Earth's surface from the sea floor. This is now explained as slabs of ocean floor moving down into the Earth at an angle. This process is called **subduction** which means *to lead down*.

Many **subduction zones** are found around the edge of the Pacific Ocean. Sometimes they are not obvious, because the ocean trenches that usually mark the top of the subduction zone can become filled by sediment.

1 As the slab of ocean floor goes down it starts to become **metamorphosed**. Why is this?

Hot fluids start to rise from the descending slab, and these help the rocks above to melt as well. This mixture is a magma.

This magma is less dense and more gassy than its surroundings, so it forces its way upwards. It erupts as a volcano. Volcanoes at ocean trenches are more explosive than the activity at ocean ridges. The different volcanic environments make it possible to fit volcanoes into two main classes: explosive and quiet (pages 49 and 54).

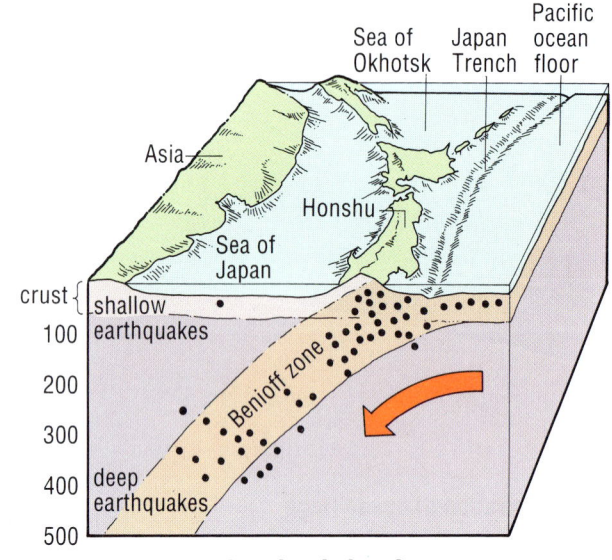

The pattern of earthquakes below Japan

a) A subduction zone where ocean plate meets ocean plate

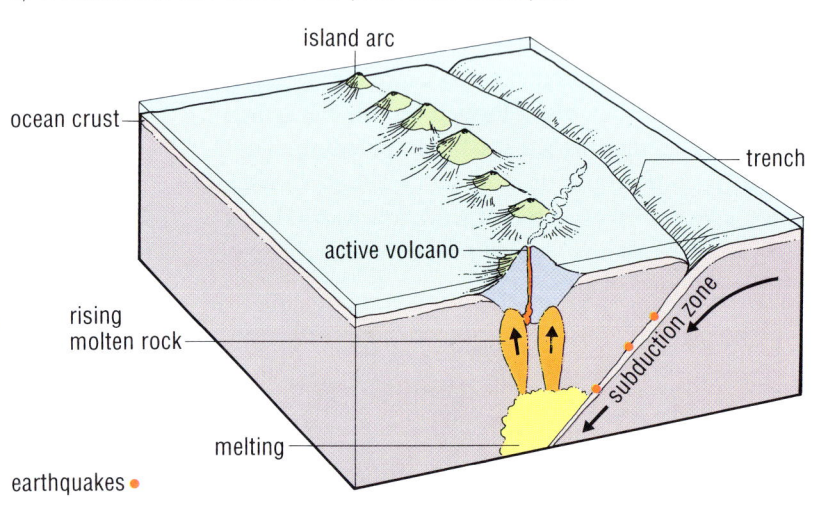

b) A subduction zone where ocean plate meets continental plate

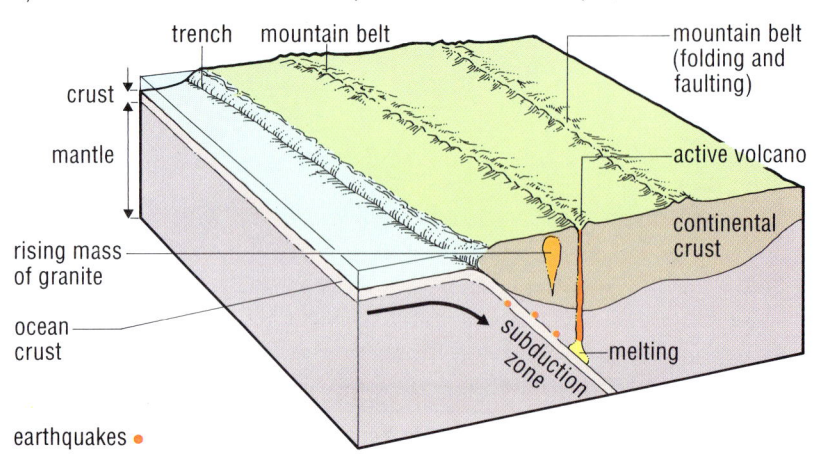

2 Volcanoes at subduction zones erupt rather sticky (high viscosity) lavas. Why would they tend to be steep-sided?

Explosive volcanoes mostly erupt **andesite**. It is named after the Andes Mountains of South America, where many andesite volcanoes are found.

3 Name the two main classes of volcano. List the differences between them.

If the subduction zone is in an oceanic area, the volcanoes will build islands. These make curved lines called **island arcs**.

An andesite volcano, in the Andes Mountains, South America

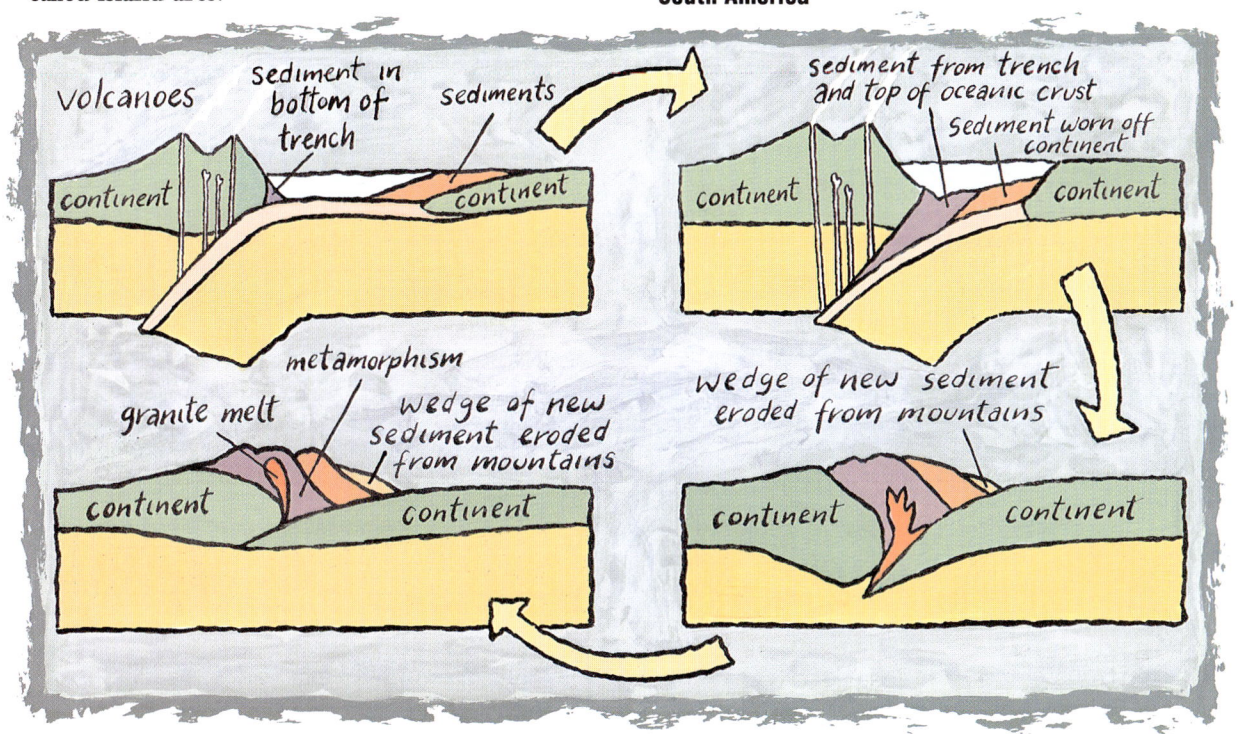

How mountain ranges form

If *subduction* is faster than *spreading* at the mid-ocean ridge, the ocean shrinks. The continents on either side of the ocean will be dragged together. Eventually they will meet.

The island arcs will be trapped between the continents as they meet.

4 What will happen to these trapped rocks?

The results of **continental collisions** are **fold mountains**. For example, the **Himalayas** in Nepal, north of India, are made of rocks pushed up when India (once a separate land mass) collided with Asia. The **Alps** are the result of Africa colliding with Europe.

Continents are built up of many ancient subduction zones and sediments. Island arcs collided with other island arcs, and made the first continents. As oceans opened and closed, blocks of **continental crust** grew larger and thicker. Because continental crust is fairly low in density it tends not to be subducted.

5 What happens to the mountain chains as soon as they rise above sea level?

Ancient chains of fold mountains have been eroded so that now we see only the deeply eroded roots. These are made of folded and faulted metamorphic rocks. Most of the Scottish Highlands are the remains of material formed at the edges of oceans, long ago.

8.3 The theory of plates

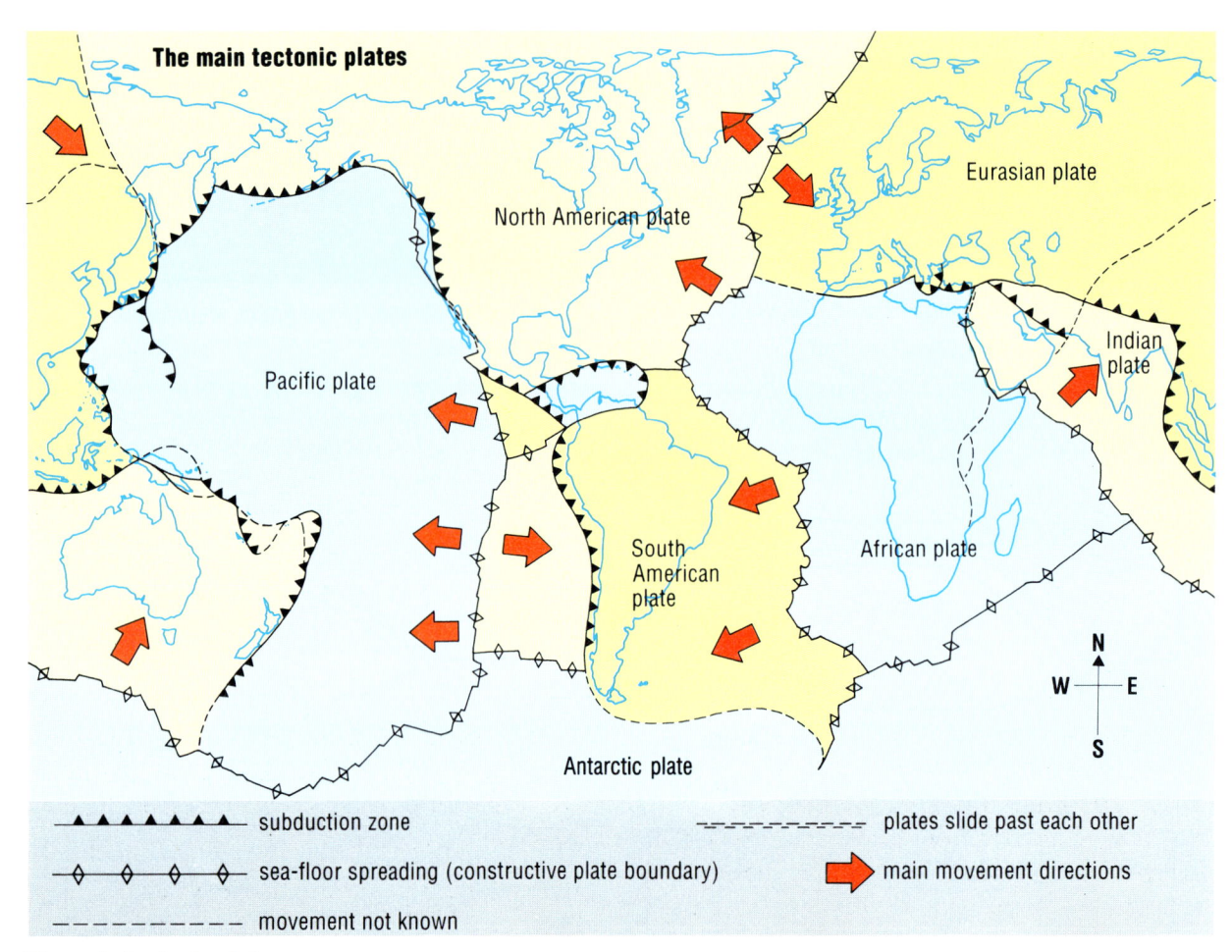

The main tectonic plates

The exploration of the ocean floors made it possible to put together a new explanation of how continental drift could happen. This theory, **plate tectonics**, was devised in the 1960s by **J. Tuzo Wilson** and others.

The theory suggests that the outer shell of the earth is made up of **plates** of various sizes. The edges of the plates are marked by earthquakes, volcanoes or both.

The plates move at various speeds in various directions. For example, the Mid-Atlantic Ridge runs through Iceland. Careful surveying by lasers shows that the Ridge's central rift valley is widening by about 4 cm per year.

Rift valleys form where the crust is widening (page 101). The Icelandic Central Rift and the East African Rift Valley are examples above sea-level, but most rift valleys are along the centre of mid-ocean ridges.

1 Iceland is about 500 km across. How long has it taken to erupt this material from the ridge?

There are various types of **plate boundary** where one plate moves against another. Because new ocean floor is constructed at ocean ridges, they are called **constructive boundaries**.

In subduction zones the plates move together. These **destructive boundaries** happen when one denser plate slides under the other and so becomes smaller.

If plates slide past each other neither gets bigger or smaller. These are **conservative boundaries** because the plates are conserved.

2 Which type of plate boundary is found in each of these places? Use the map to answer.

a) The Mid-Atlantic Ridge.
b) Along the western edge of South America.
c) Along the western edge of California.

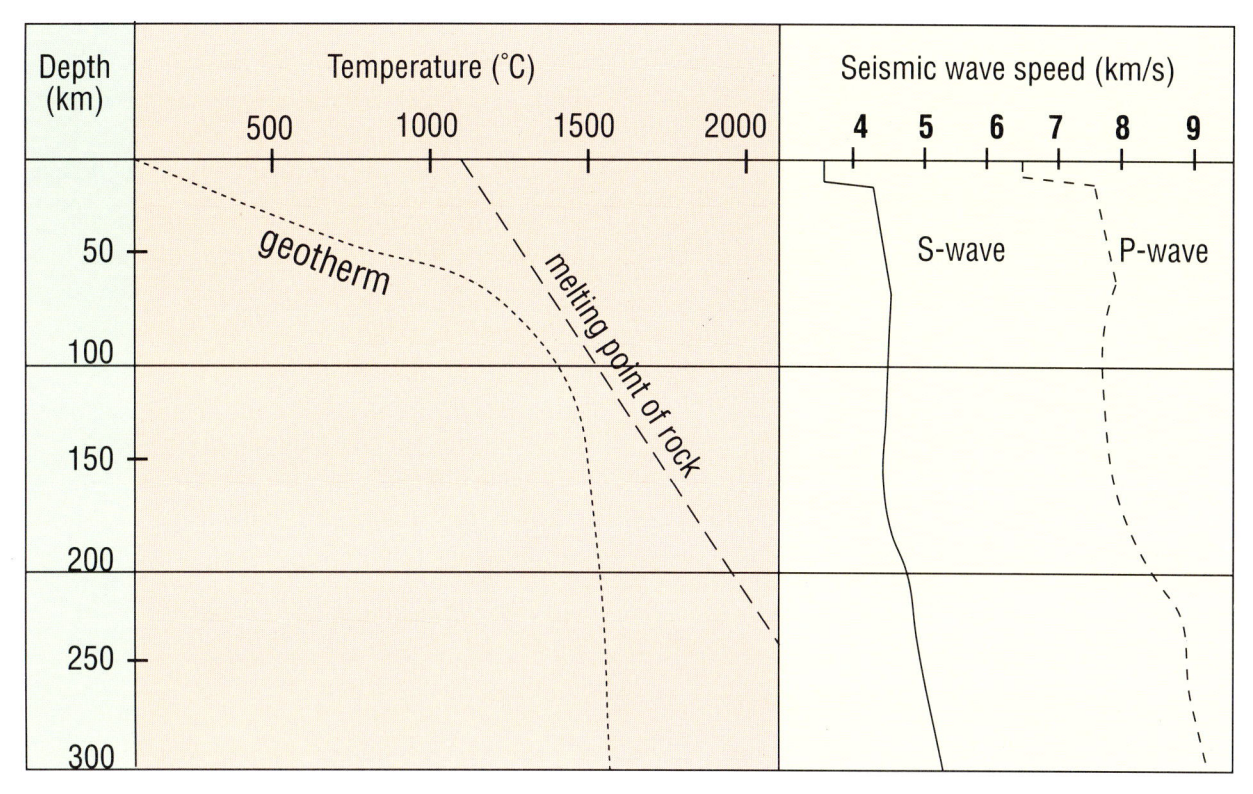

To explain how the plates can slide about over the inner part of the Earth, we need information about the detailed structure of the Earth below an ocean floor. These graphs provide some data to help interpret this structure. The **geotherm** shows temperatures at different depths.

3 What is the temperature in the Earth at:

a) 100 km; b) 200 km; c) 300 km?

The other temperature graph shows the melting point of rock. Rocks at depth melt at higher temperatures because they are under pressure from the rocks above them.

4 a) At what depth is the melting point 1500 °C?
b) What is the melting point at 50 km depth?

The speeds of seismic waves alter with depth. They increase if the density of the rock increases. At about 10 km, the speeds of both kinds of wave suddenly rise. At this point the lower density crust meets the mantle beneath it.

5 Make a copy of the graphs and draw in a line to indicate the depth to the base of the crust.

Seismic wave speeds *increase* with depth down to a certain depth, then they *decrease* slightly. This section with lower seismic wave speeds is called the **Low Velocity Zone**, or LVZ.

6 a) At what depth is the top of the LVZ?
b) At what depth is the base of the LVZ?
c) Mark the top and bottom of the LVZ on your copy of the graphs.

At the Low Velocity Zone the rocks are near their melting point. In fact, since rocks are a mixture of minerals, some of the mineral grains *do* start to melt around their edges.

The Low Velocity Zone is slightly slushy. The rocks above it form quite solid **plates**. When acted upon by volcanic forces, the plates can slide across the Low Velocity Zone.

7 Molten rock rises to erupt at ocean ridges. Can you explain where this comes from?

The theory of plate tectonics is the best explanation that we have to explain movements of the Earth's crust, but as new evidence emerges, this may be changed.

SECTION EIGHT

EGGSHELL EARTH

8.4 Looking through the Earth

We can see far out into space, but we cannot see the centre of the Earth. The deepest borehole reaches about 15 kilometres down, but what is the inside of our planet like?

Some clues come from **density**. To find relative density, we need to know **mass** and **volume**.

$$\text{Density} = \frac{mass}{volume}$$

For a sphere, volume $= \frac{4}{3} \times \pi \times (\text{radius})^3$

1 The radius of the Earth is 6371 km. Work out the volume of the Earth.

The mass of the Earth was found by Henry Cavendish in 1797, using Newton's law of gravity. His answer was almost the same as the modern figure, 5976×10^{24} kg.

2 Work out the relative density of the Earth.

If the surface rocks have an average relative density of around 2.8, the inside of the Earth must include high density material to produce this overall density.

The internal structure of the Earth was a mystery until the twentieth century when seismometers became widely spread around the Earth. Records of P-waves and S-waves arriving from earthquakes showed some interesting patterns.

No S-waves arrive at areas on the opposite side of the Earth from the source of the seismic waves. Something blocks them.

3 What material stops S-waves? (see page 59).

P-waves arrive on the far side of the Earth, but *not* in a ring-shaped **shadow zone**.

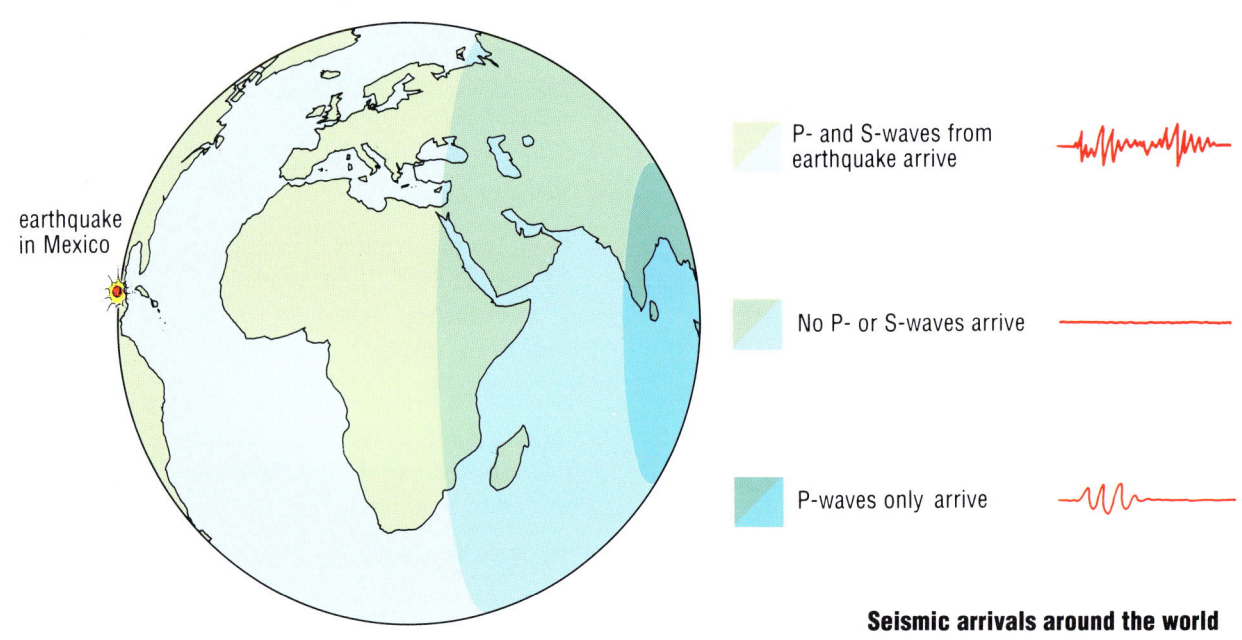

earthquake in Mexico

- P- and S-waves from earthquake arrive
- No P- or S-waves arrive
- P-waves only arrive

Seismic arrivals around the world

Modelling seismic waves in the Earth

Equipment: a ray box, a perspex disc 10 cm diameter, a card disc 18.5 cm diameter, a wooden disc 10 cm diameter

- Centre the wooden disc on the card disc.
- Put the ray box on the edge of the card disc.
- Shine light rays across the discs.
- Mark the edges of the shadow.
- Replace the wood with the perspex disc.
- Mark the new shadows in a different colour.

4 a) Which colour shows the P-wave shadow zone?
b) Which colour shows the S-wave shadow zone?

Unlike light in the experiment, seismic waves do not follow straight lines. Density constantly rises with depth in the earth, and this makes seismic waves follow curved paths.

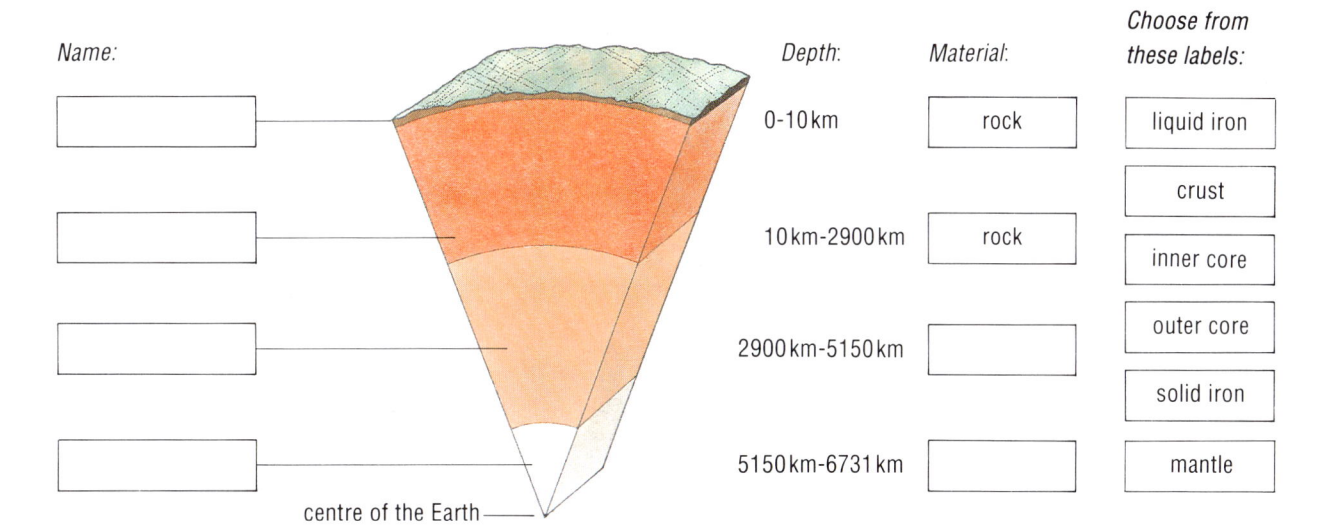

The structure of the Earth

The central part of the Earth causing these effects is the **core**. Its size was measured, using seismic wave tracing, by **Bene Gutenburg** in 1914. The radius of the core is 3473 km.

The fact that S-waves do not travel through the core tells us that it is liquid. The pattern of refraction of P-waves by the core suggests that it has a relative density around 11.

In 1936 **Inge Lehmann** studied how seismic waves travel through the core. She found that 2250 km down into the core it becomes *solid*, with a relative density over 13. The outer core is made from liquid molten iron, and the inner core from solid iron.

In 1909, **Andrija Mohorovicic** studied earthquakes in Yugoslavia. He found that seismic waves are reflected at a boundary a few dozen kilometres below the surface. He showed that the rocks below this boundary have a relative density of 3.3.

This boundary is called the **Mohorovicic discontinuity** or **Moho**. Above it are the rocks making the **crust** and below it is the **mantle**.

5 Copy the diagram of the interior of the Earth above and add labels from the boxes provided.

One important property of the Earth is its **magnetic field**. In 1600, **William Gilbert** decided that the Earth behaves as a giant magnet. The magnetic field is now thought to be caused by the effect of the Earth's rotation on the liquid iron in the outer core.

The magnetic field of the past is recorded in igneous rocks like basalt. As they cooled down and crystallized, iron particles in them lined up with the Earth's field. They show that the field has often **reversed**.

At present, compasses point to the **North Magnetic Pole**. At certain times in the past, when the magnetic field was reversed, a compass would have pointed to the South Magnetic Pole.

6 Redraw this diagram of the Earth's magnetic field to show it at a time when it is reversed.

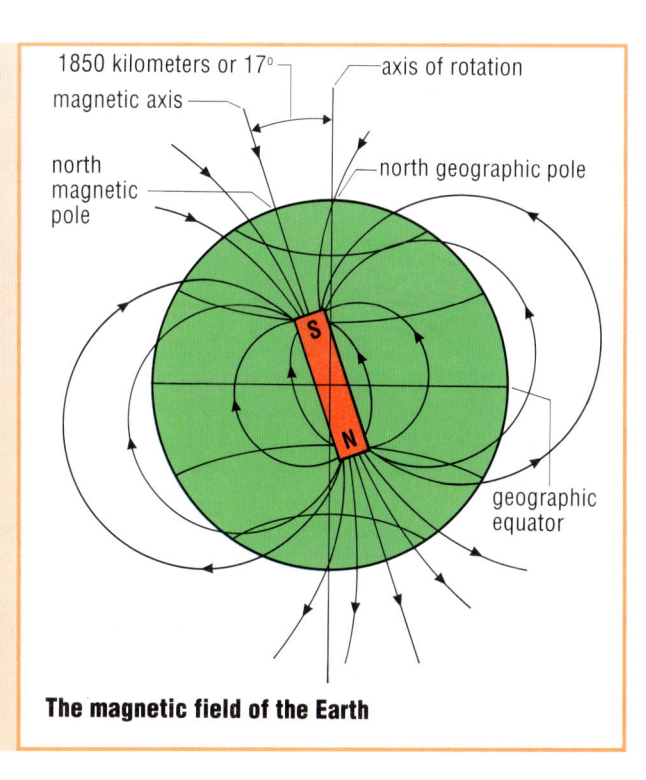

The magnetic field of the Earth

SECTION EIGHT

8.5 At the beginning

Our planet is made of elements that collected together over 4600 million years ago. The raw material came from ancient exploded stars. We are made of stardust.

Stars are atom factories. All matter began as hydrogen. Stars manufacture the other elements by **nuclear fusion**, which also makes energy (see page 95).

1 What gases are involved in fusion in the Sun?

When a star runs low on hydrogen, it begins to fuse helium into carbon. Atoms of neon, sodium, magnesium, oxygen, silicon and eventually iron can be produced in some stars, if they are big enough. To make atoms bigger than iron, fusion *takes in* energy.

2 The production of energy keeps a star hot and holds it in shape. What force is trying to make it collapse?

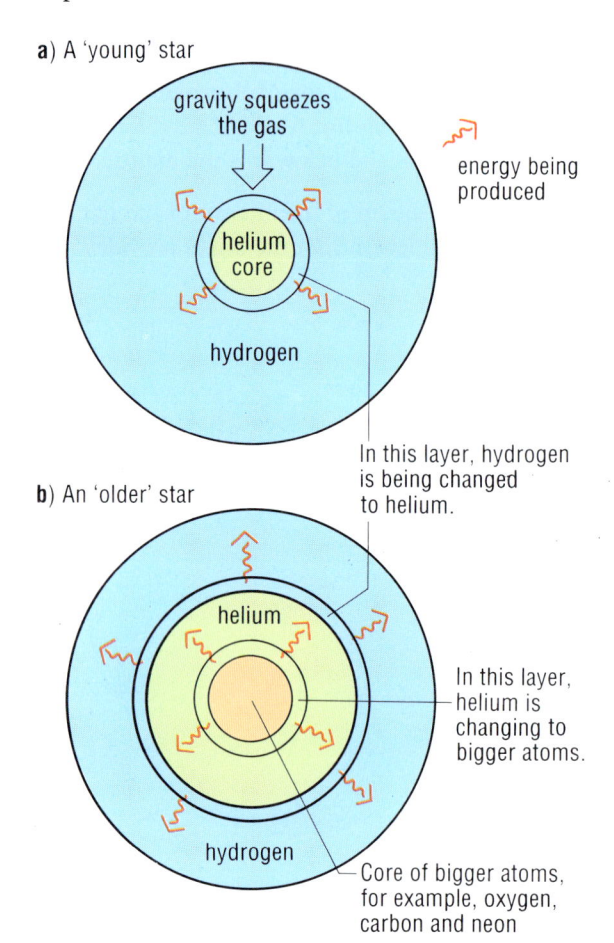

Crab Nebula - the remains of a supernova

If the star has used up most of the possible fuels, it collapses. Collapse causes stars to explode. Their atoms get a surge of extra energy. They can fuse into bigger atoms. Exploding stars are called **supernovae**.

The thin clouds blasted out of supernovae provide raw material for new stars and planets.

Our Earth started as a ball of gas and dust. Gravity pulled it together. It started to heat up as it squashed together.

3 What is the main source of heat in the Earth? (see page 34).

The Earth began to cool and mineral crystals formed. Drops of iron collected and sank through the mantle to the centre.

4 What part of the Earth was formed by iron sinking to the centre?

Volcanic eruptions broke the newly-solid crust. Gases from these eruptions started to make an atmosphere of water vapour, nitrogen and carbon dioxide.

5 What important gas was not present in this early atmosphere?

Heat caused hot rock to rise, cracking the crust and starting plate tectonics. 'Rafts' of continental crust began to be built. These collided to build larger continents.

6 What kind of plate boundary would produce the first continental crust?

Inside a star

a) A 'young' star
- gravity squeezes the gas
- helium core
- hydrogen
- energy being produced

b) An 'older' star
- helium
- hydrogen
- In this layer, hydrogen is being changed to helium.
- In this layer, helium is changing to bigger atoms.
- Core of bigger atoms, for example, oxygen, carbon and neon

Our atmosphere and oceans are all products of volcanoes. The gases from the magma include all the chemical compounds found in the first air and seas. Water vapour cooled and condensed as the first rain. Surface processes began, and the oceans started to fill.

Life may also be a by-product of volcanoes. The complicated molecules needed for life may have been formed around volcanic vents at the bottom of oceans, perhaps over 3500 million years ago.

Hot fluids can erupt from ocean ridges. The discovery of these **black smokers** has revealed some of the strangest animals on Earth. The black liquid contains large amounts of metal sulphides. These are consumed by very primitive bacteria.

The bacteria provide food for giant tubeworms and shellfish of kinds never seen before. These creatures do not rely on the Sun's energy. They live on the internal energy of the Earth. Some scientists have suggested that black smokers could have provided the environments for the first life on Earth.

A 'black smoker'

The oxygen in our atmosphere is a product of life. The first simple plant cells began using carbon dioxide and producing oxygen.

As more oxygen became available, eventually it built up to the point where new life forms could use this gas. They were the first animals. We are their descendants.

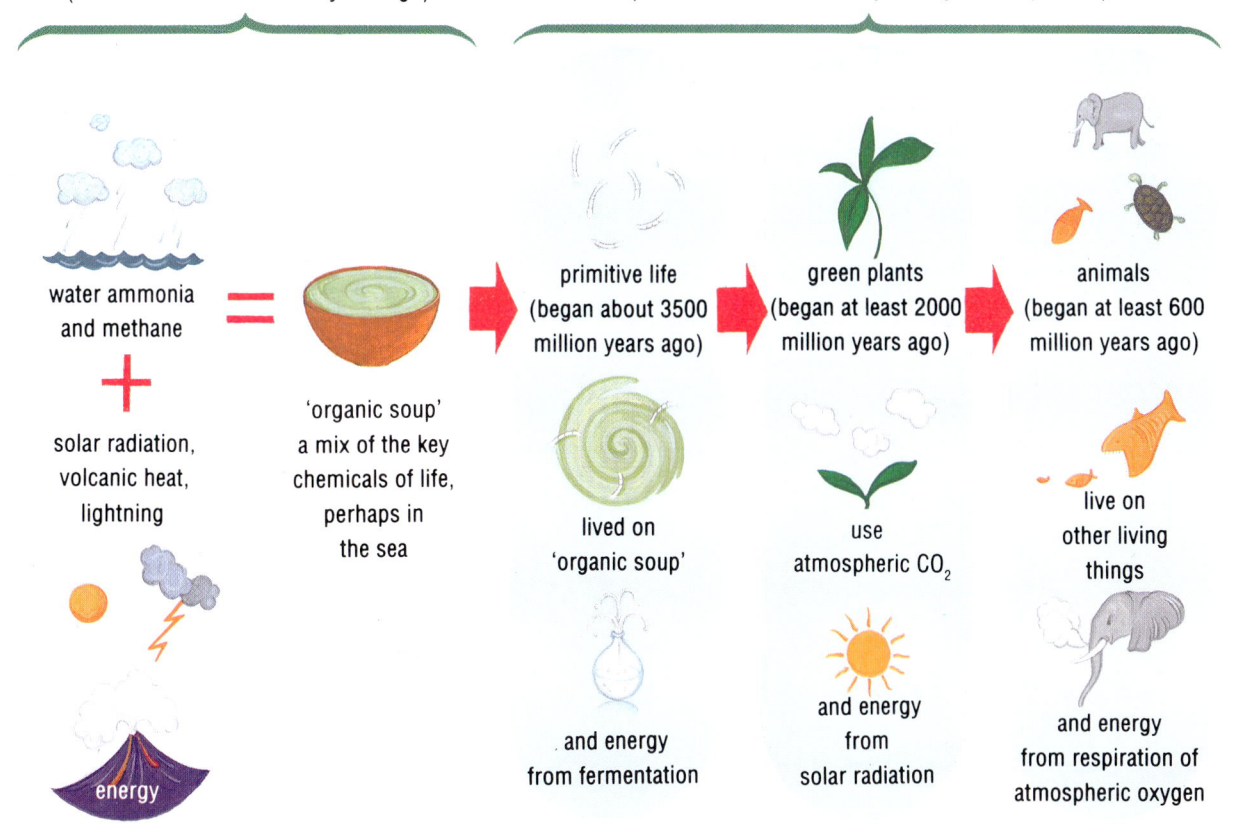

Prebiological period
(from 4500 to 3500 million years ago)

Biological period
(from about 3500 million years ago to the present)

water ammonia and methane
+
solar radiation, volcanic heat, lightning
=
'organic soup' a mix of the key chemicals of life, perhaps in the sea
→
primitive life (began about 3500 million years ago)
lived on 'organic soup' and energy from fermentation
→
green plants (began at least 2000 million years ago)
use atmospheric CO_2 and energy from solar radiation
→
animals (began at least 600 million years ago)
live on other living things and energy from respiration of atmospheric oxygen

The main stages in the development of life on Earth

Section 8 questions

1 a) Draw a labelled diagram of the formation of oceanic crust at a ridge.
b) Draw a labelled diagram to show subduction.
c) Draw labelled diagrams to show the formation of fold mountains by continental collision.

2 Boreholes were drilled to collect sediments from just above the pillow lavas under the South Atlantic Ocean. These are the results:

Distance from ocean ridge in km	Age of sediment in million years (from fossil evidence)
190	9.5
450	22
790	39
1440	73

a) Plot the results on a graph.
b) Draw in the best fit straight line.
c) On average how much ocean floor is being made per year on this side of the ridge?
d) How much is the ocean widening per century?
e) One specimen has been stored unlabelled. Fossils date it at 51 million years old. How far from the ridge was it probably collected?

3 This graph shows the speeds of seismic waves at depths in the earth down to the centre.

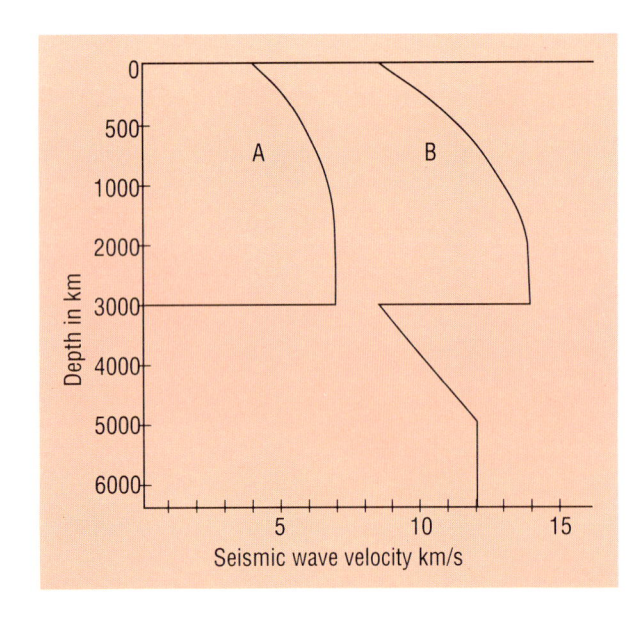

a) Which graph represents P-wave speeds? Give a reason.
b) Line A drops to zero speed at about 3000 km depth. Explain this behaviour.

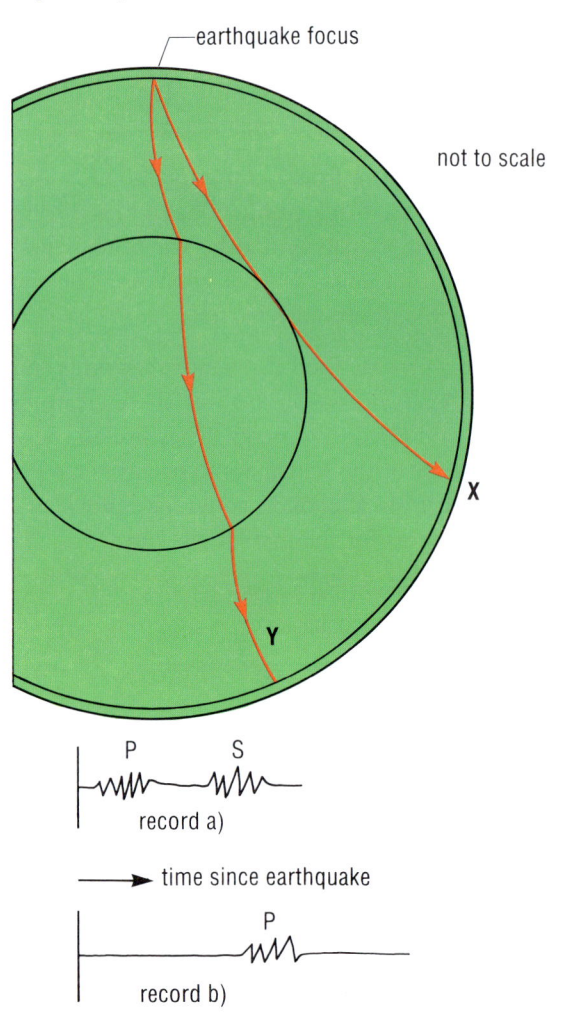

4 a) Label a copy of this diagram to show the *crust mantle core*.
b) Seismic waves from the earthquake focus were recorded at two stations, X and Y. Which record was made at Station X, and which at Station Y? Explain.

5 Using reference books and databases, describe the work of these scientists in connection with these particular scientific problems:

a) Fred Vine – sea-floor spreading.
b) Jocelyn Bell – supernovae.
c) Stanley Miller – the origin of life.

Summary: Earth processes

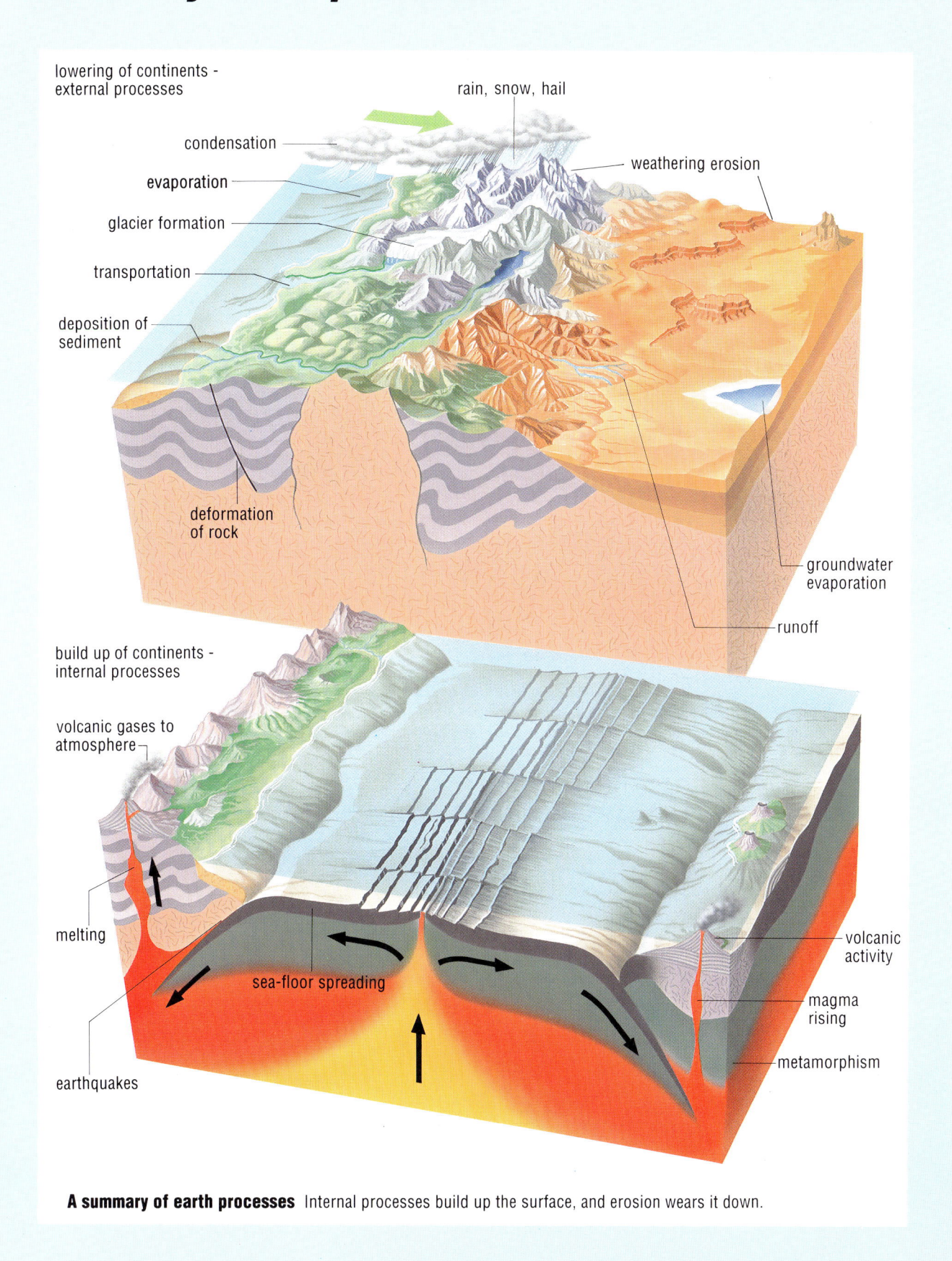

A summary of earth processes Internal processes build up the surface, and erosion wears it down.

Index

agglomerate 48
aggregates 69
air
    masses 16-17
    pressure 14-15
andesite 103
Anning, Mary 30
anticlines 61
Aristarchus of Samos 81
asteroids 94
atmosphere 6, 14, 28, 109

Bacon, Francis 100
barometer 14
basalt 12, 51, 88-89, 101, 107
basins 13
bauxite 75
Becquerel, Henri 34
Big Bang 97
bitumen 69
black smokers 109
bricks 68

Cepheids 96
Clarke, Arthur 87
climate 24-25
coal 46, 70-71
compression ratio 61
concrete 68
congomerates 41
continental
    crust 103, 108
    drift 100-105
    environment 42
continents 7, 100, 103
corals 43
craters 89
crops 25
cross bedding 43

deposition 41
dolerite 52-53, 63, 101
dunes 40, 43
dykes 101

Earth
    age 33-35
    density 106-107
    diameter 6, 80-81
    magnetic field 107
    temperature 7, 16-17, 20, 24, 105
earthquakes 54-56, 60
equinoxes 23
erosion 38
Eratosthenes 80-81
Etna, Mount 33, 48

faults 55, 57, 60
folds 12-13, 60-62, 103
fossils 30-31, 33
fronts 17
fusion, nuclear 95, 108

gabbro 101
galaxies 83, 96-97
Galileo Galilei 84
gas 72-73
geological periods 32-33
    Cambrian 33
    Carboniferous 100
    Quaternary 33
    Silurian 44
geotherm 105
glaciers 20, 40
gneiss 62-63
graded bedding 42
granite 52

gravity 81, 86, 89
Greenhouse effect 77
ground water 36, 39
Gutenberg, Bene 107
gypsum 69

Haughton, Samuel 33
Hawking, Professor Stephen 97
Herschel, William and Caroline 84
Hertzsprung-Russell diagram 96
Holmes, Arthur 34
hornfels 63
hurricanes 26
Hypatia of Alexandria 84

Icthyosaurus 30
igneous rocks 10, 12-13, 50-55, 63
intertidal environments 42
Io 92
island arcs 12, 103
isobars 15
isoseismals 57

Jupiter 82, 92, 94

Kelvin, Lord 34
kilns 68

landfill 78-79
landslip 38
lava 48-49, 51, 101, 103
Leavitt, Henrietta 96
Lehmann, Inge 107
light years 83, 96-97
Low Velocity Zone 105
Lucy 66
Lyell, Charles 33

magmas 50-53, 101-103, 109
magnetic field 107
malachite 74
Mam Tor Beds 45
mantle 107
marble 63
marine environments 42
Mars 82, 91, 94
Mauchline 44
Mercalli scale 56-57
Mercury 82, 90, 94
metamorphic rocks 11-13, 35, 60-63, 102-103
meteorites 85, 89, 94
meteors 84
mid-ocean ridges 12, 101-104
Milky Way 83
millibars 14-15
mining 70-71
Mohorovicic discontinuity 107
Moon 6, 88-89

Neptune 84, 93-94
Newton, Sir Isaac 81, 84, 86
nuclear fusion 95, 108

ocean trenches 12, 102
oil 72-73, 77
ores 67, 74-75
overburden 70-71
ozone layer 77

p-waves 58-59, 106
Pangaea 100
parallax 83
Pharaoh Neco 80
placer deposits 75
planets 6-7, 82, 84, 88-95
plate tectonics 104-105, 108
platforms 13

Pluto 84, 94
plutons 52
pollution 76-77
pressure
    air 14
    patterns 18-19
Pythagoras 80

radiometric dating 34
rainfall 24
rainwater 36
rainforest 9, 24
reservoir rocks 72-73
rift valleys 104
ripples 42-43
rockets 86
Rutherford, Ernest 34

s-waves 58-59, 106-107
salt 43, 75
sand dunes 40
sandstones 41-42, 44-45, 60
satellites 86-87
Saturn 82, 84, 93-94
schist 62-63
sea-floor spreading 101
sea water 43
sedimentary
    environments 42-43
    rocks 10-13, 33, 41-46, 60
seismic waves 58-59, 105-107
shadow zones 106
shales 41, 62
sheet wash 39
shields 13
sills 52
slate 62-63
Smith, William 31
smog 76
soils 38-39
solstices 22
spotted rocks 63
St Helens, Mount 49
stars 83, 96-97, 108
Stonehenge 23
subduction 102-103
Sun 22-23, 80-81, 90, 94-95
supernovae 108
synclines 61

tells 68
thunderstorms 27
transport 40
turbidity current 42

Uniformitarianism 65
Uranus 84, 93-94

Venus 82, 90, 94
volcanoes 10, 50-54, 108-109
    Mount Etna 33, 48
    Mount St Helens 49
    planetary 89, 91-93
    subduction zone 102-105
Voyager 93

Walker, William 30
water 6-7
    cycle 20-21
    transport 39
weather 14-19, 26-27
weathering 36-39
Wenlock Edge 44
Wegener, Alfred 100
Wilson, J. Tuzo 104
wind transport 40
winds 7, 19-19